FAN OR FOE?

One of the reasons ballplayers are fearful of people running onto the field is that they do get threats. This is not a recent development. In 1950, for example, Yankee shortstop Phil Rizzuto received a letter warning him, Hank Bauer, Yogi Berra and Johnny Mize that they would be shot if they showed up to play the Red Sox. Rizzuto turned the letter over to the FBI and told manager Casey Stengel about it. Under the circumstances, Stengel did the most prudent thing: He issued a uniform with another number on the back to Rizzuto, and gave Rizzuto's old uniform to Billy Martin. . . .

Bantam Books by Ron Luciano and David Fisher

THE UMPIRE STRIKES BACK
STRIKE TWO

QUANTITY PURCHASES

Companies, professional groups, churches, clubs and other organizations may qualify for special terms when ordering 24 or more copies of this title. For information, contact the Special Sales Department, Bantam Books, 666 Fifth Avenue, New York, N.Y. 10103. Phone (800) 223-6834. N.Y. State residents call (212) 765-6500.

STRIKE TWO

by Ron Luciano
& David Fisher

 BANTAM BOOKS
TORONTO · NEW YORK · LONDON · SYDNEY · AUCKLAND

STRIKE TWO

Bantam Hardcover edition / April 1984
2nd printing............April 1984
Bantam paperback edition / April 1985

Library of Congress Cataloging in Publication Data

Luciano, Ron.
Strike two.

1. Luciano, Ron. 2. Baseball—United States—Umpires—
Biography. I. Fisher, David, 1946–   . II. Title.
GV865.L8A36 1984   796.357′092′4 [B]   83-25707

ISBN 0-553-24549-X

Published simultaneously in the United States and Canada

PRINTED IN THE UNITED STATES OF AMERICA

H   0 9 8 7 6 5 4 3 2 1

To my sisters Bobbie and Dee Dee. For without them, I wouldn't have had any sisters at all. And I wouldn't have had my wonderful All-American niece and my @$#%$¢ nephews.

The authors gratefully acknowledge the assistance, and understanding, of the following people: John Boswell, Richard Bresciani, Karen Brinkman, Bill Brown, Patty Brown, Rose Buttino, Hank Calleo, Kathy Cofek, Barbara Cohen, Joanne Curtis, Bob DiNunzio, F.X. Flinn, John Fox, Joe Garbarino, Peter Guzzardi, Jay Horowitz, Reggie Jackson, The Jester Family, Merrie Lane, Wayne Minshew, Robert Morton, Ken Nigro, Cosmo Parisi, Richie Phillips, David Raymond, Rosemary Rogers, Jack Romanos, Lucy Salvino, Matthew Shear, Larry Shenk, Joan Sinclair, Tina Stahle, Tony Tremini, United Airlines, Vance Vetrano, and John Young.

The authors offer a special thanks to the umpires, players, and managers who willingly gave of their time, and to the many people whose stories we could not include in this book.

CONTENTS

ONE

WAS IT MY VOICE?

"Was it my voice?" I asked.

I was sitting across a cluttered desk from NBC Sports Executive Producer Mike Weisman, who had just told me the network would not be renewing my contract as color commentator on *The Game of the Week*. Weisman sighed. "Yeah, Ron," he finally said softly, "I'm afraid your voice was a little whiney."

"Be honest. Was it also the fact that sometimes I mispronounced players' names?"

Weisman pursed his lips and nodded. "That's right, Ron, sometimes you mispronounced their names."

"But was it also the fact that I didn't do enough background research on the game?"

Weisman took a deep breath. "Right again, Ron. Sometimes you didn't seem to know what teams were playing."

I was really getting into this now. "Did it have anything to do with the fact that I stopped telling stories in the middle, leaving everybody wondering what I was talking about?"

Weisman yawned. I could see this was tougher on him than it was on me. "That too, Ron. A lot of viewers wondered what you were talking about."

"But wait. Was it also the fact that I told stories while there was a play taking place on the field?"

Weisman stretched. "Ron, sometimes you did speak when you should have been quiet."

I could feel the anger rising inside me like a chocolate cake. "And you're firing me for that!"

"No," Weisman pointed out, "we're not firing you. We're just not renewing your contract."

And so my brief career as a color commentator ended. In truth, I was to baseball broadcasting what Francis the Talking Mule had been to acting. Only Francis had some funny lines. Actually, I was surprised I hadn't done better. There are many things I'm not good at. I'm not good at video games. I'm not good at yachting. I'm a terrible typist. But talking? With all the practice I've had? In fact, my reputation was based on the fact that I was the umpire who talked to players, and coaches, and fans, ushers, ticket-takers, pigeons. . . .

After leaving Weisman's office I did the first thing a man does at such a time. I looked for an excuse. I couldn't blame the technical people I'd worked with at NBC. They had always been supportive and sympathetic. I couldn't blame Merle Harmon, my broadcasting partner, who did the best possible job while working with the verbally handicapped. Finally, I looked square in the washroom mirror and found the right place to put the blame. The players.

Whenever I broadcast a game, no matter what city we were in, no matter which teams were playing, that player with the strangest, most difficult name to pronounce would have the greatest game of his career. I've seen Garth Iorg win ball games. When I did Cardinal games Joaquin Andujar was unhittable. Where were Willie Mays and Hank Aaron when I needed them?

Actually, I hadn't really been doing <u>the</u> *Game of the Week*. I was doing the backup *Game of the Week*. We would be seen in regions where the primary game was blacked out. And doing the backup game, I discovered, was something like hosting a telethon for hiccups. Nobody cared. Nobody even knew we were on. Two years after I'd broadcast my last game, people were still asking me how I was enjoying the job. So much for being missed.

I really had enjoyed broadcasting. Imagine—being *paid* to talk about baseball. Of course, after working eleven years as an American League umpire, I was happy just to have a job. Being an umpire, I had discovered, was sort of like being a King. Neither job prepares you for anything else.

Standing on a baseball diamond among grown men wearing knickers, calling safes and outs, balls and strikes, is an unusual profession. But for anyone who enjoys being screamed and cursed at and occasionally threatened, and having things thrown at them, while living out of a suitcase six or seven months a year for almost no money and absolutely no praise, this is the perfect job. Every umpire at one time or another has asked himself the same question: What am I doing here? Whenever I found myself wondering that I just closed my eyes and remembered sitting in a classroom in Endicott, New York, trying to teach mathematics to thirty thirteen-year-olds. A memory like that makes even Earl Weaver tolerable.

Men, and recently some women, become umpires for countless different reasons. All of them share a genuine love for sports. At a starting salary of five hundred dollars a month in the minor leagues, umpiring is not a profession anyone goes into for the money. In many cases umpires are former athletes who either got hurt or weren't good enough to be successful on the pro level. American Leaguer Jim McKean, for example, had been the Canadian Football League Rookie of the Year before an injury forced him to retire. Ed Montague, of the National League, wanted to play professional baseball, but his father advised against it. Since his father, a former major leaguer, was the scout who signed Willie Mays, "Fast Eddie" took his advice. I became an umpire because of my ability as a football player. I had been an All-American lineman at Syracuse University and played four years of pro football in Detroit and Buffalo. Not "played," exactly. Like all great football players, I was mo-bile, a-gile, and hos-tile. Unfortunately, I was also fra-gile. And no matter how often coaches tried to convince me that pain was the sign of a job well done, I couldn't get past the fact that pain hurt. To me, every week during what I laughingly refer to as my "professional career" was the same: We played Sunday afternoons. By Sunday night my entire body was numb.

On Monday morning I would wake up, and wish that I hadn't. Every part of my body hurt. My eyelids hurt. My hair hurt. My nails had stopped growing. Playing football ever again was out of the question. I was just hoping to be able to brush my tooth.

By Tuesday morning some feeling had returned to the left side of my body. Since that was the side that hadn't even been hit, I wasn't optimistic my right side, the side that had actually taken the punishment, was going to make a comeback.

On Wednesday morning feeling returned to the right side. I could now move all the parts of my body—rather, everything would move, but not necessarily when I wanted it to. This was also the day that the headache finally began to go away.

By Thursday I could actually pick up a glass of water without spilling more than a few drops, as well as feed myself. Every inch of my body still hurt, but at least my nails had started growing again.

On Friday I was able to hobble around. Not very quickly, but because even when I was healthy I was slightly slower than a glacier, nobody noticed. Friday was also the day the head coach would begin talking about smashing Sunday's opponent, so my headache came back.

If the sun was shining on Saturday, I almost felt like a human being. Most of the pain was gone. I could actually bend over and touch my ankles. Of course, my ankles were now located an inch below my knees, so it wasn't that tough.

On Sunday morning I felt like a new man. Then we played and the cycle began all over again.

It took me only four years of high school football, four years of college, and four years of pro ball to realize I was not having such a wonderful time. Fortunately, the Buffalo Bills shared my lack of enthusiasm. A year later I was an umpire.

American Leaguer Durwood Merrill's background was exactly like mine, except that I wasn't born on an Indian reservation in Cloud Chief, Oklahoma, and my father wasn't a hellfire and brimstone Baptist minister. Murwood, as I called him, also played football through college. His goal was to coach at the University of Oklahoma. To become a college football coach, he took a job teaching high school science. That's the kind of logic that marked him as a future umpire.

Eventually he was named head football coach at a high school in Hooks, Texas. He took over a team that had been 8–2 and turned them around—they were 2–8 his first year. "Oh, it wasn't so bad," he remembers, " 'cept I couldn't go out of the house. I didn't get a haircut for a year, either. I wasn't dumb enough to let anybody in that town near my throat with a sharp instrument." Fortunately, Durwood tied for the district championship the following year and might have been on his way to a successful coaching career. Then came the afternoon that led him to umpire school.

"My assistant coach, Charlie Phillips, was also the assistant principal of the school, and when he moved up to principal, he made me his assistant. One afternoon a boy from our rival high school walked in and started beating on one of our kids. Charlie and I dragged this troublemaker outside and told him not to come back. This took place during lunchtime, so all of our students were watching.

"The kid we threw out was so mad he tried to punch out a brick wall. He gave it some shot. I winced. Didn't seem to bother him at all, though. Then he turned around and started walking back toward the main entrance. Now, the front walk to the school was lined with tall, lovely cedar bushes. When Charlie and I saw this kid coming back we stood shoulder to shoulder in front of the door. We made quite a formidable pair; I was 6 feet, two hundred fifteen solid pounds, and Charlie was a little bigger and a little stronger. The kid was maybe five-nine, a hundred fifty pounds. I said to Charlie, 'What we'll do is block him from getting into the school. If he lays a hand on either one of us, I'll pop him and we'll get him under control.' Sure enough, this kid took a swing at me. And missed. I then hit him hard enough to spin his head around. I mean, this was my knockout punch. Twenty years of football went into it. I assumed the fight was over.

"Seems all I'd done was get this boy really angry. He promptly picked me up and tossed me into the cedar bushes. I was flying through the air thinking, 'This can't really be happening.' What made it even more embarrassing was that all my kids were watching. The only thing that made me feel a little better was that as I was scrambling out of the bushes, Charlie sailed over my shoulder. I mean, he was launched.

"Naturally, this called for some rethinking of our plan. I helped Charlie onto his feet and we decided to grab the kid together. I got him in front and Charlie had him in back. I was really afraid we were going to hurt him. Turns out we had him just the way he wanted us. I was just about to tell Charlie to ease up on his hold when that boy flipped me over his shoulder back into the bushes.

"Not only my pride was hurt, my hands were bleeding, I had stickers all over my body, my shirt was just ripped apart and, I believe, if I hadn't been wearing a pop-on tie he would have strangled me. I got back on my feet and Charlie and I just started whaling away. This kid whipped us all the way down the walk to the street. Next thing I know he had me down and was holding my face in a mud puddle maybe two inches deep. I saw my whole life passing before me. I thought, 'I'm drowning in a mud puddle—and all the students in the high school are watching.' It would've been hard to convince anybody I died a hero's death.

"Then I saw the most beautiful sight I've ever seen. We had one lawman in town, and someone had called him. He came roaring up to the school in our police car and slammed on the brakes. That car went sliding sideways to a stop. Right at that moment I was mighty thankful we'd had a winning football season. Then our police force got out of the car—he stood six-four, a big, strapping guy. He put on a weighted glove, pulled the kid off me, held him at arm's length, and just blasted him. He sent him somersaulting backward over the hood of the police car. I took a deep breath and started getting up. Charlie asked me if I was all right and I told him I'd have to think about that. Just then our policeman bent over the kid to make sure he was still alive. Next thing I see is our policeman bouncing down the street on his rump. Then the kid got up again. I felt like I was on the receiving end in a horror movie. Eventually two carloads of Texas State Highway troopers arrived and subdued him.

"A few days later somebody sent Charlie and me a paper bag with our names written on it and the challenge, 'See if you can fight your way out of this.' Now, that was demoralizing. I figured it was time to get out of Hooks.

"About a week after the bag arrived I was watching *The Game of the Week* and saw a commercial for the Umpire Development Program. I had always been a baseball fan. Each year, in fact, my wife and I would go up to St. Louis to see the Cardinals. The umpires always fascinated me. I remember telling my wife that if I were trained, and if I knew the rules, I could umpire. She never discouraged me. Then again, deep down she probably thought I was crazy. So when I saw the commercial I decided umpiring had to be easier than wrestling with that paper bag."

For Kenny Kaiser, the decision to become an umpire came to him like a shot. Literally. Kaiser, later to be aptly named "The Incredible Heap" by Thurman Munson, had been a bar bouncer, a professional wrestler, and a banker—he repossessed cars and furniture for a bank in Rochester, New York. Kenny is a person who defies description. His body looks like a barrel on which two arms had been stuck backward, so that his palms faced away from the rest of him. He doesn't walk as much as waddle, so much so that if you watch him too long you can actually get seasick. His face? Promoters made him wrestle with a mask on. Many people have said that Kenny and I resemble each other, something neither of us takes as a compliment.

Even before he became an umpire, Kenny had a subtle sense of humor. Once, for example, he had to repossess a set of living-room furniture. "Well, Mr. Kaiser," the man who had defaulted told him, "you just can't get blood out of a stone."

"You're absolutely right, Mr. Johnson," Kenny agreed, "but I bet I can get your furniture out the front door."

His specialty, however, was reclaiming automobiles. He was a legal car thief, breaking into cars on which loans had not been repaid and hot-wiring them started. He was hard at work one evening when a delinquent owner took a shot at him. "That's when I decided to get out of the banking business."

A friend of his was getting ready to drive to

Florida to attend umpire school. Kenny decided that was a good way to take a Florida vacation and went with him. "I never dreamed it would be that easy to get a job in baseball," he remembers. And he was right. He had to go through the course a second time before finally getting a chance to work in the minor leagues.

Stevie Palermo's career began when he worked a Little League All-Star Game. "That game had everything in it—great plays, bad plays, arguments. We were supposed to go six innings and ended up playing eight. I was working home plate and I remember one kid tried to score by leaping right over the catcher's head. I was so startled I didn't even make a call. That turned out to be the right call to make, because he flew right past the plate and the catcher never tagged him. We got that worked out eventually. Barney Deary, who was in charge of the Umpire Development Program for the major leagues, happened to be in the stands that day. He liked the way I took control and suggested I think about umpiring as a career." Palermo has since become one of the best young umpires in baseball today.

Dick Stello learned to umpire in the Army. After being discharged, Dick worked semipro games in the Boston area while holding down a full-time job for the phone company. One afternoon he was playing golf with a friend of his, who had once pitched for a Red Sox farm club, and Neil Mahoney, at that time Boston's minor league director. They were in the clubhouse after finishing the round when Stello's friend ran down the aisle and made a beautiful hook slide into a garbage can. "It wasn't even close," Stello claims, "he was out by twenty feet. I gave him the big 'out' call. He got up and started arguing. He claimed the can dropped the ball."

Mahoney liked Stello's style. "I didn't know you umpired," he said.

"A little," Dick admitted. Two months later

Mahoney helped him get a job in the Basin League, one of the best amateur leagues in the country. A year later Stello attended umpire school and began calling his way to the major leagues.

The National League's soon-to-be doctor, Jerry Dale, one dissertation away from his Ph.D. in education, had been a successful pitcher in the Washington Senators organization before a bad arm forced him to quit. While going to college in 1958 he was working as a clerk on the Santa Fe Railroad as well as coaching a Little League team. One day the umpire didn't show up and Jerry was asked to fill in. Like an ex-ballplayer, he refused. Then they told him the job paid five bucks.

And so another umpire was born.

"While working Little League," Jerry recalled, "I heard that Pony League paid seven-fifty a game, so I worked my way up to that league. Then I learned that the Colt League was paying nine dollars. Eventually I got up to the high school level. That was fifteen dollars a game." After becoming an excellent college umpire, he wrote to the presidents of every minor league asking for a job in professional baseball. He was hired by the Class C Pioneer League, becoming one of the very few umpires working today who never attended umpire school.

Umpire schools first opened in the late 1940s. Before the creation of these schools, umpires were either ex-ballplayers or men with guts who learned the trade in the very rough amateur leagues. The famed Beans Reardon, for example, worked as a boilermaker's apprentice in the San Pedro, California, shipyards and began umpiring in the yard league. Both Al Barlick and Larry Goetz, two great, tough umpires, started in the coal fields, where miners were known to get drunk during ball games and shoot at fly balls. "That never bothered me," Goetz once remarked. "It was when they started talking about shooting at grounders that I got nervous."

It was a lot easier for major leaguers to become umpires. Former White Sox manager Clarence (Pants) Rowland became an umpire after leading the Sox to the World Championship in 1917—a story that makes me believe there is still hope for Billy Martin. After widely respected pitcher Big Ed Walsh retired as a player, in 1922, American League President Ban Johnson simply made him an umpire. Thirteen years later American League President Will Harridge did the same thing for Fred (Firpo) Marberry after the Tigers released him. The famed Jocko Conlan made the transition from player to umpire between innings. He was a White Sox outfielder in 1935 when a base umpire fainted from heat exhaustion. The Sox and St. Louis Browns agreed Conlan should umpire the rest of the game. He did, wearing his Chicago uniform.

Actually, Jocko had already decided he wanted to become an umpire. On another blistering afternoon a few months earlier he'd hit a hard ground ball to the shortstop. He ran as hard as he could. The first-base umpire, Clarence (Brick) Owens, had his hands in his pockets, with just his thumbs sticking out. As Conlan crossed the base, Owens just wiggled his right thumb. He didn't even take his hands out of his pockets. Jocko couldn't believe it was that easy. "I've got to hit and run and sweat," he yelled at Owens, "and that's all there is to that play, the little wiggle?"

Owens nodded.

At that moment Conlan knew he wanted to umpire.

New York Yankee pitcher George Pipgras pitched and won the second game of the 1927 World Series; seventeen years later he was umpiring in the Series. But he might be most remembered for a White Sox–Browns game in 1941, when he ejected seventeen players by clearing the bench. Will Harridge called him the next morning to find out if he had gone crazy. "No, sir," Pipgras told him.

"But, George, seventeen?" Harridge whispered. "*Seventeen*?"

Paul Pryor, who umpired 20 years in the National League, was another player who found the calling overnight. In 1948 he was a pitcher in the Class D Georgia State League. The day he was given his unconditional release, one of the league's umpires had a bad auto wreck. Pryor called the league office to ask for the job. "You ever umpired before?" the league president asked.

"Are you kidding?" Pryor responded.

The next night he was working home plate. "I remember calling a strike on a kid and he turned around and said, 'You couldn't get me out pitching, so now all you have to do is raise your right arm?' I grinned at him. 'Nice, isn't it,' I said. 'Strike two.' "

Today, with rare exceptions, all umpires in professional baseball are graduates of an umpire school. To answer the two most often asked questions about umpire school: Yes, you do have to go to school to learn how to be so dumb, and no, you do not have to be blind to pass the entrance exam.

I believe most people are born to be umpires. You're born, and somebody smacks you. You haven't even had time to do anything wrong and someone's hitting you. Perfect training for an umpire. The schools just fill in the details.

Umpire school consists of a six-week course during which you learn the rules and regulations, the mechanics of working the two- and three-man systems used in the minor leagues, how to handle the equipment, and how to handle game situations, including just when to eject a player, manager, or the entire press box, if necessary. There are currently two schools in operation: the Joe Brinkman Umpire School has branches in Florida and California, and the Harry Wendlestedt Umpire School is in Florida.

People find out about the schools in various

ways. The National League's popular Eric Gregg was trying to make his Philadelphia high school team as a catcher when he realized he wasn't ever going to make the major leagues. "Coach asked if I could hit the fast ball. 'Hit it!' I said, 'I can't even catch it.' "

Weeks later he was watching *The Game of the Week*, the prime *Game of the Week*, when announcer Curt Gowdy did a promotional piece for the major leagues' Umpire Development Program, an umpire school then in operation. "Gowdy came on and said, 'Be a major league umpire and earn thirty thousand dollars for six months' work,' " Eric recalls. "And I thought, that's for me! I called the telephone number they gave and spoke to Barney Deary, who was setting up the program. Barney explained that applicants had to be at least twenty-one. I was only nineteen. But he offered to help me get started doing Little League games in the Philadelphia area, and in two years I could reapply.

"Little League? I thought, 'Where's my thirty thousand dollars?'

"The following Saturday Gowdy came on again, but this time he said, 'The age is now nineteen.' I knew they did it just for me. I called Barney Monday morning. I was working in a print shop at the time and the people I was working with were incredibly supportive. They threw a going-away party for me and bought me all kinds of presents—but they wouldn't give me anything real nice because they were so sure I was coming back."

I never saw that commercial, so I went to the Al Sommers Umpire School, now Harry Wendlestedt's, Class of 1964. Among my classmates were Larry Barnett, basketball official Jake O'Donnell, and Baby Davey Phillips. I remember umpire school being much like Army basic training but without the charm. Instead of the usual calisthenics, like jumping jacks and deep knee bends, we did safes and outs. Safes and outs consist of putting your hands on your knees and standing absolutely still, running as hard as you can for five or ten yards, stopping, putting your hands on your knees again, and either spreading out your arms and screaming "SAFE!" or jerking your right arm into the air at a right angle and calling "OUT!" Every day started and finished with safes and outs. And if you did anything wrong, the instructor would order you to do twenty, fifty, or even a hundred safes and outs. Kenny Kaiser supposedly holds the all-time record for safes and outs, but it deserves an asterisk because he also holds the record for the number of times going through umpire school.

Inevitably you'd have the entire class of 150 students running down the field, alternating safes and outs every five yards, and one guy would stop, snap his arm straight into the air, execute a perfect "out" movement, and call "SAFE!" That was one of the people you just knew didn't have a big future in baseball.

There is no such thing as the typical umpire school student. Applications come from all over the country, South America, even Japan. They come from tall people and short people, thin people and fat people, ex-ballplayers, people with good jobs, bad jobs, and no jobs; married, divorced, and single people, rich people who fly down in their own airplanes and are chauffeured around, poor people who hitchhike to school, people with loud voices and soft voices and squeaky voices and lisps, women and men, even people with physical defects. Joe Brinkman recently had 1,800 applications for the 161 openings in his Florida school. What he looks for are men and women with some sort of stable background, ideally between 23 and 27 years of age—young enough to have a future in baseball but old enough to understand what they were getting into.

The instructional staff of an umpire school is made up of major and minor league umpires. I taught at both Al Sommers and in the Umpire Development Program, now Joe Brinkman's school. At school, each umpire teaches that aspect of the game at which he is best. Nick Bremigan, for example, teaches the rules. John McSherry works with students on the field. My expertise was in being big. Good size is one of the most important things an umpire can have, so I tried to teach students how to be big. I did a good job with some of them, too, mostly the tall ones. However, they had to be ugly on their own. I couldn't teach them everything.

I also served as an example for other teachers. "There are two ways of doing things," McSherry might say, "Luciano's way and every other way. Every other way will be correct."

Not every student goes to umpire school hoping to have a career in professional baseball. A lot of people work in Little League, semipro, school, or softball leagues in their hometowns and simply want to improve their skills. When I was instructing at the Umpire Development Program, for example, we had a 62-year-old retired optometrist in one class. This was the first student who could really see what I'd been missing. And there's no question in my mind that attending umpire school made Brent Musberger the sports broadcaster he is today.

Although all applicants are screened, some unusual people do end up in class. Recently Brinkman had a Las Vegas card shark. He would spend his free time throwing playing cards against a wall—and they would all land face up. No matter how he threw them, face up. I wasn't sure whether that skill would make him a better umpire or not, but it certainly was impressive.

And almost every class has its own phantom, a student never identified who leaves strange items in unusual places. My personal favorite was the jellyfish phantom. He would smuggle huge, ugly jellyfish into the dormitory and leave them next to people's beds or on the shower room floor. There's something deliciously indescribable about getting up in the middle of the night and stepping into the middle of a jellyfish.

Perhaps my most memorable student was a dog trainer who brought his German shepherd to school with him. The shepherd later went on to star in the television series *The Littlest Hobo*. While his trainer was sitting in the classroom or working on the field that dog would lie still watching everything. And he did incredible tricks. His owner would say, "Gee, it's dark in here," and the dog would trot over and turn on the lights. Or we would put an umpire's mask, brush, and indicator on the floor, and the owner would spell b-r-u-s-h, and the dog would go get it. Not only was it entertaining for everyone, it also worked out better than anyone expected. The dog finished Number One in that class.

There is no way of looking over a class and knowing who's going to make it in professional baseball and who isn't. The student who looks so good the first week may never be able to master the incredible pivot, or he may fold up like a wilted flower when John McSherry challenges him on a call, while the kid who is hesitant or shy at the beginning may grow into a fine umpire. Even Joe Brinkman, who has been teaching since 1974, can't pick out a prospect with certainty. "We had a kid in school one year that I was sure couldn't miss. He was six-five, handsome, intelligent, and handled himself extremely well on the field. I was going to recommend him for a job in professional baseball at the end of the session. I was sure he was going to have a fine career. Unfortunately, one night I got a telephone call from the St. Petersburg police telling me he was on the corner of Forty-ninth Street directing traffic in his underwear."

The very first thing every student is taught is that ballplayers and managers are the worst people ever put on this earth. They are lower than old bubble gum stuck to the soles of shoes. Most instructors—experienced major and minor league umpires—never use the word "ballplayers." They are "$#%@¢#$%" or "rats" or "$#%@¢#$% rats." Anybody who calls them ballplayers gets to do safes and outs for an afternoon. "They're out there for only one reason," I always told my students, "to make you look bad. They're gonna eat you alive. A $#%@¢#$% can be your best friend for five years and eight innings. Then in the ninth inning, with the score tied, you'll call him out on a pitch he doesn't swing at. Whose fault is that? I guarantee you the $#%@¢#$% doesn't think it's his. He isn't going to walk back to the dugout dragging his bat and tell his manager, 'Gee, what a great call my pal just made.' And if you think $#%@¢#$%s are bad, they're nothing compared to managers. Managers are evil."

The problem is that most people who come to school are baseball fans, and they refuse to believe $#%@¢#$%s could be bad. They've spent years watching Tom Seaver do television commercials for sick kids. How could he be a bad guy?

Invariably, during an early classroom session, the instructor will set up a hypothetical rules situation, using real players to make it easier to understand. "Say the Cardinals are playing the Phillies," I might begin, "and Mike Schmidt hits a ground ball to Ozzie Smith. Smith fields it but throws it over George Hendricks's head at first base into dead territory. Schmidt makes it all the way to third. Okay, where does the umpire place Schmidt?"

Hands'll go up in the air, and I would call on a student. "That would never happen," he would reply, "because I've seen Smith play and he would never throw it away."

Before ordering a hundred safes and outs I would take a deep breath and ask my trick question: "You're a Cardinal fan, aren't you?"

The student would smile and admit, yes, he was.

"NO, YOU'RE NOT!" I'd scream. "YOU'RE AN UMPIRE. THE ONLY THING YOU ROOT FOR IS A FAST GAME!" *Then* I'd give him the hundred safes and outs.

The textbook for the classroom is the *Official Baseball Rulebook*, but Nick Bremigan, probably the most knowledgeable rules man in baseball today, has put together a supplementary pamphlet umpires refer to as *Rules for Idiots*. I like to think of this as the book written especially for me. This breaks down the most complicated rules into related circles and makes them easy to understand. For example, the circle in the center of one page reads: "Two base awards from time of pitch." There are four circles around it, and written inside each of them is a situation in which the runner is permitted to advance two bases from the pitch, among them, "Thrown ball into dead territory on first play by an infielder." So, to answer the earlier question, the umpire would put Schmidt on second base, because he was at home plate at the time of the pitch, and throw out the Phillies' manager, who would be loudly arguing that Schmidt should stay on third.

The rulebook is divided into ten sections, each covering a different aspect of the game. Section 9.00, for example, pertains to the umpire and contains the two most important rules in the book: 9.01c, "Each umpire has authority to rule on any point not specifically covered in these rules," and 9.01d, "Each umpire has authority to disqualify any player, coach, manager, or substitute for objecting to decisions or unsportsmanlike conduct or language, and to eject such disqualified person. . . ."

Tests are given after each section is taught in the classroom. Rule 6.00 concerns the batter. A test question on that rule would read, "Tagging up on a deep fly ball to right center, the runner from third takes off for home as soon as the center fielder touches the ball. The ball, however, jumps out of

the center fielder's glove and is finally caught by
the right fielder. When the ball is actually caught,
the runner is already one-third the way home and
scores easily. The defense appeals at third base that
the runner left too soon. Should the umpire uphold
the appeal?''

One of the most important lessons I learned at
school was that the world would be a better place
to live in if we would only eliminate the ''buts''
and ''howevers.'' The best answers to that question
would be (a) hope it never happens, (b) hope that it
is not your call to make, and (c) hope that the
runner trips before reaching home plate and is tagged
out. The correct answer is that a runner can tag up
after the ball is *first* touched by any fielder, but
managers simply do not know the rules, so there
will be an argument on a play like that one. Therefore the follow-up question should be, ''After making your decision on the previous play, will you
have to eject both managers and the outfielder, or
just the manager who uses abusive language and
kicks dirt on you?''

I thought I knew the rulebook when I graduated.
After teaching at the Sommers School and in the
Umpire Development Program, I knew I knew
the rules. But knowing them, I discovered, was not
same as applying them. Somehow I always had situations that didn't seem to fit inside the idiot circles.
My basic philosophy on the field became: Penalize
the team that caused the problem. If an infielder
made an error that resulted in a complex situation,
his team suffered. Later, I simplified that to the old
umpires axiom: When in doubt, call 'em out! Finally,
in particularly difficult situations, I would invoke
the Bluff Rule. That meant sounding like I knew
what I was talking about and doing so loudly and
firmly. ''GEES, BILLY, WHY DON'T YOU LEARN
THE #$@¢$%$& RULE? EVERYBODY KNOWS
IT'S RULE SIXTEDYUN POINT BLUMBLE. IT
SAYS RIGHT THERE HE ONLY GETS ONE BASE

ON THAT PLAY. HOW CAN YOU EVEN ASK ME THAT QUESTION?" If a runner was trying to advance a base more than I felt he should be awarded, I would physically stop him before he got there and scream, "YOU! SECOND BASE!" I knew once he got to the next base he wasn't going to give it up without an argument. I could be completely wrong in my call, but if I grabbed a runner and led him to a base, it certainly looked like I knew exactly what I was doing.

The first weeks on the field at umpire school are used for drills. The instructors would hit ground balls and fly balls, and the students would practice being in game situations. The setup was always the same, one out and a man on first, or men on first and third. That permitted a double play to be made. During these drills students are taught to yell every call they make on the field. Nothing is a "ball," it's a "BALL!" When a player is placed on a base after an overthrow he is not told, "You, second base," but "YOU! SECOND BASE!" The inevitable results of this are laryngitis and sore throats. Every year, almost every student and instructor loses his voice during the early weeks. Naturally, these are the most enjoyable weeks of the session.

Sometime during the second or third week the class is divided into groups and actual games are played. And no matter how often the students had been told that they were umpires, not $#%@¢#$%s, no matter how often they had been told that $#%@¢#%s are worse than the dust that collects underneath a bed, worse than the mud from the Delaware River used to rub up new baseballs, they revert. They show up on the field dressed in their high school or college baseball uniforms, they start arguing every call, they even keep batting records and won-lost standings. I'd be teaching a student to call balls and strikes and the pitcher would break off a curve ball, so I'd stop the game and patiently explain to the pitcher that the object was not to win but to create situations in which the students could learn. The pitcher would nod his head and throw a knuckle ball.

When I was a student I never had this problem. As a football player I had gone entire seasons without ever touching the ball—and footballs are so much larger than baseballs. So I didn't even bother bringing a baseball glove to umpire school. Of course, I knew I couldn't catch, anyway. When we played they would stick me in right field and then make a rule: No hitting to right field.

Joe Brinkman had been a fine college athlete, and he had trouble making the transition from player to umpire—even after he owned the school. "During a session in California I was managing one team and John McSherry was managing the other. Without realizing I was doing it, I really got into the game," Brinkman said. "We were losing and had a runner on third base. I thought their pitcher was balking, but I couldn't get the umpire to call it. I was screaming at him. Of course, McSherry was yelling from the other side, 'Don't listen to him. I'm your instructor.'

" 'Yeah, but it's my school!' I'd shout back. Later in the game one of the students on my team hit a long fly ball that clearly bounced over the fence. 'Home run!' I screamed, and by that time I had the umpire so intimidated he actually called it a home run. McSherry went crazy, while I sat calmly on my bench. As an instructor, I was appalled; as an umpire, I was embarrassed; but as a manager, I was absolutely thrilled.

"It was unbelievable. Winning that game had actually become important to me. I was hollering at the umpire, trying to gain the slightest advantage, just like one of the $#%@¢#$%s."

The hardest movement to master on the field is the incredible pivot. Because students are being trained to work in amateur baseball or in the minor leagues, where usually only two umpires work a game, they have to learn how to spin around in the infield on one foot. Anyone with the dexterity of a ballet dancer can pick this up right away. Everybody else gets to fall on their face a few dozen times. Each night in the dorm hallways, as students tried to learn how to pivot, you'd hear a thump or a splat, then "Oommph" or "Oowww."

The last few weeks of the course are the most difficult mentally, because the instructors try to give the students a slight taste of what they can expect in professional ball. They scream and curse at the kids, kick dirt on them, push them around, challenge them to fights, and do all the other things that make umpiring the wholesome profession it is. Everybody who has been through the course has some idea how to call balls and strikes and safes and outs or knows when a pitcher is balking or how to fill out the basic forms—but learning how and when to argue is a vital part of the curriculum. Brinkman teaches that if you give a man the right answer you might not have to eject him. If you say, "I made the call and that's the way it's going to stand," you'll be okay. But if you say, "I think I got it right," you're going to have problems.

"Umpires aren't supposed to think," he says, "they're supposed to know. Any umpire who believes a manager or player has come out to politely discuss the situation is going to have problems. If an umpire believes in reasoning with them, he's gone."

Eric Gregg, presently one of only two black umpires in the National League, proved his ability to take abuse in school. The instructors poured it on, and Gregg didn't blink twice. "I'm black, poor, and from the ghetto," he told them. "You don't think I've heard the word @%#&$% before?"

Probably the most difficult pieces of equipment students had to learn how to use were the outside chest protector, known as the balloon or the mattress, and the ball-strike indicator. The mattress used to be mandatory for all American League umpires, while the National League used the inside protector, which is strapped to the body and worn beneath the coat. Since students might eventually work in either league, they had to learn how to work with both protectors.

Basically, the mattress is held in place by sticking both arms through shoulder straps, then grasping a handle near the bottom. Whenever the home plate umpire had to move away from the plate he was supposed to swiftly slip off the protector and gracefully tuck it under his left arm and run with it. As complicated as that sounds, it was much more difficult to actually do it. There was no way to look coordinated with that thing. Perhaps because I had extensive experience with football equipment, I never actually tripped over it. But I was fortunate. The first few weeks of school, students would spend much of the night walking up and down the halls taking it off and putting it on and falling over it, and taking it off and putting it on and walking into a wall, and taking it off and putting it on and smacking into other students trying to learn how to pivot.

One of my students came up with the most ingenious way of discarding a protector I've ever seen. During a school game the base umpire went running to the outfield to cover a fly ball. When this happens the home plate umpire is supposed to tuck the mattress under his arm and call any plays on the bases. This student simply flipped the protector straight back over his head and left it lying there on the ground. It might not have been correct, but it was creative.

The best I've ever seen at handling the outside protector was Harry Wendlestedt. He looked like he had been born with that big balloon attached to his chest. Naturally, he was purchased by the National League and never used it.

Compared to conquering the outside protector, learning to use the ball-strike indicator was easy.

Of course, compared to mastering that mattress, catching Nolan Ryan's fast ball with a boxing glove was easy. When I started school I didn't even know what an indicator was. It looked more like a little plastic toy than anything else. I figured anything that small had to be easy to handle and fun to play with. (Later in my career I made the same mistake about Earl Weaver.) The indicator is a piece of plastic shaped to fit comfortably in the palm of the left hand. It contains three plastic wheels with numbers on them that are rotated to keep count of balls, strikes, and outs. It is made for the left hand because the right hand is raised to signal strikes and outs, and if umpires held the indicator in that hand they would undoubtedly be throwing it all over the field.

An indicator is really a small scoreboard. The thumb is used to move the strike counter, the extended index finger registers balls, and the pinkie moves the out wheel. Rather, the pinkie is supposed to move the out wheel. No human being has ever had a left pinkie strong enough to move the out wheel. How do you strengthen your pinkie? Move the out wheel. How do you move the out wheel? Strengthen your pinkie. If you ever desire to drive an umpire insane, or more insane, just put one drop of glue on the out wheel of his indicator and watch what happens when he tries to register an out.

There are umpires who work for years without becoming comfortable with the indicator. Students always had a tough time getting used to it. We used to tell them to learn how to use it by registering their steps as they walked around the dormitory. And every night those students not falling over practicing their pivots or tripping over the outside protectors were trying to learn how to use their indicators by counting their steps—and bumping into people spinning onto the floor or trying to stick their legs through an arm strap.

I was never very good with an indicator. I had pulled a tendon in my pinkie playing football and it never healed right, so for 15 years I was never really sure how many outs there were. In the minor leagues I learned that I could never, ever depend on the scoreboard to have the correct count. The visiting team's best hitter would come to bat and before the first pitch I'd glance at the scoreboard: two strikes! Or the high school kid operating it was studying for an organic chemistry test between pitches. On occasion I did lose track of the count or number of outs during a game. I might have had a difficult call on the previous play or pitch and was still thinking about it, a manager might have come out to argue and I let him distract me, maybe I was hit by a foul ball and was in pain, or maybe I just forgot. Whenever I lost the count I'd pray for a foul ball because the batter couldn't walk or be struck out, then I'd immediately challenge the batter or catcher, demanding, "I'll bet you don't even know the count." If someone asked me the count or number of outs and I wasn't sure I had it right, I'd reply sarcastically, "Now, how should I know that? You know how dumb umpires are." Or, "I'm only a rookie and they never tell me anything." Or I'd shake my head in disdain and sigh, then say, "How do you expect to be successful in this game if you can't even keep track of the count?"

Another thing umpire school students had trouble with was taking off the big steel mask. This was supposed to be done with two fingers of the left hand, because anyone holding the mask in his right hand while calling an out could easily smack a sliding ballplayer on the head with it. The tricky part about taking off the mask was that the umpire's hat was not supposed to come off with it. Because the straps of the mask fit over the hat, accomplishing this move is similar to pulling a tablecloth out from beneath a set table without disturbing the wine. We always had a few students in the hallway at night learning how to take off the mask without their hat falling over their eyes, bumping into people pirouetting onto the floor on top of people falling over their balloons who tripped over people counting their steps with an indicator. That was one dangerous hallway.

Nick Bremigan could never understand why students couldn't keep their hats on and was constantly threatening to tack them on. I remember one student, the son of a minister, who was so determined to keep his hat on his head that he actually glued it on with Super Glue. It stayed on all day, all night, when he took his mask off, when he took a shower, through hurricanes, tornadoes. . . . When the hat started to mildew, he finally had to cut his hair to get it off. The day after he did, Bremigan was on him again.

Although umpire school requires a tremendous amount of hard work, it can also be an enjoyable, memorable experience—as long as you don't let the instructors intimidate you and you pay no attention at all to the curfew. My roommate at Sommers School was an ex-ballplayer. While I spent the first few nights trying to figure out the protector, he went out. Finally, I asked him where he was going. "To an antiques auction," he told me. "Gee," I said, "I don't know much about antiques, but I'd love to learn." He invited me to go with him the next night.

Turns out his idea of an antique was a woman over twenty-five. Whenever the instructors asked us why we had missed curfew the previous night, we would tell them we'd gone to an auction to bid on an item and it had been auctioned off very late. The important thing to remember was to always come back to the school with a vase or a candelabrum, or, as we did one night, with a wine bottle with candle drippings all over it, from a restaurant that served very old pasta.

As with any large group, there are always some

people who don't fit in, and there are occasional problems like theft or turning over somebody's van and pushing it down the side of a hill into the river. Durwood Merrill remembers being asleep one night when the door to his room opened and policemen came in with flashlights, looking for a stolen wallet. "I was watching them and saying to myself, I'm a married man, I've been a successful football coach and the assistant principal of a high school. Now, here I am at umpire school for one week and they're about to take my fingerprints and a mug shot."

Eric Gregg's class had a gentleman bandit. One day a student from Venezuela screamed he had been robbed. He claimed he'd had four twenty-dollar bills in his wallet and somebody had taken them and in their place left eight ten-dollar bills. Eric knew that victim was going to make a fine umpire.

The most exciting moment for every student is his first real game. The schools have arrangements with local high school and semipro leagues, and when spring training starts the best students are sent to major league camps to work the early games. John McSherry remembers walking toward home plate at Tigertown, in Lakeland, Florida, feeling confident that he and his partner could handle the game—until he looked into the Tiger dugout and saw his partner getting the Tiger manager's autograph.

I also worked my first game at Tigertown, not because I was an outstanding student but rather because I had played pro football with the Detroit Lions. Spike Briggs owned both the Lions and the Tigers, and had paid my football salary for two seasons. This was his chance to get even.

I really felt umpire school had prepared me for this day. I'd learned how to use the protector, indicator, and mask, I missed only two questions on the final rules exam, I could pivot on a quarter, I had great size, and I really sounded pretty confident when I shouted, "YOU! SECOND BASE!" Unfortunately, there was an overflowing crowd for the game and they had strung a rope across the outfield. People without seats were going to sit behind it. Nowhere in school did anybody say anything about a rope with people behind it. People were supposed to be in the stands. At the pregame meeting at home plate the Tiger manager said, "Okay, we've got to make a special rule for the people on the field." A special rule? I hadn't even used the regular ones yet! We finally agreed that any ball hit into the crowd on a fly was a home run, but if someone reached over or under the rope and touched a ball in play it would be a double.

I was working the bases, so it would be my call. Naturally, in an early inning somebody hit a line drive, rope high into the fans. I didn't know if it had been touched before or after it went past the rope. Maybe it was a double, maybe it was a home run. Maybe it was the end of my career if I made the wrong call. So I did the best thing under the circumstances. Nothing. I didn't make any call. That turned out to be the right decision. The hitter trotted into second and stopped, and the home plate umpire threw a new ball to the pitcher, and we started playing from there. "Hey," I thought, "this is easier than I thought."

Usually, of the 150 or more people who start the umpire school class, less than 20 get jobs in professional baseball directly out of school. But before that first season is over at least another 20 would be hired to replace those people who did get jobs, then learned that being yelled at was not for them and quit. Because almost all minor league umpires are hired out of school, many students who don't get a job at the end of the first session return for a second time. Or third time. Take Kenny Kaiser, for instance. He failed to get a job out of school—twice. And both times he was hired after students who did get jobs quit. Although Kenny claims he won the Least Likely to Succeed in Anything trophy at the end of each session, he was always a good umpire and worked hard to become possibly the best ball-strike umpire in the big leagues today. His problems early in his career stemmed from the way he handled people on the field. His idea of a convincing argument was a body slam.

Some of the most important things a student learns in school are not found in the rulebook or taught on the field. They are the practical lessons passed along from the veteran instructors to their students, the facts of life as an umpire. Perhaps the ten most important things every young umpire should know are:

1. Always cash your paycheck the day you get it, particularly in the minor leagues.
2. Never kill a spider in your dressing room. This has nothing to do with superstitions. Spiders will eat all the other bugs that live in umpires' dressing rooms. Exceptions to this rule are made for all poisonous spiders and any spider with legs over three inches long.
3. During an argument, never clean home plate while the manager is still on the field. (This is known as the "Weaver Doctrine.") If a manager covers home plate with dirt and you clean it while he is within kicking distance, he will cover it again. Every time you clean it, he will cover it. Do not clean it until he is safely in the dugout, preferably in the clubhouse.
4. During an argument, always stand on the in-field grass—or the infield plastic in those ball-parks with artificial surfaces. This is to prevent dirt being kicked on your uniform. American Leaguer Dale Ford claims Jim Frey taught him this when Frey was managing Kansas City. The Royals were playing the Yankees, and Frey started complaining on every pitch. Ford had no choice but to eject him from the game. "When I did," he remembers, "Frey charged out of the

dugout at me. I knew he was a student of Earl Weaver's, so I expected him to try to kick dirt at me. I moved onto the infield grass. He started kicking, but the best he could do was raise a wisp of dust. I could see he was getting very frustrated. Finally, he began scraping together a pathetic little pile of dirt, but while he was doing that I maneuvered around so that I was standing between him and Yankee catcher Barry Foote. When Frey drew back his foot for the big kick, I stepped to the side, and he just covered Foote. Foote started kicking right back, and I let them go at it."

5. During an argument, never respond to the question "What did he say?" This is a trick question. After an umpire has ejected a player for abusive language the manager will invariably ask exactly what it was the player said. If the umpire replies, "He said I was a dumb %#$@&%*¢," the manager will undoubtedly reply, "Well, he sure got that one right."

6. During an argument, move as close as possible to the stands. Whenever a player is ejected, the umpire has to file an ejection report with the league office. It is always beneficial to be able to write in that report, "The player swore audible to the stands." At school, we would teach students how to ease over near the stands. Of course, the first time someone came out to argue with them, they'd put their heads down and run over to the stands as fast as they could.

Doug Harvey, the veteran National Leaguer, is considered the umpire's umpire. But when he was in the California League, C-ball, the home team had a runner on third with one out. The batter hit a short pop-up. In anger, he flipped his bat. Trying to avoid the bat, Harvey accidentally pushed the catcher away from the plate. The runner on third saw this and scored after the catch. Harvey felt he had caused the problem so he ordered the runner back to third. The manager of the home team came out and started yelling.

Harvey had seen the wife of the team's owner in the stands and wandered toward her seat. The manager was screaming a stream of obscenities at him. He leaned on the fence and listened, then asked the owner's wife, "Can you believe the manager of your team would use language like that?"

The manager was so incensed he refused to leave the field when Doug ejected him. Instead, he stood on home plate and would not move. Finally, Harvey ordered the batter into the batter's box and directed the pitcher to throw. The pitcher hesitated, but when Harvey ordered him to pitch a second time, he whistled one right by the manager's head.

"Strike one!" Harvey called. Two seconds later the manager was in the clubhouse.

7. Never, ever refer to a manager or a player as a "good guy." This is similar to lighting a match to see if there is gasoline in the fuel tank, or being foolhardy enough to comment out loud that there is no traffic while driving home from the beach on a sunny Sunday afternoon. Historically, absolutely every time an umpire has called a manager or a player a "good guy" he has had to throw that person out of the game the next time they were together.

8. Always clean home plate with your back to the pitcher. Bill Klem once instituted this as a rule for National League umpires, supposedly as a courtesy to the fans, but the real reason is that the umpire does not want to be embarrassed when he bends over to clean the plate and splits his pants, which he will, he will.

9. Don't eat meatloaf before a game; don't eat meatloaf after a game.

10. Don't drink any water, ever.

There are additional hints that will be helpful, such as always carry your wallet on the field so people will know who you are in case of an accident, and never eat at any restaurant called "Mom's," but these are the ten guaranteed to make an umpire's life easier.

Finishing umpire school is only the end of the beginning. But with perseverance, ability, and luck, the student who is willing to work unbelievably long hours under poor conditions and take incredible abuse can end up just like me: overweight and looking for a good job.

TWO

THE DENVER HAMBURGER

Whenever an umpire settles down to reminisce about his career, he will invariably begin with the six most accurate words in the English language: It wasn't funny at the time. Basically, that describes life in the minor leagues.

Every professional umpire starts in the minor leagues; most of them finish there. For an umpire, life in most minor leagues consists mainly of long automobile drives between small towns to work games under lighting too dim to brighten a porch, dressing in closets, sleeping in hotel rooms so small that if you eat in the room and gain weight you can't get out, and surviving on cold hot dogs and warm soda. There is an old saying I've recently made up that says an umpire who lasts five years in the minor leagues deserves to be immortalized; an umpire who lasts ten years deserves to be institutionalized.

Kenny Kaiser spent thirteen years in the minors.

Describing Kenny Kaiser's road to the major leagues as a rocky one is something like calling the Grand Canyon a drainage ditch. Kenny was in trouble from his first day in professional baseball. Actually, it was the night before his first day. He may hold the record as being the only player, coach, manager, or umpire to be fined by a league president *before* being in his first game.

The night before he was to work his first professional game, in the Class D Florida State League, he discovered a pool hall across the street from his hotel. "I was just a young kid," he explains, "but I was a pretty good pool player. I asked this guy for a game, and he agreed, and one thing led to another and he hit me with his cue and cracked my rib. I did the only thing I could do, I hit him over the head with the table. How could I have known he was the catcher for the Cardinals' farm club? George McDonald, the league president, fined me twenty-five dollars and warned me that if I threw one more pool table he was going to send me home."

For an umpire, the only really good thing about the minor leagues is the memories. The players and managers are all trying desperately to get to the major leagues, and every call an umpire makes is going to hold back half of them. The ball parks are small and the playing fields are terrible. But worst of all are the hometown fans. Minor league fans are serious about their local teams. American League umpire Rocky Roe summed it up by noting, "You've had a great night if they're not waiting for you after the game with tar and feathers."

Which brings us back to Kenny Kaiser. After a colorful season in the Florida State League, he was fired. The next season he was hired by the Class D Western Carolina League. The Western Carolina League was tough on umpires—once, in fact, its entire staff quit on the same day.

Kaiser's first day in that league, he admits, was the closest he ever came to being killed. "I had not met the man I was to work with that season before I got there, and he came to the hotel to pick me up. I heard a knock and opened the door, but I still couldn't see any light. I realized it was being blocked out by the biggest man I'd ever seen, about six-ten, two hundred seventy-five pounds. 'I'm your partner,' he said.

"I said, 'Anything you say is all right with me.' I was only nineteen years old and serious about making it to twenty.

" 'Get your bags,' he told me. I said, 'Yes, sir,' and carried them to the car. We drove to Greenville, South Carolina, to work our first game. On the way down we spoke about a lot of things and I could see he wasn't too happy with life. Hey, he wasn't too happy, I wasn't too happy.

"He was going to work home plate that night and I was on the bases. Normally, before the season starts, the umpires shake hands with the opposing managers and wish them luck. After our pregame meeting one of the managers stuck out his hand and my partner said, 'I don't shake hands with managers.' Right then I knew it was going to be a long season. I just didn't realize it was going to be a long season that night.

"It took me about three innings to figure out that my partner was not a great umpire, but I knew I was not going to break that news to him. We had a 1–1 game going into the ninth inning. In the top of the ninth a runner from the visiting team tried to score on a short fly ball. I thought he was out by maybe twenty feet, but my partner called him safe. That was good enough for me. In the bottom of the ninth inning, with two out, a Greenville runner tried to score on a base hit and looked safe to me, but then again, I'm not six-ten. My partner called him out, and the runner went crazy. He jumped up yelling and stood face to chest with my partner. Finally my partner said softly, 'Get out of my way, boy.' The runner continued arguing. 'Get out of my way, boy,' my partner repeated. The Greenville player said he wasn't moving. That was probably a mistake. My partner shrugged and hit him with a short left, breaking his nose. There was blood all over the place. I guess that was actually the start of the riot.

"We managed to fight our way to the dressing room. As soon as we got inside I started piling suitcases, equipment, benches, anything I could find, in front of the door. While I was doing this my partner calmly got undressed and got into the shower. 'I'll wait till you're finished,' I told him.

"Greenville's manager started banging on the door, shouting, 'He hit my ballplayer, lemme in there.' This man was about six-six, two-fifty himself. I didn't want him in there. My partner was still trying to take a shower and I think all the noise was disturbing him. 'Open the door,' he said. 'Yes, sir,' I answered and quickly removed the suitcases, equipment, and benches and opened the door.

"The manager and about six other men stormed in. 'Where is he?' the manager demanded. I pointed to the shower. He walked over there and ripped open the curtain. That was probably a mistake, too. My partner leveled him. The six guys carried him out and as soon as they got out the door I piled the suitcases equipment, and benches behind it again. I never knew baseball could be this exciting.

"By this time a large crowd had gathered outside the door and I could hear parts of things they were threatening—words like 'tar' and 'too good for them.' My partner finally finished his shower. He went over to his overnight bag and pulled out a .45. I thought he was going to shoot me. Instead, he took two shots at the top of the door, put two very big round holes right in the top of it. 'Get the bags,' he said. 'Let's go.'

"I opened the door. There wasn't a person within twenty-five miles. But when we got near our car, I noticed five state police cars surrounding it. 'This is it,' I thought, 'I've read about what happens in these small towns. Fifteen years on the road gang.' I swore if I got out of this I would never umpire another game. Umpire? I wouldn't even go to a city that had a ball park. A state policeman came over to me and said, 'We're gonna help you get out of this, boy.'

They put two police cars in front of us and two behind us—and behind them were eighty-seven cars and trucks.

"My partner was whistling as we drove along, but I guess he noticed I was disturbed. 'Oh, don't worry about them,' he told me. 'They're just trying to scare us.'

"It certainly was working.

"When we reached the state line the trooper in front of us got out of his car and leaned in the window of our car. 'All right, boys,' he drawled, 'I'll tell you what I'm gonna do. I'm gonna give you a five-minute head start, then I'm gonna let them people come.'

"I was feeling pretty wonderful about being alive, so I told the trooper how much I appreciated everything he had done for us.

" 'Don't thank me, son,' he said. 'If I wasn't working today I'd be right at the head of that pack.'

"The next day my partner was fired and I was transferred to the New York–Penn League."

Just about every umpire who has spent time in the minor leagues has at least one riot to his credit. Durwood Merrill remembers the night in Amarillo, Texas, when some fans broke down the door to the umpires' dressing room to register a complaint about a call that had cost their team the game. "There were about twenty-five of them, and right in the front was this woman. She was threatening the worst things of all. I knew if there was a fight one of two things were going to happen: Either I was gonna get hurt, or I was gonna get hurt bad. There was just no way we could get through them. Finally, I walked up to this woman's husband. I had a towel wrapped around me, and said to him, 'Maybe I'm gonna get hurt, but I'm gonna take you with me. You ain't gonna get out of this alive either.'

"He looked me right in the eye, and I believe he knew I was serious. Then he grabbed that woman's arm and said, 'C'mon, honey, let's get out of here. These @$#$#%#s aren't worth the trouble.'

"I didn't know whether to be pleased or insulted. But he pushed her out the door and that crowd dispersed."

Of course, that was probably better than the night Durwood was in Bakersfield, in the Class C California League, and somebody snapped closed a lock on the umpires' room after a game, trapping him and his partner inside. They hollered and pleaded for almost three hours before a night watchman cut off the lock to free them. Then they discovered some fans had let the air out of all four tires on their car.

Joe Brinkman didn't have a real riot his first season in professional ball, although he did get punched in the mouth after a game one night by the father of the losing pitcher. And the first night Davey Phillips's family and future wife saw him work, his partner did open somebody's skull with his mask and was beaten up by an entire team.

But minor league baseball is not just good times.

At some point, most minor league umpires will have to deal with every conceivable situation—as well as many inconceivable situations. A game in Wilmington, North Carolina, once had to be called on account of whale, for example. A fan spotted the whale surfacing offshore and the rest of the fans, as well as the players, left the field to see it. And veteran minor league umpire Dick Phillips was working in the Class C Sunset League in the West when a home run ball became an out at second base after hitting and killing a nighthawk. A major league umpire may never have to deal with whales or nighthawks, but he will have to know how to handle unusual situations without having the ball park collapse around him, and he gets that experience in the minor leagues.

Many of the problems a minor league umpire faces are caused by poor facilities. Because the own-

ers of farm clubs, particularly in the lower classifications, do not make enough money to properly
maintain their ball parks, the conditions are often
terrible.

Joe Brinkman got into trouble one night in A-ball
because the ground crew, the town wino, had laid
down what might best be described as creative foul
lines. A ball that would ordinarily have been fair
landed outside an S-curve in the line, and Joe called
it foul, leading to a long argument.

Jim McKean had a near riot in Rochester when
Orioles farmhand Jim Fuller, batting with the bases
loaded, hit a long drive that disappeared through a
hole in the fence. "People were running all over the
place and there was no ball," McKean remembers.
"Now I know it should have been a ground-rule
double, but at that time I'd never seen anything
like it." McKean ended up putting Fuller on second,
then ejecting him and his manager, Joe Altobelli,
for demanding a home run.

Davey Phillips was working home plate in the
Class D Midwest League when a batter hit a 400-foot
shot into the darkness. It sailed over the left-centerfield fence, hit a telephone pole, and bounced back to
the shortstop, who tagged the runner out.

Rain is always a problem in the minor leagues
because few clubs can afford a tarpaulin that covers
more than the pitcher's mound and the home-plate
area. Doug Harvey had a game in which part of the
outfield was so saturated it had to be roped off.
Doug suggested calling it a water hazard and penalizing anyone who hit into it two strokes, but instead the home team decided it would be a ground-
rule double.

In order to get a game in after two days of rain
in Spokane, management soaked the infield with
gasoline, then set it on fire to burn the field dry.
Larry Herndon was catching that night and Eric
Gregg was calling balls and strikes. "The fumes
were unbelievably strong," Herndon recalls. "After

the first hitter made out I stood up and said, 'Eric, this is ridiculous, I can barely breathe.' Eric was huge then, really big, and he said, 'Yeah, I'm not feeling so good either. Let's just try to finish the inning.'

"So I got down into position and gave the pitcher a sign. Suddenly, wham! The whole world fell on top of me. All of Eric Gregg had just passed out and keeled over on my back." That remains the only baseball game called because of gas fumes.

One of the minor league umpire's greatest adventures is opening the door to the umpires' room. There is no way of knowing who or what will come walking, flying, or crawling out. Actually, the umpires' room is misnamed. These spaces were never intended to be used by umpires and they never have any room. This is the very last place the owner of a minor league team is going to spend any money. When automobile manufacturers did away with running boards they eliminated most of the better minor league dressing rooms.

Usually, umpires dress in areas not suitable for any other purpose because they are too small, too difficult to reach, or too dangerous to be in. Many are tiny spaces next to the boiler room or just behind the rest rooms. About the only advantage to the two-man system used in the lower classifications is that three men could not fit into most of these rooms at the same time.

A classy dressing room was one that had hooks on which to hang your clothes, rather than rusted nails hammered into the wall. The shower was rarely more than a nozzle, and one of the umpires usually had to dress beneath it. Most of the time it leaked. I was damp for entire seasons. I never left my clothes in these rooms because of the insects. If I left a pair of my size 15 shoes sitting there, by the time the game was over something would have nested in them.

Eric Gregg had to share his first minor league

dressing room with ducks. This was an old shed next to a duck pond and it had a hole in the wall, so ducks were constantly walking in and out. To get to the field from this duck room, Eric had to climb over the left-field fence.

Doug Harvey killed twenty-eight black widow spiders in the umpires' room in Bakersfield one night, then marched into the general manager's office and told him he was going to dress right there.

For Doug, that was only an introduction to minor league baseball. By the time the season ended he wasn't sure if he was learning how to be an umpire or a veterinarian. Doug Harvey's Wild Kingdom began in Bakersfield a few weeks after the spiders incident. "I was working the bases when an infielder called time out and pointed to this large furry thing walking across the field. I thought it was a beaver or something. I nudged it with my foot, trying to get it to move a little faster. It turned around and I was suddenly looking at the biggest teeth I had ever seen. It was a rat maybe two feet long, and it snapped at me.

"The infielder said to me, 'You gotta get him off the field.' Naturally, I laughed. Then I told him, 'Don't look at me, kid, I'm no big-game hunter.'

"Ray Perry, manager of the Reno club, came out with a first baseman's glove, picked this rat up, and carried it off the field. That still remains the best move I've ever seen a manager make.

"Two weeks later I was in San Jose and I was beginning to wonder about this . . . spiders, rats. Again I'm working the bases, and suddenly I hear the first baseman screaming, 'Whoa! Time!' And there is a jackrabbit running in from right field. The first baseman spooked him and he ran toward second, then made a sharp left and headed for third. This was the most incredible thing I've ever seen; the jackrabbit ran the bases in the correct order—twice. Then someone on the San Jose club sailed his glove across the field and hit the rabbit. The rabbit rolled over twice, then turned around and whang! It took off and jumped over the right-field fence.

"Now I figured I'd seen just about everything. Turned out I figured wrong. Within a month I was working home plate in Las Vegas. It started raining and thundering and lightning and I called time out and cleared the field. The wind started swirling and just ripped a hole out of the left-field fence. Then the field lights went out, leaving only the dim emergency lights in the stands. I knew we weren't going to play anymore, but according to the rules I had to wait thirty minutes before calling the game. As I was sitting in the dugout waiting, there was a great flash of lightning, and in that instant I saw this beautiful white stallion run through the hole in the fence. 'That's it,' I said. 'Game's over. No way am I waiting thirty minutes.' I knew then I had seen everything. After spiders, rats, rabbits, and stallions, what could a Giant or a Cardinal do to me?"

Ducks in the dressing room, horses in the outfield, why would any sane person put up with these things? The dream is the same for umpires in the minor leagues as it is for players and managers. The big leagues. Beautiful, well-lit ball parks in great cities, filled with thousands of live fans. Real dressing rooms, warm hot dogs. Like every other umpire in the minors, I used to read the obituary column in *The Sporting News* every week in hopes some umpire in the classification above mine had died.

And the minor leagues do prepare an umpire for the majors. He has seen horses in the outfield, whales in the bay, fans breaking down the dressing room door, everything but pine tar on a bat. And he has been confronted with more complex situations in one season than he will see in his entire major league career. Minor league players are just as inexperienced and inconsistent as minor league umpires, and they make unbelievable mistakes. It is the ability to apply the correct rule in difficult situations, or at least fake it, that helps an umpire get to the major leagues and stay there.

Rocky Roe, for example, had the bases one night during his first year in A-ball. Young Ricky Henderson was on first base. Henderson took off for second, the catcher made a tremendous throw to beat him, the shortstop caught the throw and put his glove down to make the tag. Henderson came sliding into the base—and with his spikes pinned the shortstop's glove to the base. The shortstop lifted up his hand, leaving his glove—with the ball still in it—wedged between Henderson's foot and second base. "I could see this was going to be a problem," Rocky says.

"Henderson, seeing the glove on the ground, immediately put his other foot on the base and I called him safe. That brought Stump Merrill, the manager of the other team, running onto the field. 'How can you make that call?' he screamed at me.

" 'Well, Stumpy,' I told him, 'unless they've changed the rules in the last few weeks, when a fielder comes up after making a tag he'd better have a piece of leather on the other end of that appendage.' When I said 'appendage' that sort of confused him a bit, because he asked me what I was talking about. I said, 'He's gotta have control of the ball.' Stump looked, and the glove was just lying there in the dirt, the ball still nestled in the pocket. He shrugged, turned around, and walked back to the dugout shaking his head."

Chuck Cottier, now a coach with Seattle, was managing Clinton, Iowa, when he witnessed one of those bizarre plays that give umpires nightmares. Perhaps the most difficult call for a major league umpire is the trap play in the outfield; in the minor leagues, with inadequate lighting in most outfields, it can be an impossible call. Cottier's Clinton team had the bases loaded with one out. Arturo Bonito, his center fielder, was the runner on second. The batter hit a looping fly ball into the darkness, and all the runners took off. The runner on third scored, Bonito rounded third and headed home, the runner from first base was on his heels, the batter was racing into second. Then the third baseman screamed, "He caught it!" Cottier was coaching at third, and he remembers it being like someone had put a movie projector in reverse. "Everybody turned around and started racing back. When everything settled down, three of my players were standing on third base and the batter was on second. I looked at these three guys and tried to think of something helpful to say. Then Bonito sized up the situation and pow! He took off across the infield toward first base. He ran right over the pitcher's mound and slid into the base, just beating the throw. So we were a little better off, we had two men on third, the batter on second, and the runner who started on second on first. I didn't have the slightest idea what was going on, so I figured the umpires didn't either.

"Finally they called it a double play. They called Bonito and the batter third out. I have no doubt that if there hadn't been any outs in the inning they would have called it a triple play. Heck, if they needed four outs they could have found them somewhere on that play.

"After the game I sat down with Arturo and asked him, if he had started on second, how did he end up on first on a double? He said, 'Chuck, I looked around. We had three men on third, one man on second, and nobody on first. I figured maybe they would forget where I started!' "

Cottier wanted to protest the game but gave up after trying unsuccessfully to write out a protest report.

Ray Miller, now the Orioles' pitching coach, was on the mound in Dubuque, Iowa, when he helped test an umpire. Again the bases were loaded. The batter hit a grounder back to Miller, who fired a one-hopper to the catcher to force the runner on third. Just as his throw got there the runner slammed into the catcher. The umpire looked on the ground for the ball and couldn't spot it, so he couldn't call the runner safe; then he looked in the catcher's glove—it wasn't there either—so he couldn't call him out. For about one second everybody stood absolutely still, then the whole field erupted.

The catcher knew he didn't have the ball, so he got up and started searching for it. The base runners, seeing the catcher looking around frantically, took off. Miller came running in to try to find the ball. The runner from second slid across the plate. The runner from first slid across the plate. Then Miller saw the ball—in the collision at the plate the first runner had slashed a hole in the catcher's pants with his spikes, and the ball had gone into the pants. So as the hitter was rounding third trying for an inside-the-pants home run, Miller was grabbing the catcher. Eventually the plate umpire allowed all runners to advance only one base from their position at the time the first part of the play was made, quoting the rule that states, "Time shall be called when the ball lodges in the catcher's mask or paraphernalia and all runners shall be permitted to advance without liability one base from their position when the first part of the play was made." That satisfied both managers.

This is a perfect application of the Bluff Rule, which every umpire must learn in the minor leagues. In fact, no such rule exists. The ball should have remained in play, in the catcher's pants. Years ago a casebook of unusual plays was included at the back of the rulebook. This situation was covered in that. The casebook was extremely helpful to umpires, so naturally it was discontinued.

One of the first things an umpire will learn in the minor leagues is that the managers and players don't know the rulebook at all, which makes the Bluff Rule all the more important. Julio Cruz, for example, the fine second baseman, learned his baseball on the streets and sandlots of the Bronx, New

York. During his first season in the minor leagues he was leading off second base when the pitcher suddenly whirled around and fired to the shortstop. It was a tricky move, but legal. Julio didn't budge. "Oh, no," he yelled, "in stickball they don't move around like that!" The umpire called him out, but Julio insisted that move was illegal in the Bronx.

Umpires are going to make mistakes in the minor leagues; that is an important part of the learning process. Because I knew I was smart enough not to make the same mistake twice, I spent most of my minor league career trying to make every mistake once. There are managers who will tell you I succeeded. But every umpire makes mistakes. Nick Bremigan, for example, was not born holding the official rulebook. In fact, he may be the only umpire who called the same player out twice on the same play.

The bases were loaded with no outs. Bremigan was working third base in a three-umpire system. The batter slashed a hard grounder to third. The third baseman caught the ball, then stepped on third to force the runner coming from second, then fired home. The catcher dived and tagged the sliding runner for the second out. Meanwhile, the runner coming from second had rounded third base too far and the catcher whipped the ball back to third. Bremigan was right on top of the play. Instinctively, he called the runner out.

Again.

In the middle of all this action, Nick overlooked the fact that this runner had already been put out on the force. He had done exactly what he was supposed to do: On the original part of the play he watched the third baseman touch the bag, so he never saw the runner coming from second, then moved around the base to get the best possible angle if the runner from first kept coming and there was a play at third. This is what is properly called "a learning experience."

Every one of these plays had something in common: They all resulted in an argument. Unusual plays always lead to arguments and ejections, while usual plays lead to arguments and ejections only some of the time. Learning how to run the ball game, meaning how to survive an argument with a manager, coach, player, spectator, club owner, or passerby, may be the most valuable lesson an umpire has learned in the minors. One thing is for certain: He will have plenty of learning opportunities.

Sometimes it's easy to decide what to do—the manager or player does something so blatant he just has to go. When Steve Boros was managing Waterloo in A-ball, he objected to an umpire's decision by coming out of his dugout carrying a folded-up sign, walking across the field in the middle of the game, and tacking it to the scoreboard in the outfield. Then he stepped aside for everyone to see what he had written: The scoreboard read Appleton 2, Waterloo 1, Umpires 1. Now, that man just had to go.

The National League's Joe West had no choice but to run Joc Sparks, a fiery minor league manager, before the game began in Iowa City one night. West and Sparks had had some problems the night before, but Sparks was polite when he came out to exchange lists of starting lineups. In a friendly manner, he asked West where the umpires were staying while in town. West told him it was a Holiday Inn. "Figures," Sparks replied. "That's the only place in town with braille numbers in the elevator." Throwing Sparks out of the game was as easy as dumping Frank Lucchesi the night he ripped up third base and wouldn't give it back, then tried to climb the flagpole in center field.

If an umpire is going to survive, he has to establish his authority. The moment he appears indecisive or allows a manager or player to show him up, he's finished. He's as vulnerable as the rich sky-diver who allows his only heir to pack his parachute.

Paul Nickoli, one of my partners in the minors, handled a tough situation as well as anyone. About the only thing Paul and I had in common was a dislike for Earl Weaver. Earl has brought a lot of people together that way. One night when Nickoli was working with Davey Phillips, Nickoli had an argument with Weaver and ejected him. Weaver refused to leave. Nickoli gave him ten seconds to get off the field, then counted by fives. Then he ordered Weaver's pitcher, Gene Braebender, to pitch.

Weaver ordered him not to pitch.

Nickoli shrugged, then stepped behind the plate. Braebender was standing on the mound, caught between a rock and a hard face. "Ball one," Nickoli called. "Ball two" . . . Braebender was getting desperate to pitch.

"He can't do this!" Weaver yelled to him.

"Ball four, take your base," Nickoli said. The next batter stepped up. "Ball one . . ."

Earl finally realized Nickoli intended to walk the ball park and left. I'd like to say that this lesson changed Earl, that after this he realized that umpires have a difficult job and did his best to work with them in harmony. But then this book would be fiction.

The object is to throw out the right people at the right time, and that is not as easy as it sounds. Ejecting that first player is very traumatic, because you feel you've lost control, but the fortieth man is simple—by that point you just don't care. Throwing people out of a game is like learning to ride a bicycle—once you get the hang of it, it can be a lot of fun. Most minor league umpires, in fact, go through a period where they throw out people too quickly.

When veteran American Leaguer George Maloney was working in Orlando, in the Class D Florida State League, he and his partner once ejected so many players the game ended in a forfeit. "The teams had a twenty-man roster," George remembers.

"We had a close play at first and the entire Orlando team charged us, so we started picking them off. By the time we'd finished we'd run nine of them. That left eleven. Then an Orlando player got hurt. That left ten. What I didn't know is that somebody had to take that player to the hospital, leaving nine. So when I got the center fielder the next inning we had no choice but to call the game."

It doesn't take long to get used to the power. I liked it. There were times I imagined how nice it would be to have the same power off the field. I thought it would be fun to be walking down a crowded street and say to somebody, "You! You're off the sidewalk."

The theory is that good umpires will eventually learn the difference between right and gone. Sometimes, however, the line between them is thin. Perhaps the most important thing to a minor league umpire is food. He is not paid enough to eat well, or often, and he comes to depend on the warm hot dogs delivered to the umpires' room by the home team after the game. The hungry umpire is the tough umpire.

Eric Gregg and his partner were in Cocoa Beach, Florida, and they were hungry. Cocoa Beach was making a pitching change, and Eric's partner wandered down to the bullpen. The players in the bullpen were eating hot dogs and popcorn, drinking sodas, smoking cigarettes, just like real life. Eric's partner looked at the players forlornly, then gently asked for one small bite of a hot dog.

The player with the hot dog refused.

Eric's partner asked again, this time a little more forcefully. Again the player refused. This was not gold he was asking for, it was one bite of a hot dog . . . a hot dog with loads of mustard and sauerkraut and relish. Finally, the umpire warned the player, "Give me a bite of that hot dog or you're gone." The player stood up and refused—and was immediately ejected for eating in the bullpen.

Probably the one thing no umpire will ever forgive Billy Martin for took place when he was managing Denver. Usually, at the end of every game there, umpires found a big hamburger waiting for them. Among umpires, Denver was known for that hamburger.

One night Jerry Dale had the plate. In the late innings of a tie game Martin started complaining over almost every pitch. He was shouting the usual clever remarks umpires hear all the time: "Punch a hole in that mask" and "He couldn't have hit that pitch with a ladder." Finally, Jerry booted him. Then Martin came out and really let him have it. Jerry remembered his schooling and stood near the stands so he could write in his report to the league president that Martin's language was "audible to the stands." Finally, Billy departed.

The game went fourteen innings. Denver lost. As Dale and his crew walked toward the gate leading to the umpires' room he saw Martin standing there with his arms crossed. Oh, gees, Jerry thought, now I'm gonna have to go through another battle just to get off the field. But Martin never said a word. In fact, he smiled.

Dale found out why when he reached the umpires' room. The hamburgers were gone. Billy had stolen the umpires' hamburgers! Cursing, kicking dirt, throwing equipment, smashing water coolers, climbing flagpoles is one thing . . . but stealing the Denver hamburgers? Martin was a marked manager.

Before the game the following night there was a knock at the umpires' room door, and Billy Martin asked permission to come in. He entered and stood there sheepishly, then apologized—not for complaining, not for his abusive language—but for stealing the hamburgers. There was a manager who had realized the way to an umpire's strike zone is through his stomach. The umpires graciously accepted his apology, although, in truth, they would have preferred a platter of hamburgers with ketchup and onions.

As umpires get more confident in their ejections, they each begin to develop a personal style. Eventually, most umpires draw a line in their mind, and any player or manager who goes over the line gets ejected. It can be a curse word, a motion, an offensive nickname. The important thing is to establish that line, let the managers and players know what it is, and be consistent. For example, anyone who mentioned my weight was gone. "Fatso" was the key word, but it got so that any word starting with "fa" was close enough. Durwood Merrill actually drew his line on the field, which I thought was innovative.

He was working in Evansville in the Triple-A American Association with Stevie Palermo, when manager Fred Hatfield came out for a heated discussion. Durwood let Hatfield have his say, then suggested he go back to the dugout. Hatfield had more to say. And even more. Finally, Durwood had heard enough. He picked up a bat and drew a line in the dirt, then warned Hatfield he would be ejected if he crossed that line. This was an old but effective technique first used by old Bill Klem.

Hatfield was a little too smart for any umpire. He decided to go around the line. Durwood was too quick for him. Before Hatfield could move Durwood drew a second line in the dirt at a right angle to the first and warned him again. Hatfield turned the other way. Durwood drew a third line. Finally, before Hatfield could retreat, Durwood cut behind him and completed the box.

When Hatfield stepped out of the box, Durwood ejected him.

By the time an umpire has reached Triple-A, he has at least learned how to maintain control. The growth of Kenny Kaiser is a perfect example. He was a gun in the low minors, throwing out anybody who looked at him with both eyes simultaneously.

Once, when he was in A-ball, the public-address announcer told the crowd after a close call at home plate, "The score is Lynchburg 1, Salem 1, Kaiser 1." Kenny then ejected the entire pressbox. Everybody went; the public-address man, sportswriters, maintenance people, electricians, everybody who laughed at the joke. But only a decade later he had calmed down considerably. He had learned to think before reacting.

In Pawtucket one night Kenny called a runner out for interference going into second base. Joe Morgan, the manager, came out to put his two cents in. Kenny listened, then offered some change. Morgan did not appreciate that. "You didn't even see the play," he complained. "I'm gonna show you what the runner did."

"Uh, don't do it, Joe," Kenny warned.

"I'm gonna show you," Morgan repeated, backing up about thirty feet.

"Please, Joe, don't do it," Kenny repeated.

Morgan ignored him. He took off for second and made a beautiful slide into the bag. "There," he said, "that's how he did it!"

"You're sure?" Kenny asked. Morgan nodded. "Good," Kenny told him. "Then I got it right. Now you're both out. He's out on the play and you're out of the ball game."

Not all arguments in the minor leagues end with the manager or player ejected. Sometimes they just have their say and leave. At other times, on a few memorable occasions, they don't even have their say. Spencer Abbott was the minor league version of Earl Weaver. Abbott's bouts with umpires were legendary. Once, when he was managing the old Kansas City Blues, his team was trailing by a run in the ninth inning but had the bases loaded with two out. The count was three balls, no strikes on his hitter. The opposing pitcher went into his stretch, then whirled and picked the runner off first to end the game. Abbott was incensed by the umpire's call. He leaped off the bench—and smashed his head against the concrete roof of the dugout. He knocked himself out cold. By the time he was revived, the umpires were long gone.

A similar thing happened to Chuck Cottier when he was managing in the New York–Pennsylvania League. Eric Gregg called Cottier's runner out on a close play at third base. "I knew Chuck was going to be coming after me," Eric recalls, "so I took a deep breath and got ready to meet him. I was already angry. I had made a good call and he was going to try to burn me. Sure enough, here he comes. He started running out of the dugout, but before he got up any momentum he tripped over the bat rack and broke his leg. I was really sympathetic. I went after him. He was lying there on the ground and I started screaming, 'Get up and argue like a man!' Then I threw him out of the game. I just loved it."

Later in both their careers, Cottier's leg healed sufficiently for him to become Gregg's first major league ejection.

These arguments are really not funny at the time they occur, and the riots aren't funny, and the hotels are ridiculous, and the food is usually tasteless—and when it does have taste it's bad. That's why most minor league umpires consider quitting at some point in their careers.

For me, it came after my fourth season. I had just had it with the minor leagues. But Barney Deary told me to stay with it a while longer, promising me that if my contract was not purchased by a major league he'd find a job for me in the Umpire Development Program. Fortunately—for the Umpire Development Program—the American League bought me at the end of the following season.

Rocky Roe almost quit his first month in professional ball. He worked Lakeland against Winter Haven six nights in a row and had long arguments each night. "Finally," he remembers, "I asked my partner, 'Is it like this every night? Maybe I'd better think about making a career move!' "

Durwood Merrill had his crisis in the California League. Fresno had a Japanese pitcher on the mound and a 14–2 lead in late innings. The other team had runners on first and third. "All of a sudden," Durwood recalls, "this pitcher faked a throw to third, leaped straight into the air, whirled around, and threw to first. I had never seen anything like it before. I didn't even have the regular balk rules down yet and he was showing me a double gainer. Who was he kidding, besides me? I figured he would've picked me off, so it had to be a balk. Fresno's manager came out and let me have it. 'I don't know where they found you,' he said, 'and I don't know where you've been, but I can tell you where you're going. Nowhere. You'd better find yourself another profession.'

"I ran him out of the ball game, but I kept thinking, maybe he's right, maybe I'm not very good at this. It took me a long time to get my confidence back. I'll tell you, I was lucky I was a little older or I would've quit. You take kids nineteen or twenty years old just out of umpire school and throw them up against these grizzled old baseball people that've been around for twenty years and they'll just carve 'em up neat as a Thanksgiving turkey. That's why there's such a big turnover of umpires in the low minors every season."

The thing that keeps most umpires going in the minor leagues is their partner. A partner can make or break a young umpire. If two guys work well together, they really believe that they can conquer the world, or at least a minor league baseball team. "I was a terrible umpire my first season in A-ball," Jim McKean admits, "and the managers were all over me. Once I threw Woody Smith, a veteran manager, out of the game. He got dressed and sat in the stands, and I threw him out of the

stands. Then after the game he came to the umpires'
room and I threw him out of there, slamming the
door on his hand as he left. That was just an average day. But I was working with Nick Bremigan and
he was always there when I let things get out of
control. I believe that if it wasn't for him, I would've
gone home. There were times when things got so
bad I started to pack my bags and he would tell me
I was crazy. I mean, I knew that was true, otherwise I wouldn't have been there in the first place.
But without his support I believe I would have gone
home."

Of course, it's a good thing that Jim never realized he was listening to someone just as crazy as he
was.

Davey Phillips feels working with veteran umpire Frannie Walsh helped make him a major leaguer.
Frannie was as tough an umpire who ever called a
game. He had two years in the National League and
a lot of years in the minors. Davey was with him
one day in Little Rock when Walsh, working the
plate, called a strike on a half swing. Vern Rapp,
Little Rock's manager, questioned the call, and
Frannie looked to Davey for confirmation. Davey
nodded his head, meaning the batter had swung.
Rapp yelled at Phillips, "Yeah, you didn't see it
either."

Before Davey could open his mouth to reply,
Walsh stormed over to the dugout and pointed a
warning finger at Rapp. "You got something to say,
say it to me, you hear?"

Rapp replied that he hadn't been talking to
him.

"Well, I'm talking to you, Rapp."

"But, Frannie, if I say anything to you, you'll
run me."

Frannie took that as a compliment. "You bet
your life I will," he said, smiling. But by taking all
the abuse, he let Davey concentrate on becoming a
better umpire.

Of course, the following season Davey had a lot of Frannie's confidence, but he didn't have Frannie. One afternoon in Richmond Davey tried to eject Rochester's first base coach, Herm Starett, for arguing on a strike call, and Starett refused to leave.

At first Davey didn't know what to do. Everybody he'd ejected throughout his minor league career had left. Then he looked over toward the stands where two friends of his, Richmond police officers, were watching the game. He whistled to get their attention. "Fellows!" he shouted, waving them onto the field. As soon as Starett saw them coming he departed quietly. I guess he figured that a seventh-inning stretch is one thing—and a two-year stretch is something else.

In the minors, umpires don't just work together, they live together. They drive from city to city together, eat meals together, share hotel rooms . . . and get to know each other's smallest habit. Eric Gregg and Steve Palermo worked together one season in the New York–Pennsylvania League. Steve's family lived in the area, and the two young umpires would often stay at his house after a game to save expenses. "Stevie had so much ability even then," Eric remembers, "but he was so intense. He couldn't bear to make a mistake. Usually, after a game, we'd get to his house and his sister or mother would make us a big, hot dinner. I mean real, human food. But whenever Steve felt he had had a bad game, he wouldn't want to eat. He would just sit quietly, then get up and go to bed. If he wasn't going to eat, it made no sense to prepare a whole dinner, so I'd just have a sandwich.

"So we'd be driving back after a game and I'd finally get up enough courage to ask, 'Well, what'd you think?' I knew my dinner depended on his answer. If he started to say something about it being a bad day, I'd interrupt, 'Bad day! Are you kidding? You were great out there.'

"He'd mention a play in the fifth inning and I'd

be thinking about my steak. 'What a call that was,' I'd tell him, 'a great call, and I loved the way you hustled into position to make it.' The reason Stevie became such a tremendous umpire is that he really worked hard at it, he was really dedicated. Of course, the reason I was so overweight when I came up to the majors was because I convinced Stevie he was such a good umpire."

As terrific as a season could be when teamed with the right partner, it could be worse than a bad marriage with the wrong person. Sometimes partners just don't jell. They might both be fine umpires, but instead of working well together they just missed, sort of like Abbott & Hardy. Sometimes they missed by a lot.

Joe Brinkman was a really tough kid when he started in the minor leagues. He had been a star athlete in the Army and still believed he could play better than some of the ballplayers he was watching. He had what is known as a "short fuse," meaning he did not take a lot of abuse. One night, for example, a pitcher was complaining about his ball-strike calls, so Joe decided he would never call another strike for that pitcher. He told the batters not to swing and called every pitch a ball.

Unfortunately, Joe ended up with an extremely religious partner one season. He was a good man, but his interests were exactly opposite Brinkman's. Joe would be trying to go to sleep at night and his partner would be reading the Bible aloud or reciting the rosary. After a few months of this, Joe was thinking about requesting a transfer. Then one night they were driving from Columbus, Georgia, to Asheville, North Carolina, in the Blue Ridge Mountains. They were on a curving mountain road and Joe was asleep in the passenger seat. Suddenly he heard his partner scream, "I can't hold it, Joe!" and the car went off the road.

"I opened my eyes just as we swerved by the guardrail by about two inches," he recalls, "and then we headed straight down that mountain. I thought this was it for me. We were completely out of control, skidding around trees, barely missing boulders, about to flip over. Finally we hit an embankment, and the car got jammed right between two huge trees. I couldn't have picked that car up and placed it between those trees. I just couldn't believe we were alive.

"That night I made it to the game on time, but my partner was late. At the pregame meeting one of the managers asked me where he was. 'He's in church,' I told him, 'and if you say one word about it I'll throw your $@#%$ %$@¢$ outta here!' "

A few seasons later Brinkman did ask for a transfer. "I tried everything to get along with my partner, but it just wasn't working. He wasn't a very good umpire and we were always in a jam. The final straw came one day at the pregame meeting at home plate. While the home team manager was reviewing the ground rules, my partner took his wallet out of his pocket and started passing around a wedding announcement. The two managers looked at it, but they had no idea what was going on. I didn't either, but nothing this guy did surprised me, so I was ready for anything. Finally he explained, 'That's my girlfriend. She's marrying my best friend today and I'm here umpiring this game, so please don't argue with me.' Everywhere we went for the next few weeks he made the managers read this tattered wedding announcement, and we didn't have any trouble. The guy was either insane or a genius. I just couldn't work with him."

To me, the mark of a good partner was someone who had a car and would do most of the driving. John McSherry and I lived together in Florida while we were working in the Instructional League. Between the two of us we topped six hundred pounds. I'm six-four, and John is about the same. We needed a car to drive to the ball parks, so we bought the most inexpensive thing we could find. It was a

Nash Metropolitan, sort of a tiny Volkswagen bug. We paid 95 bucks for it, cash. And it was worth every cent. We used to make a pop! sound when we squeezed out. That car was in such poor condition we couldn't make a left-hand turn—when we had to turn left one of us would climb out and kick the front tires to the left, then kick them straight after the turn. We always tried to plan our trips so we would make only right-hand turns.

At the end of the Instructional League season we just left that car on the street with the keys in it. We figured anybody who took it deserved it. But when we came back the following year it was parked exactly where I'd left it. I turned the key and it started. We used it again, and then left it on the street again. That was in 1967. So if anyone finds a Nash Metropolitan parked under a tree on Melrose Avenue in Lakeland, it belongs to John McSherry and me. But it will be all right with us if they keep it. Actually, it has to be all right—the car doesn't turn left.

The long drives between games may well be the most grueling aspect of life in the minor leagues. There's nothing like a little eight-hundred-mile jaunt between cities in the Texas League to really get an umpire excited about a game. Rocky Roe disliked driving as much as I did, but he decided to do something about it. He and his partner, Pete Calieri were driving from Reading, Pennsylvania, to Bristol, Connecticut. It was Calieri's car, so he did most of the driving. "We were coming into the New York City area," Rocky says, "which meant we were going to hit a lot of traffic. Pete said he was just too tired to drive any farther, so I told him I'd take over.

"I don't know what came over me, but I realized this was my opportunity to get out of driving for the rest of the season. So when Pete stretched out in the passenger seat I watched him out of the corner of my eye. Just as he was ready to fall asleep,

I yanked the car onto the shoulder of the road and screamed, 'Oh, no!'

"Well, Pete woke up. Somehow, I managed to wrestle the car to a stop. I sat there, both hands on the wheel, breathing as heavily as I could manage. 'Gee, I'm sorry, Pete,' I told him, 'but I can't seem to get the feel of your car.' That was the last time I drove that year."

Davey Phillips finally learned to live with Frannie Walsh's driving. Walsh would hold the wheel with a death grip, lean forward, and occasionally take his hands off the wheel to wipe the sweat off his brow. Watching this used to frighten Phillips, so he did the most practical thing under the circumstances—he leaned back, put his coat over his head, and went to sleep.

Naturally, Kenny Kaiser had the worst partner of all in the minor leagues. (Of course, many of Kaiser's partners in the minor leagues make the same claim.) Kenny was working in the Northern League and his partner that year had a dog, a big, friendly German shepherd, that traveled with them. "It was a nice dog, I liked him, but I just didn't know why he had to be around everywhere we went. He was there when we had dinner, and at night he used to sleep on the floor between us.

"One night I woke up and turned on the light. There, on the night table, was this marble. Looking at me. Only it wasn't a marble, it was a glass eye. I found out my partner was legally blind and the shepherd was his Seeing Eye dog. I didn't care that we had been getting into fights on the field every night, I expected that. What bothered me was just that this guy had been doing all the driving."

When the major leagues are scouting minor league umpires they look for knowledge and application of the rules, hustle, the ability to maintain control, a good appearance on the field, good judgment, and courage. Courage, the ability to make the tough call because it's the right call is the one

thing that can't be taught. An umpire either has it
or he doesn't, and without it he'll never be a good
umpire.

Eddie Montague proved early in his career that
he had enough of what is needed to make the major
leagues. During his first season of professional baseball he was in Modesto, California, working third
base in a Modesto–Reno game. The score was tied
in the bottom of the ninth inning, but Modesto had
loaded the bases with no outs. The batter hit a fly
ball to center field. Reno's center fielder caught it,
the runner on third tagged up and scored. Game's
over. The home team wins. Everybody goes home
happy. Then Reno appealed that the runner on third
base left third base before the ball was caught.

This is the kind of play that makes an umpire.
If Montague rejected the appeal he would get a mild
protest from Reno; if he called the runner out the
entire ball park would fall on top of him. But the
runner *had* left too soon in his judgment, so he
jerked his thumb into the air.

"It looked like an army attacking," he recalls.
"They came at me from everywhere. Modesto's manager, Tommy Burgess, called me every possible terrible name. Finally my partner, Bill Malone, jumped
in to help me. He got in front of Burgess, calmed
him down and warned him to stop screaming at
me. So Burgess started screaming at him. 'What're
you yelling at me for?' Malone demanded. 'Eddie's
the guy who made the call.'

"It got more complicated. The runner on second had gone to third on the play, and Reno wanted
him sent back to second. In fact, we really weren't
sure what to do, so we decided to go off by ourselves and get the situation straightened out. Everybody was screaming at us. Then Bill put his arm
around my shoulder and summed up life in the
minor leagues for me. 'Fast Eddie,' he said, 'it may
look like we are here on a beautiful afternoon in

Modesto, California, umpiring a baseball game—but where we really are is in the outhouse!' "

The most enduring lesson of all taught by life in the minor leagues is that an umpire has no friends. Most people become umpires believing that if they are honest in their hearts and fair in their judgment they will be respected by the managers and players and appreciated by the fans.

Oh, are they wrong.

The minor league umpire never can win. No matter what he does, he's wrong. Max Stone—"Mad Max," as he was affectionately known—was once given a day in his honor. On Max Stone Day in Lincoln, Nebraska, the ball club and fans chipped in to give him a used car with an eight-hundred-dollar lien on it. But he had earned it. One day he was working in the Western League and ended up ejecting a ballplayer. Just as he was ready to resume play, he got the ultimate vote of confidence from a fan: "Stone, I don't know what he called you, but if he called you what you is, you were right to throw him out of the game."

THREE

THE DICTATOR IS ALWAYS RIGHT

By 1967 I had worked my way up to the International League, just one major league umpire's broken leg away from the big leagues. I considered myself reasonably tough. I had been an All-American lineman on a football team that played in the Orange Bowl. I had played championship lacrosse with Jimmy Brown. I had gone head to stomach with Big Daddy Lipscomb in pro football and survived to tell the story to all the doctors and nurses in the hospital. And I had spent three years in various minor leagues with Earl Weaver. I thought I was ready for anything. Then the American League asked me to go to the Caribbean to umpire in a winter baseball league.

I laughed. I may be dumb, I told them, but I'm not stupid. They told me I was too big to get hurt; I told them my size just made me a bigger target.

American baseball is to Caribbean baseball as Tom Selleck is to Ken Kaiser. They have a few of the same parts, but they are arranged *so* differently. At the end of each American baseball season baseball officials ask top minor league umpires to work winter ball to "polish themselves up." "Finish themselves off" is what they really mean. Baseball in Latin America can be reduced to three basic tenets:

(1) The dictator is always right; (2) never argue with an armed outfielder, and (3) it's a good game if everybody leaves the ball park alive.

Supposedly, the way they laid out the baseball diamonds in Puerto Rico, the Dominican Republic, Venezuela, and Cuba was to put some veteran fans in the first row of seats and have them toss empty rum bottles as far as they could. The foul lines were put down two feet beyond the best throw. Nevertheless, Durwood Merrill claimed that after working two seasons in the Dominican Republic he could tell the difference between a bottle of Don Q and a bottle of Ron Rico by the sounds they made whistling past his ear.

Probably the most important thing that working in winter ball does accomplish for an umpire is to make him really appreciate life in the American minor leagues. After a season in the Caribbean an umpire will accept just about any sort of treatment. You want to reduce my salary? Sure. Who wants money? Thousand-mile overnight drives? A pleasure. Food? Who needs to eat?

Joe Brinkman's introduction to winter ball in 1971 was typical. Three days before he was to fly to the Dominican Republic he received a letter warning him he was going to be assassinated. Either a leftist or a rightist revolutionary group did not want four Americans taking jobs away from local umpires and wrote that they would be killed when they arrived in Santo Domingo.

Because Brinkman's career as a minor league umpire had enabled him to build a savings account in the high single figures, he decided to go. The FBI was called in and met with the four Americans in Savannah, Georgia. Agents told the umpires that their plane would be met in Santo Domingo by U.S. government agents who would provide security.

The umpires' plane landed in the Dominican Republic in the middle of the night and, instead of pulling up to a terminal, parked on an unlit, deserted runway. The umpires sat there, waiting. And waiting. No agents showed up. Finally, and carefully, they got off the plane and immediately telephoned the American embassy. Brinkman explained that he was one of the four American umpires who had received the assassination threat and asked where they were supposed to meet the agents assigned to protect them.

Umpires? an official at the embassy asked. What agents? The official claimed to have no knowledge of any agents or umpires. He advised the group to check into their hotel and phone the embassy again from there. They did. Don't go out alone, the official suggested. They didn't; they didn't go out at all.

That night another State Department official told them it would probably be safe for them to go to a nearby restaurant to get something to eat. "What should we watch out for?" Brinkman asked. "The hot sauce," the official said.

The restaurant, The Lucky Seven, was about three blocks from the hotel. After a full meal and some drinks, they were beginning to feel a bit more relaxed and made all the usual jokes about being kidnaped, tortured, and killed. By the time they were ready to leave the restaurant, they were laughing at their earlier nervousness. A light breeze had started blowing as they walked outside. Suddenly some tree leaves parted and, almost in unison, they spotted a man with a rifle on horseback. They dived onto the sidewalk, burying their heads in their arms, waiting for the first shots.

There were no shots. The local citizens just walked around the four Americans lying on the sidewalk without paying too much attention. Gradually, the umpires summoned enough courage to crawl forward a few feet—and behind the tree found the statue of the revolutionary rifleman on horseback.

Eventually, they learned, U.S. government agents

had been keeping them under surveillance—but from a safe distance.

It did not take Brinkman long to learn that Caribbean baseball is played under different rules from American baseball. Tommy Lasorda, for example, is one of the most popular figures in Latin baseball. But one day he had committed a terrible sin—he was managing the visiting team. It had been a relatively quiet game; the umpires had only been forced to gather around second base—out of range of the fruits and bottles being thrown at them from the stands—once, and it hadn't been necessary to call the armed soldiers out of the dugouts onto the field. Then, in a crucial situation in a late inning, a home-team batter hit a routine ground ball to shortstop and was thrown out easily at first base. But umpire Pete Caron, who had worked in the Caribbean before, called him safe. Brinkman couldn't believe it. Lasorda came out to argue and Caron told him, "I may be an umpire. I may look stupid. But I'm smart enough to want to get out of this country alive."

This line of reasoning made a great deal of sense to Brinkman. Sometime later he was working with Caron, Terry Cooney, and Richie Garcia. There were about thirty thousand people in the ball park, meaning there were about forty thousand weapons. It turned out to be a tough game, and by the late innings the umpires had ejected about ten players, among them local heroes such as Orlando Cepeda, Rico Carty, and Jay Alou. Charlie Sands, a major league catcher at that time, told Brinkman, "You guys are crazy. You've thrown out all the stars. If they don't play, these fans are gonna be really upset. They might even come and get you guys."

"TIME!" Brinkman called, then declared a general amnesty. He allowed every ejected player to be put back in the game.

"You can't do that," Garcia told him.

"Watch me," Brinkman replied.

Eventually, Joe Brinkman claims, he got to like working in the Caribbean because he couldn't understand a word the fans were yelling at him and there was always a line of armed soldiers between the umpires and the fans. And, except for the day the fans climbed over the barbed-wire fences and started throwing rocks, breaking his big toe, he had very little trouble.

Dale Ford's introduction to Latin baseball was similar. In Puerto Rico, every game is a celebration. The fans dress in their team's colors, mariachi bands wander among the crowd, everybody has something to throw at the players and umpires, people dance in the aisles and on dugout roofs, and in one city a woman sprays the home-team players with holy water. Everybody has a great time. Okay, the people who get shot probably don't have a great time.

Dale made his debut in Puerto Rico at first base. Nick Bremigan, who had worked in the country the season before, was at second base. In the fourth inning of the Opening Day game two fans behind first base suddenly leaped up and pulled pistols. Everyone around them scattered. They exchanged shots and one of them was hit. Within minutes stretcher-bearers arrived and carried away the wounded man. The rest of the fans quickly returned to their seats and continued cheering as if nothing unusual had happened. Dale Ford could not believe he had actually witnessed a shooting and the game hadn't even been halted. It was beginning to occur to him that umpiring in Puerto Rico was not the vacation it was supposed to be. Finally he walked over to Bremigan, who didn't seem bothered by the incident. "Uh, Nick," Dale asked, "how often does this sort of thing happen?"

Nick shrugged. "You've got nothing to worry about, Dale," he explained. "They've got a city ordinance down here . . . it's illegal to shoot toward a sporting event." Then he turned around and walked back toward his position.

For many people living in poverty in some of these countries, baseball is the most important thing in their lives, and local ballplayers and managers are practically worshiped. The first year Doug Harvey was in Puerto Rico he worked a game at Luis Olmo Stadium. He might have anticipated some problems—Luis Olmo was managing one of the teams. The playing field was about 430 feet down both foul lines, but the outfield fence cut straight across so that it was only about 260 feet to straight-away center field. Harvey was working first base, Herman Schmidt was at third base, and Ishmael Guasp, was behind the plate.

Olmo's team was winning by a run in the eighth inning when their best hitter drove a long, high fly ball to center. It looked like a home run. The batter went into his home run trot and just jogged around first. But the ball actually went higher than it did far, and it bounced off the top of the center-field fence. The outfielder played it well and threw the batter out at second on a close play. It is well known that in Puerto Rico, if you make a call against the home team, particularly against the home team managed by the man the stadium is named after, you can open a fruit stand. Apples, oranges, pineapples, rum bottles, game programs, shirts, everything came flying out of the stands at the umpires. Harvey, Schmidt, and Guasp gathered at second base until the barrage ended, then returned to their places and resumed play.

Unfortunately, in the top of the ninth inning, two more close plays went against Olmo's team, enabling the visitors to score twice and win the game. As soon as the last out was made, Olmo came racing onto the field screaming at Guasp. Harvey went over to help Guasp and, as he did, noticed the groundskeeper, a man in his late fifties, also walking toward the plate umpire. "That's all right," Doug thought, "the groundskeeper is supposed to be on the field after the game." Except this groundskeeper was about to slug Guasp from behind. Harvey tackled him before he could throw a punch. Instantly, the groundskeeper's son jumped into the fight, and Harvey turned around just in time to hit him in the nose with a forearm. Blood started spurting all over.

The fans were already incensed that Olmo's team had lost, and this was adding injury to insult. "The field was surrounded by a heavy chainlink fence," Harvey recalls, "and I looked out to left field and they had peeled it back like a piece of tinfoil. There had to be fifteen thousand people pouring out of the stands.

"I yelled for Schmidt and Guasp to stay with me and we got ready for the brawl. One of the fans took a swing at me with a two-by-four. I stuck my arm out—and that board just broke in half lengthwise. With all the adrenaline flowing inside my body I felt no pain, and the two-by-four didn't even bruise my arm. I was feeling pretty good, ready for anything they wanted to come after us with.

"That's when a piece of cement about eight inches in diameter went sailing by my head. I thought, 'Doug, these people are serious about this.' The adrenaline flowed out of my body and I realized we were in a tough situation. I didn't know how we were going to get out of there.

"Then I heard it. This booming voice from way above, this commanding voice ordering, 'GET BACK THERE!' I couldn't believe it. 'Did I really hear that?' I wondered. Everything stopped. Then I heard it again. 'I SAID, GET BACK THERE!' I thought I was hearing the voice of God. The crowd separated, opening a path for us.

"I looked up just in time to see the biggest hand I'd ever seen in my life go by my head. And then I saw Frank Howard standing behind me. Frank six-foot-eight-inch-two-hundred-ninety-pounds Howard. He put one arm around my shoulder and the other arm around Schmidt and Guasp and escorted us into our dressing room.

"The room had no roof, so we spent the next two hours pressed against the front wall because people were lobbing rocks and bottles at us. The police finally drove us safely out of town."

When George Maloney had his riot in Puerto Rico the police had to bring in a bus to get him and his partner, Frannie Walsh, out of the stadium. The umpires had to lie on the floor as the bus made its getaway, because the fans were shooting out the windows.

Unlike the U.S. minor leagues, where a home team victory usually guarantees the umpires safety, in the Caribbean a home team victory only makes the post-game riot more enjoyable. The fans there root for the home team and popular players on both sides. Kevin Walton is an excellent young umpire, and I would believe that even if he weren't my nephew. Kevin was working in Arecibo, in northwestern Puerto Rico. The visiting-team manager, Jose Pagan, the former Giants shortstop, has played on or managed just about every team in the country, so fans in every city love him. The game had progressed without serious incident, although right fielder Bobby Tate had been hit on the head with a rock and play had been halted twice to get fans off the light towers, until the bottom of the ninth inning. With the score tied, Mookie Wilson singled. The pitcher then walked two men to load the bases. The batter hit a chopper to shortstop, and Wilson raced home. The throw to the plate actually beat him, but catcher Ellie Rodriguez juggled the ball, and home plate umpire John Hershbeck called Wilson safe to end the game. But nobody else saw Rodriguez bobble the ball. Before Hershbeck could turn around, much of the world was coming after him. They were coming out of the dugout, over the fences, through the gates. He was just buried. And this was after the home team won! Everybody was upset because Pagan's team lost.

Finally, Hershbeck and Kevin Walton, my nephew, the excellent young umpire, managed to fight their way to the dugout. But just as they reached the entrance to the umpires' room and safety, they heard a loud bang, and a split second later Kevin was slammed backward by a thud to his shoulder. "John heard the bang and saw me clutch backward," Kevin Walton, my nephew, the excellent young umpire, explains. "He turned absolutely white and yanked me down, then dragged me into the locker room. I was in real pain. I didn't know what hit me. I could feel something oozing down my chest. 'You okay?' John screamed. 'You okay?' I didn't think I was. I thought I was dying. Finally we managed to get inside and get the door bolted, and I looked at my shoulder. A bright orange stain was spreading across the front of my chest.

" 'An orange,' John said, 'it's an orange.' I was sorry to disappoint him. It's hard to be a hero when somebody gets hit with an orange. What had happened, obviously, was that somebody had drilled me with it just as the firecracker exploded.

"Meanwhile, two thousand fans were banging on the door and throwing things against the walls. There was practically a battle taking place outside our dressing room, and we were in there laughing. We just wondered what would have happened if the home team had lost and the fans had *really* been angry."

Because my nephew, the fine young umpire Kevin Walton, spent more than one season in Puerto Rico, he had more than one riot. He was working a playoff game in Viamo with American umpires Tim McClellan and Steve Ripley and one native umpire. Viamo had finished first during regular-season play but was losing 3–1 in the bottom of the eighth inning to the team that finished fourth. A loss would eliminate them from the playoffs. This prospect did not please the local fans at all. With one out and Viamo runners on first and third, the batter hit a double-play ball. The play at first was close, and Viamo manager Art Howe snapped. He was bumping McClellan all over the field. Twenty minutes later, after the field had been cleared of rum bottles, orange peels, and managers, play was resumed.

With two out in the bottom of the ninth, Viamo's last batter hit a lazy fly to right field. McClellan took two steps toward the outfield, to make sure the fielder caught the ball, then stopped. "Am I crazy?" he wondered. He stuck his thumb up in the air and raced for the dugout. He was safely in the umpires' room before the right fielder caught the ball.

So the riot started. It was a good one as far as riots are rated. The fans were trying to break down the door, the umpires had piled everything they owned against it, and two policemen were trying to keep order. In the middle of all this, the native umpire picked up his bag, told the Americans that it had been nice working with them, and walked out of the room. The mob opened up for him, allowed him to walk past, then resumed the riot. Finally, the policemen had had enough. "One of them said to me," Kevin remembers, " 'Come on, let's go. We'll take you to your car.' I looked at these two cops, and I listened to the two thousand people outside ripping chairs out of the cement.

" 'Maybe we'll just wait a little longer,' I told them."

Additional police arrived and decided the umpires would be safer inside the visiting team's locker room. Since the mob was waiting outside the stadium, the police hustled Walton, McClellan, and Ripley through the doorway to the playing field and started walking them across the diamond. About a hundred fans had remained in their seats. Just as the umpires reached the pitcher's mound these people realized who they were and a split second later realized where they were going. The race began for the visiting team's locker room. The umpires barely beat these fans to the door, but some of the others went to get the rest of the rioters.

Inside the dressing room, the victorious team was pouring champagne over each other's heads, newspaper reporters were screaming questions at the players, the team owner and his entourage were moving about the room shaking hands, people were getting thrown in the showers, and the three umpires sat huddled in a corner while two thousand, one hundred fans tried to break down the door.

"By this time there were about thirty policemen with us," Kevin continues, "and they kept trying to convince us, 'Come on, you'll be fine.' Then, every time the door would open, we'd see an ocean of fans threatening to rip us apart. Finally, Steve Ripley said, 'I'm not going out there ever. I don't care how long I have to sit here. I'll stay here for days.' He kept asking, 'How do you say "I'm not going out there" in Spanish?'

"After an hour, the cops brought our car right to the entrance, linked arms, and made a cordon for us to get out. We ducked our heads and dived into our car. Six policemen on motorcycles with sirens whining led us out of there at full speed. We had an escort until we got ten miles out of town, then they let us go.

" 'Wow,' I kept thinking, 'that was some ball game!' "

In most games played in the Caribbean, two American umpires are teamed with two local umpires. Because these locals have to live in the country after the season, they try to be so fair that they often take both sides of an argument. These native umpires would make a call and, when the team the call went against came out to argue, change it. Then, when the other team complained about him changing his call, he would change it back again, then again, until the American umpires intervened and made a definitive ruling. Joe Brinkman remembers the night a native umpire kept changing his call until he was literally backed up against the outfield fence.

Since these local umpires are so easily intimidated, the American umpires rarely let them work home plate. One afternoon, at the end of the winter league season, Jim McKean and Mike Fitzgerald decided to make an exception for the noted Poopie Alazondo.

He was called Poopie because he was very short. He was also a very poor umpire. In view of what happened, both of these points are worth noting.

San Juan was to play Santurce on the nationally televised Sunday afternoon game. The final standings had already been determined, so the outcome had no importance. Poopie had been asking all season to work the plate, and McKean thought this would be a good time for it. He called the league president and asked permission to put Poopie behind the plate. "What can happen?" McKean asked.

After a meaningful pause, the president gave his permission. Then he wished them very good luck.

Frank Robinson was managing Santurce, and Les Moss was managing San Juan. Before the game McKean went to see Robinson, a man known to be rough on umpires. "I said, 'Frank, this is Poopie's hometown and he's been dying for this opportunity. The game has no meaning, so please, tell your players to just let him go. Whatever he calls, just leave him alone.' Frank agreed. Then I went to Les Moss and told him the same thing. And he agreed. So it actually looked like it was going to be okay. It did look that way."

At game time Poopie walked up confidently to home plate. The very first thing McKean heard was a fan behind first base yelling, "Get that Communist out of there!" "*Communist*?" McKean thought, "Frank Robinson *and* a Communist?" Hey, Poopie might be short, but not a Communist. He took a deep breath.

The first three innings passed quietly. Poopie did an adequate job, and Robinson hadn't said a word. "In the fourth inning," McKean recalls, "he made his first really bad call. He called a high pitch, I mean an over-the-batter's-head high pitch, a strike. For the first time I heard a few peeps out of Santurce's dugout. This situation is the real test of an umpire: Can you maintain your concentration when they start yelling at you? Unfortunately, Poopie couldn't.

"The next pitch bounced on the ground. 'Strike two!'

"I thought, 'Uh-oh, here we go.' Poopie's next call was just as bad, so I called time and walked slowly to the plate. 'Look, Poopie,' I told him, 'just concentrate on what you're doing. Take your time. Don't worry about those guys in the dugout, I'll take care of them. Just keep your mind on what's in front of you. Just the pitcher, the batter, and the catcher, nothing else. Got it?'

"Poopie looked at me and snapped, 'You jus' get back to your base. I take care of myself.'

" 'Why, you Commie,' I thought, 'here I'm giving you a break and you're yelling at me.'

"That was the beginning. Poopie didn't get another pitch right. Both dugouts were all over him on every pitch. But nothing they said bothered him, he just kept calling them wrong. Finally, in the fifth inning, he called Felix Millan out on another sky ball. Millan just dropped his bat on home plate and walked away. Poopie threw him out of the game.

"Then I looked over into the San Juan dugout and saw it. They had gotten a ladder somewhere and were holding it up so Poopie could see it. The point they were making was obvious—Poopie was so short he needed a ladder to see over the catcher's shoulder. I just knew Poopie was not going to react well to this.

"He did not. As soon as he saw the ladder, he went wild. He threw everybody in the dugout out of the game—the manager, coaches, all the players, even the trainer. The fans were going wild. I couldn't even hear myself think, which, under the circumstances, was probably a good thing. I was the one who had thought this was a good idea. I remembered asking the league president, 'What can happen?' Now I was finding out.

"Poopie ejected fifteen players besides the assorted managers and coaches. I walked in and got his attention and told him, 'Poopie, you can't throw out fifteen players. We need nine to play.'

" 'Game's over,' he told me. 'Game's over. We go home.'

" 'No, we don't,' I explained. The game was not yet official and there was a sizable crowd in the stands. If we allowed the forfeit San Juan would have to return all the ticket receipts. I went over to San Juan's dugout and told Les Moss, 'Give me nine, any nine you want. Send the rest of them home.' Moss did this and we started playing again.

"Frank Robinson had been remarkably quiet. But the following inning he came over to me and began yelling. 'You're starting to make a joke out of this game', he complained.

"I looked over at the San Juan dugout and saw Les Moss sitting there all by himself. 'No kidding, Frank,' I said.

"We still had two innings to go. I was praying, 'Please let the home team win so we don't have to play the last half inning.' Somehow we all survived. Even the fans were great, they understood the situation. I think they also knew Poopie would have cleared the park if they gave him a hard time. But that was the last game I know of that a local worked home plate in Puerto Rico."

Durwood Merrill decided during his first weeks on the island that managers, players, and fans would leave him alone if they thought he was crazier than they were. So he set out to prove that. He and his partner, Steve Palermo, both dyed their hair blond and let it grow long and shaggy. Durwood told everyone he was the wrestler Gorgeous George. Unfortunately, the blond dye in Palermo's hair turned orange. Actually, that may have added to the impression the two umpires were trying to create. When Durwood got in a jam he would say incredible things such as, "If you don't get out of here right now I'm gonna have to pull your lungs out of your chest." He found that this cut down on arguments.

One evening, though, he ejected a relief pitcher for taking too many warm-up throws after being warned to stop. Following the game the team's owner burst into the umpires' room with a drawn .45. Merrill and Palermo were scheduled to work in the same ball park the next night. The owner warned them not to show up.

"We'll be here," Palermo told him defiantly.

"Oh, no, we won't," Merrill told him intelligently.

They did return and worked the game without incident. They had been in the country too long to be frightened by a gun. Bullets, however, continued to scare them.

Players in the Caribbean, like the fans, take their fights seriously. They rarely mill around the pitcher's mound threatening each other. When pitcher Pat Underwood hit Benny Ayala in the back in retaliation for an earlier throwing incident, Ayala chased Underwood off the field, through the dugout, into the clubhouse and later followed him to his home. In fact, he'd probably still be chasing him if Underwood hadn't left the country the next day.

One night 175-pound Rick Dempsey went after 220-pound Jerry Johnson. Durwood Merrill got between them and tried to keep them apart. Now, which one of the three made the dumbest move? Durwood was doing his best to hold Johnson back while Dempsey was throwing long-range bombs. Suddenly Dempsey yelled, "Durwood, duck!" It sounded so ridiculous to Durwood that it made sense. He ducked, and Dempsey just blasted Johnson, knocking him down. Unfortunately, Johnson pulled Durwood down with him. "Durwood, get up!" Dempsey ordered, but Johnson was tripping all over him, and by the time Johnson got up, other players were there to hold him back.

Umpire Larry Young was working his final game in Puerto Rico after three seasons when Ishmael Okendo and Al Wiggins brawled. It took about eight players to separate the two of them. After being ejected, Okendo climbed into the left-field stands to wait until Wiggins came out to play left the next inning. Young tried to get a policeman to arrest Okendo, offering to swear out a complaint. After the game Okendo told reporters he wanted to kill Wiggins. And Wiggins wasn't even an umpire.

Nobody appreciates Caribbean baseball more than Tommy Lasorda, and no one is more appreciated there. He played in Cuba, the Dominican Republic, and Panama, then managed five seasons in the Dominican Republic. The people in those countries like him and respect him. He has become the kind of person who is able to get done whatever needs to be gotten done. When Eric Gregg met and married a Dominican citizen, for example, he had difficulty obtaining a visa for her to leave the country at the end of the winter league season. Officials at the American embassy told him it would take months, possibly a year for him to get that visa. The president of the league told him he might be able to get the necessary papers in two weeks. Tommy Lasorda got him the visa the next morning.

My mother, Josephine Teresa DiNunzio Luciano

of Endicott, New York, has an old Italian expression to describe a man who becomes as popular and powerful as Lasorda is in the Caribbean. A lucky bum, she would call him.

Tommy's introduction to Caribbean baseball took place in Cuba in the early 1950s. He was pitching, American umpire Tom Gorman was working the bases, and Cuban umpire Ormando Maistri was behind the plate. Before the game began, Gorman took Lasorda aside and told him, "This guy working behind the plate today? Don't get on him."

"The game began," Lasorda says, "and I threw a pitch that I thought had part of the plate. He called it a 'ball-a!' I thought it was a terrible call. So I started hollering at him. I just got all over him. But he never said a word, so I just assumed he didn't understand English.

"I threw the next pitch right down the heart of the plate. It just split the plate in half.

" 'Ball-a two!' Now I was really angry. I took about a dozen steps in toward home plate and gave it to him with both barrels. Maistri still didn't say a word. Finally he had had enough. He slowly took off his mask and started trudging toward me. When he was about five feet away, he stopped.

" 'Lasworda!' was the only word he said. Then he opened his jacket. There was the biggest pistol I had ever seen holstered inside his coat.

"I looked at that gun, I looked at him, I looked at that gun again, then I said, 'Maistri, you're the best damn umpire I've ever seen!' He nodded agreement, turned around, and trudged back behind the plate. I took a deep breath and started walking back to the pitcher's mound. The first thing I saw was Tom Gorman standing near second base grinning from ear to ear."

That was the beginning of Tommy Lasorda's education about baseball Caribbean style. He didn't earn his degree until 1970, however, his first year managing in the Dominican Republic.

The team he was managing was beating Santiago, in Santiago, by two runs in the bottom of the ninth. Doyle Alexander was pitching for him. With two outs, the Santiago hitter, Tom Solvario, hit a line drive over left fielder Von Joshua's head. The ball hit the fence and bounced back, and Joshua fired it into third base. The Dominican umpire at second base started twirling his index finger above his head, the signal for a home run. Alexander, Rico Carty, Tito Fuentes, and Lasorda converged on him. "How the @$#%%&%& can you call that a home run?" Lasorda demanded. Fifteen thousand Santiago fans were cheering as Solvario circled the bases.

"The player hit it out of the ball park," the second-base umpire replied in Spanish.

"Then where did Joshua get the ball to throw back in?" Lasorda asked.

The umpire thought about that for a moment, then replied, "He took it out of his pocket!"

Lasorda finally convinced him to ask for help from the American umpire working home plate, confident that this umpire would straighten out the situation. The American umpire shrugged and claimed he hadn't seen it. That was sort of like dropping a lighted match in a dry barn. "Why, you !#@$%&¢* needle-nose *&¢%!" Lasorda screamed, "I always knew you were a #$%¢%$# ump, that I knew, that was established a long @$ #%$¢%& time ago, but I never realized you were a gutless @$%&*$¢@! You are the biggest @#¢$#%#%$-¢%#*¢(##$#$@%#$ I've ever seen in my life. You haven't got the @$#%$¢%& guts to tell the truth. You know the $#%$¢&% ball bounced, you just don't want this crowd on you!"

Unfortunately for Lasorda, this umpire understood @$#%$¢%&. "All right, Lasorda," he said, "you're gone!"

Lasorda screamed, "You're @$#%$¢%& right I'm gone." Then he took off his hat and whipped it into the stands. Then he took off one spike and threw it as far as he could, then heaved another spike after it. He ripped off his shirt and threw that into the stands. Because he had pitched batting practice before the game he was not wearing a sweatshirt under his jersey, so he was standing there bare to the waist, wearing only pants and socks. He received a standing ovation as he marched to the clubhouse.

Alexander got the last out and Lasorda won, 2–1. He was in the shower room after the game, singing, joking with his players, when fifteen armed soldiers marched into the clubhouse. Tommy remembers thinking, "They must be visiting Carty or Fuentes," as if it were an everyday occurrence to have a platoon of soldiers with carbines drop by after the game to say hello. "Where's Lasorda?" the sergeant in charge demanded.

Naturally, his players did everything they could to protect him. "In the shower," about six men instantly replied.

"He walked into the shower room and said to me, 'Get your clothes, you're coming with us,' " Tommy remembers. "I thought Rico Carty or Jay Alou was having some fun with me, so I decided to go along with them. I got dressed and marched right out the clubhouse door with these soldiers. When we got outside there were twenty more soldiers waiting, and they had roped off an area leading to a patrol truck. I was beginning to think that this was some elaborate practical joke.

"They put me in the truck and drove me to the town jail. When we got there they escorted me into a small room. One of the directors of our club arrived within a few minutes and I thought this was all over. It had been a funny joke but, admittedly, it was starting to wear a little thin.

"The director started talking calmly with the

police captain, then their voices got a little higher, then they started screaming at each other. I felt like I was watching a tennis match, with me as the prize. By this time it was after midnight. After perhaps a half hour, the police captain called in a guard and made a motion of a man turning a key. My Spanish still wasn't perfect, but I knew what that meant. They were going to lock me up.

"Now, I knew these people took their baseball seriously, but this was getting ridiculous. I was fully prepared to admit that maybe it was a home run.

"They put me in a cell with five or six other people and locked it. This was the first time in my life I had ever been in a jail, even to visit someone, and I didn't like it one bit. I figured it would be just a little while before the team bus showed up to get me for the drive back to the capital, Santo Domingo. That would be the punch line to the joke. All of a sudden, this woman sitting on a bench against the back wall of my cell started shrieking. A guard came right over. I assumed he was going to make sure she was okay. Instead, he just knocked her out cold. *That* was the punch line.

"A few minutes later I heard a bus outside. It was the greatest sound I'd ever heard. They had come to get me. Then I heard Rico Carty's voice and I knew I wouldn't be in that cell too much longer. Rico was a national hero, and if anyone could get me released, it was him. Then I heard the bus leaving. I'm not that brilliant, but I knew I wasn't on it.

"I spent the night standing up in that cell. I wouldn't sit down. I had a lot of time to think, but the one thing I couldn't figure out was why I was in jail. Arguing with an umpire just isn't a criminal offense. Finally, the captain came to see me and I asked him what I was doing in jail. He explained that the General had been at the baseball game and had bet on Santiago. When he saw me arguing with the umpire he got upset that his manager didn't argue like that. So when I took my shirt off, he had me arrested for indecent exposure.

"I nodded. That made a lot of sense. I was in jail in the Dominican Republic for indecent exposure. I had come a long way in my baseball career, but this was an unexpected direction. Finally, one of the owners of the Santiago club arrived and got me out. The league president suspended me for two days, telling me, 'Lasorda, the whole country's talking about you.' 'Good,' I said, 'because then they're talking about baseball, not revolution.'

"The story became front-page news. For the rest of the season, every time I came out of the dugout, the fans would start yelling at me to take my shirt off again. Finally, on the last day of the season, I got into a really good argument with the umpire. I took off my hat and threw it into the stands. I took off one spike and threw it, then another. Then I grabbed the front of my shirt with both hands, like Superman, and paused. The fans were on their feet screaming, 'Take it off! Take it off.' I teased them for a minute, then ripped it right off my back—exposing the second shirt I was wearing beneath it. They just loved it. I loved it. I'm not sure how the General felt about it."

As Lasorda, and every other manager, player, or umpire who has worked in the Caribbean has learned, politics plays an important role in the baseball season. Traditionally, games are always canceled during a revolution and postponed for elections. Graig Nettles remembers winter league players in Venezuela being told to stay out of sight for almost a week during presidential elections. And Lasorda saw the Cuban government change hands twice, the first time when tanks rumbled through Havana as Batista overthrew the government, then again in 1959 when Castro overthrew Batista.

Preston Gomez was managing Havana in the

International League when Castro took over. "The celebration was supposed to begin at midnight," he explains, "and, unfortunately, our game with Rochester was a long one. At midnight, the soldiers in the ball park started shooting their automatic weapons in the air. I've never seen a field cleared quicker in my life. Frank Verdi, coaching at first base, was hit in the helmet by a falling bullet and started running around yelling, 'I got shot! I got shot!' Leo Cardenas at shortstop was hit by a ricochet. That became the first game I know to be called because of revolution."

Luckily, Castro was a baseball fan. The minor leagues' championship, the Little World Series, was played in Havana and Minneapolis that year. Castro came to every game in Cuba. The first night he sat in the right-field stands, the next night he sat behind first base, and for the final game he sat on the bench. Want to talk about pressure on an umpire? I'll guarantee you no close calls went against Havana. Smart umpires do not say "out" to a bearded guerrilla either.

That was not Fidel Castro's first time on a baseball field. Although he failed a tryout with the Washington Senators, he did pitch in professional baseball. Almost. In 1951 he was a well-known student leader. During a game in Cienfuegos, about three hundred university students started blaring horns and setting off firecrackers, then marched onto the field. Don Hoak, who later became the fiery leader of the Pittsburgh Pirates and Cincinnati Reds, was just getting ready to step into the batter's box.

Castro walked directly to the pitcher's mound and took the ball and glove from the pitcher. He was wearing a blousy white shirt, black trousers, and black suede shoes with pointy toes. He toed the rubber, went into his windup, and pitched. The other students stood along the foul lines cheering. Hoak stood nearby watching. Castro threw about six pitches, then indicated Hoak should step into the batter's box.

Hoak hesitated, then looked at the students. They wanted him to step up to bat. That was good enough for him. Castro threw an inside curve ball. Ormando Maistri, the umpire, one of the truly brave people of our time, called it a ball. Castro walked in a few steps and glared at Maistri. The students started jeering.

Maistri then told Hoak the next pitch was going to be a strike. That was not a prediction, it was a guarantee. It was a fast ball, head high, and inside. Hoak fouled it into the stands. The third pitch was another inside fast ball, and again Hoak fouled it off. That made two pitches too close for him. He stepped back and told Maistri, "Listen, I've got a good career and big money and big times ahead of me, and I'm not gonna let some silly punk in a pleated shirt throw at my skull. Get that idiot out of the game. If there's trouble, as long as I got a bat in my hands I'm not the only one who's gonna get hurt."

Maistri called the police onto the field to clear off the students. Riot clubs held at shoulder level, they pushed Castro and the student demonstrators back into the stands. Compared to Bill Veeck's Disco Night at Comiskey Park, it was no trouble at all.

However, I doubt Hoak would have been so defiant if Castro had already become dictator. Joe Pignatano was coaching in the Dominican Republic when Generalissimo Trujillo ruled that country. A pitcher named Smith, in the Phillies organization, hit Giants shortstop Andre Rodgers with a fast ball. The two of them fought briefly. Just as the fight ended, Trujillo's brother, accompanied by about forty soldiers, marched onto the field. He went first to the pitcher's mound and told Smith he was ejected from the game. Then he walked over to Rodgers and, without a word, slapped Rodgers across the cheek. Rodgers drew back his hand to hit back, and forty rifles were raised simultaneously.

Pignatano mostly remembers the colors of the shoes people were wearing during this incident, because as soon as he saw the soldiers raise their rifles he dived onto the ground and crawled quietly into the locker room.

Communication and transportation were always a problem for players and umpires in the Caribbean. George Maloney remembers being lost most of the time he spent in Puerto Rico. At game time he would be driving somewhere in the mountains, asking everyone he met, "Baseball place?"

Missing a game was a minor problem compared to that of Eric Gregg. Usually, after working a game in San Juan, Eric, Palermo, and Richie Garcia would relax at a bar that also sold rocking chairs; hence it became known as "the rocking chair place." One night, however, Eric left them to go to a party with some Puerto Ricans, making plans to join Garcia later at the rocking chair place. But when the time came to leave the party, Eric realized he did not know the actual name of the bar. "Rocking chair place?" he asked the people at the party. "Where?" They smiled. He smiled. They smiled. He pretended to be sitting in a rocking chair. They nodded, they seemed to understand. They brought him a rocking chair.

He wandered the streets of San Juan that night, looking for a familiar landmark, asking people, "Rocking chair place?" Everybody smiled. Nobody had the slightest idea what he was talking about. It took him a full day to find his way back to the hotel.

The Caribbean is not the only place outside the original forty-eight states where baseball is played, and in Japan, Taiwan, Germany, even Alaska there is one common element: The umpire always gets the blame. Many people have come to believe that

Japan is an umpire's paradise. Supposedly, the Japanese managers and players treat umpires with the respect due their honored position, bowing when handing over the starting lineups and discussing contested plays calmly and politely rather than screaming.

Not true. Not true at all. Not the slightest bit true. I have an original Rembrandt painting to sell to anyone who believes that; it's one of the rare ones on which he typed his signature. Japanese managers and ballplayers treat umpires worse than minor-league fans do. Arguments in Japan last so long that managers bring their players off the field to rest while they're making their point. And they have been known to punctuate their points with their fists.

It is possible, however, that they learned this behavior from American ballplayers. Don Zimmer played there in the mid-1960s and remembers seeing six-two-and-a-half Daryl Spencer turn around after a five-five umpire called him out on strikes, pick up that umpire by the mask, hold him in midair, and just shake him.

By now, the Japanese players have learned their lessons. When Davey Phillips was getting ready to go on an exhibition tour of Japan with the Kansas City Royals in 1981, he was warned that Japanese players will shove, kick, slap, and punch umpires. "I heard all of that stuff," he said. "I was going over there to have fun and represent American baseball, but I wasn't about to let anybody push me around."

In America, he explained, when a manager is making multiple changes in his lineup, he'll use hand signals to indicate that the substitutes will either bat in the same places as the people they're replacing— straight up—or that he is switching them in the batting order—flip-flop. The hand signals are used to save time and inform the people in the pressbox of the changes. Phillips believed this was

an international language. However, he also believed
in the essential goodness of man, the possibility of
peace on earth. . . .

Phillips was working the plate in Tokyo and he
called a Japanese hitter out on strikes. The batter
turned around and glared at him but didn't say a
word. Davey was purposefully even louder and more
demonstrative than usual, and the Japanese managers and players had left him alone. But just as the
next hitter started coming to the plate, Davey heard
Royals manager Dick Howser warning, "Watch out,
Dave, here he comes!" Phillips whirled around to
find the Tokyo Giants manager no more than five
feet away.

"I ripped off my mask," Davey explains, "and
screamed, 'Don't you take another step!' Then I
really laid into him good. I was boiling. I was doing
an excellent job and I wasn't going to let him argue
a strike call in front of fifty thousand people. Well,
he didn't say a word. I didn't give him a chance to
say a word. I just raked him up one side and down
the other. It was a truly remarkable performance.

"Finally he had had enough. He turned around
and walked back to his dugout. Never said one
word. Not that I would have understood one word
anyway. 'Yeah, go on, get back there,' I thought,
'and don't come out again.'

"I yanked my mask down and got into position
to call the next pitch. The hitter stepped up to the
plate and took a few practice swings. Only then did
I notice that he did not look familiar. That's when
reality began to hit me. 'Uh, John,' I said to Royals
catcher John Wathan, 'this, uh, this is a pinch-
hitter, isn't it?'

" 'Yep,' he said.

"I paused again, then sort of whispered, 'And
that's what the manager was trying to tell me,
wasn't it?' Unlike the U.S., Phillips suddenly realized,
Japanese managers tell the umpires they are mak-

ing changes. Or, as in this case, try to tell umpires they are making changes.

" 'Probably,' he said. I closed my eyes. Perhaps, it occurred to me right there, my future does not lie in foreign diplomacy."

In fairness, foreign players have just as much difficulty playing baseball in the United States as our players, managers, and umpires have in their country. It never surprised me that Spanish players had no idea what I was talking about because American players and managers were telling me for years that they couldn't understand me at all.

American managers often have difficulty conversing with their foreign ballplayers. Herman Franks was managing the San Francisco Giants when Japanese pitcher Masanori Murakami was with them. Franks complained that he was unable to talk to Murakami on the mound, so Willie Mays and Orlando Cepeda volunteered to tutor the pitcher. A few weeks after the lessons had begun, Franks walked slowly out to the mound to speak to Murakami. But before he opened his mouth, the young pitcher looked at him, smiled, and said politely, "Take a hike, fatso!"

When Mariners pitching coach Frank Funk was managing in the minor leagues, he had two Japanese players, a six-four first baseman and a five-ten pitcher. The first baseman carried a sword with him and practiced samurai movements with it in his hotel room. The pitcher had a fifth-degree black belt in karate. Funk remembers, "They understood enough English to know what I was talking about, and I understood enough martial arts to know that whatever they wanted to do was okay with me. When the pitcher had a bad game, he'd wait outside the team bus until everyone was aboard, then he'd stand in front and apologize to the whole team for his performance. The first baseman never apologized. It wasn't that he didn't make any mistakes, it's just that no one dared criticize a six-four first baseman who carried his own sword."

Eventually, though, those players who play baseball in countries other than their own learn enough of the local language to get by with more than hamburgers and tacos. Sometimes much more than get by. Dominican Republic natives Juan Marichal and Felipe and Matty Alou were with the San Francisco Giants when Generalissimo Trujillo was assassinated. One of the reporters traveling with the team was instructed to get comments from the three of them on the assassination. After questioning each of them, he cabled to his paper: "They say they didn't do it."

FOUR

WHERE THE @$#%# IS PIRATE CITY?

For a very few lucky umpires the years spent squinting under minor league lights, the riots of the winter leagues, the months of indigestion, the thousand hours of anxiety, the days and nights of loneliness and despair become worth it. One day the telephone rings and they are told that their contract has been purchased by the American or the National League. After a moment of complete disbelief, everybody's reaction is the same: satisfaction. Finally, I've made it. I'm going to the big leagues. Me.

Once the initial shock has passed, the second reaction sets in: "Me? Going to the major leagues? There must be some mistake. I've spent only eighteen years in the minors. I barely know the rules."

That feeling too passes, replaced by a strange sort of confidence: "If I'm good enough for the major leagues, those umpires can't be so good either, so I won't look too terrible."

Finally, though, all doubts disappear, and an indescribable feeling of happiness takes over. The umpire tells his family, friends, people he meets on the street, friends of people he meets on the street. Only then does the final thought take hold: "What if I screw up? It's not just Buffalo anymore. Now I'll be making a fool of myself in front of the whole country!"

Durwood Merrill was sleeping in a Wichita, Kansas, hotel room, waiting to work a game that night, when his call to the major leagues came. "Durwood," said a mellow voice, "This is Lee MacPhail [American League president]. How would you like to come to the big leagues?"

Durwood responded with the only reasonable answer. "Sure, Mr. MacPhail," he said, "and this is Dwight Eisenhower."

Rocky Roe and his partners had defied the oldest rule of minor league travel—there is no short cut between cities—and were lost on a wooden bridge, examining a map and trying to figure out what state they were in, when the announcer of the game on the car radio mentioned that a major league umpire had been hurt and would miss some games. Rocky's partner and friend Bob Davidson said to him, "Maybe you're going up to the major leagues." This was only Rocky's third season in baseball, so he knew that wasn't possible.

They finally reached their hotel at 3:00 A.M. "At ten the next morning my phone rang," Rocky explains, " 'Rocky,' the person on the other end of the phone said, 'this is Dick Butler. How are you?' Dick Butler was the American League's supervisor of umpires. I knew it wasn't really him. I knew it was someone Davidson had put up to it.

" 'I'm fine, Dick,' I said casually. 'Nice to hear from you.'

" 'How would you like to come to the big leagues?' he asked.

" 'Love to,' I told him. He then started repeating all the details I'd heard on the radio the previous day. An umpire had been hurt and I was being called up as his replacement. I didn't pay any attention to anything he said. Then he started giving me travel details. 'Are you writing this down?' he asked. 'Sure am,' I told him.

"Then he started telling me things that hadn't been mentioned on the radio, who I'd be working with, what cities I'd be going to, details about my pay. I started listening closely. Finally, after perhaps ten minutes, I stopped him in midsentence and asked, 'Excuse me, is this really Dick Butler?'

" 'Yes, who did you think it was?'

"I made him repeat everything. If this was a practical joke, it was certainly working. As soon as we hung up, I burst into Davidson's room. He looked innocent enough. 'Did you just call me?' I demanded. He said he hadn't. 'This is important. Did you just call me?' 'Honest,' he said honestly, 'I didn't!' Then he asked why. ' 'CAUSE I'M GOING TO THE BIG LEAGUES!' I screamed."

Eric Gregg was lounging poolside in Tucson, Arizona, when Fred Flagg, the National League supervisor of umpires, reached him. "What are you doing September twenty-third?" Flagg asked.

"Nothing that I know of," Eric told him.

"Think you can be in Cincinnati for the Reds game that day?"

Eric replied very calmly, "I can be there in an hour!" Flagg then gave him all the details. When he had finished, Eric promised solemnly, "I'll do my very best, Mr. Flagg."

"I don't want you to do your best, kid," Flagg told him, "but, please, just don't screw up!"

Perhaps the most unexpected call to the major leagues came to Harold Siroca. He wasn't even in baseball at the time. Siroca had worked three years in the low minor leagues, then quit and returned to his Queens, New York, home. He was umpiring local college games and working at Crazy Eddie's, a budget audiovisual equipment store, when the major league umpires went on strike in 1981. Because most minor league umpires refused to fill in for the

striking big leaguers, major league baseball was forced
to recruit amateurs. Siroca, having had three years'
experience, was asked to work Yankee games. "I
went to my boss at Crazy Eddie's," Siroca recalls,
"and I told him I needed Saturday off because I was
going to be umpiring at home plate at Yankee
Stadium. He looked at me a little strangely, then
said, 'Harold, we've got thirty television sets in this
store. Saturday afternoon, I'm gonna turn them on.
You'd better be on every one of them!' "

John McSherry was packing his bag to go to his
second spring training when Barney Deary called
him. "This year you'd better bring your good clothes
with you," he suggested.

"I told him, 'Mr. Deary, those *are* my good
clothes,' " John remembers. "Then I heard him sigh.
People are very subtle in this game. I asked him
why I needed good clothes and he told me he couldn't
tell me. I thanked him for a very wonderful conversation and threw my shirt into the bottom of my
suitcase.

"A few days after I got to Lakeland Fred Fleig
came by to see me. 'I've heard good things about
you,' he told me, then asked, 'Do you intend to
make this your profession?'

" 'Do I intend to make this my profession?' I was
staying at the Toffanetti Hotel, a marvelous place.
The Toffanetti had an ancient pulley elevator oper-
ated by a hunchback. Going down wasn't so bad,
because he'd just have to let the rope out. But by
the end of the day, the hunchback was tired and it
would take an hour to get up to the third floor.
Wednesday night they served spaghetti, all you could
eat for a dollar. Elderly people from all around would
come over, take out their teeth, and slurp down
dinner. You put your ring on the table for a second,
whupp . . . it was gone. I was working seven days a
week and getting paid forty bucks. Do I intend to
make this my profession? It took everything inside

me to resist blowing my entire career with that answer.

"I took a deep breath and said, 'Yes, sir, I do.'

"He told me not to get too excited, but the National League was going to take a good look at me during spring training. He said I probably wouldn't even work the plate. I just kept nodding my head. I was afraid what I might say.

"I was supposed to have my first day off the next day, so that night I went out to celebrate. I celebrated. It was 3:00 A.M. when I got back to the Toffanetti and there was a message waiting for me. I was scheduled to work home plate, teamed with Ken Burkhart, for a 10 A.M. game between Cincinnati and Pittsburgh at Pirate City. I didn't realize it at the time, but I was about to answer one of baseball's most perplexing questions: Where the @$#%# is Pirate City?

"A friend of mine, another minor league umpire, had come down to spend a few days with me before he had to start work. I woke him up and told him he was driving me to Pirate City the next morning. He asked, 'Where the @$#%# is Pirate City?' 'Don't worry,' I told him, 'we'll find it.'

"We got up early the next morning, which was still late the preceding night for me. I was not feeling too wonderful, but this was the first day of my major league tryout and I was not about to mess it up.

"I knew the Pirates trained near Bradenton, so we drove there. When we got to what looked like a town, we started asking people, 'Where's Pirate City?' Everybody seemed to know. Back to the main street, take a right, first left, you can't miss it. We missed it. Back to the main road, two traffic lights, a left, the third left. You can't miss it. We missed it for almost two hours. Finally, we made a left onto this deserted road and there it was. Pirate City is a city like a bank's free gift is a gift. It looks like one of those outposts where people with long beards and tattered clothes wander out of the woods after being lost for years, take one look, and walk back into the forest.

"But I didn't care, I was going to the big leagues. And I figured Kenny Burkhart would have gotten there in plenty of time to rub up the baseballs and get things ready. We walked into the clubhouse at five minutes before ten. The Pirates trainer looked at me and asked, 'Where've you guys been?'

"I said, 'You mean Burkhart isn't here yet?' I wasn't feeling so great to start with. Now I was feeling really miserable.

"He told me, 'You're the first guys I've seen.'

"I turned to my friend and said, 'Listen, you'll work the bases with me.'

" 'Fine,' he said, 'I'll be right back.' That was the last time I saw him.

"I got ready as quickly as I could and went out on the field. I called over Pirates coach Don Leppert and told him I needed a ballplayer to work with me. A few minutes later he came back and I asked, 'Where's the ballplayer?'

" 'Right here,' he said.

" 'Right where?'

" 'Here I am,' I heard someone say. I looked down and standing in front of me is the oldest Pirate I have ever seen. I looked at him and thought, 'The whole career ends right here today. . . .'

"His name was Lorenzo Lanier, and he turned out to be one of the nicest people I have ever met. But a rotten umpire. I told him, 'Lorenzo, just go down behind first base and do what I tell you to.' Seemed simple enough to me.

"Jim Bunning was pitching for the Pirates, Chris Cannizzaro was catching. Two sweethearts. If a poll were taken among major league umpires to determine who the nicest players in the game were, these two would finish second. Everybody else would finish tied for first. Bunning was near the end of his

career and didn't really have too much left. But that
day he did have me behind the plate, and that was
almost all he needed.

" 'Okay,' I told myself as I got into position to
start the game, 'so things haven't gone too good so
far, I was late for the game, my partner hasn't shown
up, and I got the oldest living Pirate in the world
working at first base.' Besides that I was beginning
to feel a little seasick. But it was still early. If I
concentrated and didn't screw up, I still had a shot
at getting a job.

"The Reds' first batter, the immortal Cinco
Diaz, stepped to the plate. Bunning's first pitch was a
foot outside. Close enough for me. I yanked my right
hand up in the air. 'Strike one!'

"Diaz stepped out and gave me a nasty look.
Cannizzaro loved me, though. He was yelling to
Bunning, 'Atta way to throw, Jimmy boy, you still
got it, just keep chucking like that. . . .'

"That next pitch was a curve ball that started
outside, then broke further outside. 'Strike two!'
Again Diaz stepped out of the box and walked around
muttering, 'I can't hit that, I can't even reach that.'
Cannizzaro was really pumped up. 'Beauty pitch,
Jimmy baby, how to throw that breaking ball.'

"Bunning threw again. Not even close. 'STRIKE
THREE!' Diaz just went crazy. He started jumping
up and down, cursing in Spanish. I finally told him,
'Hey, kid, you wanna go to the big leagues, you
gotta hit that pitch.'

"He shouted at me, 'You wanna go to the big
leagues, you gotta *see* that pitch.' So I'm really
doing well, one batter, one argument. Bunning likes
me, though, he thinks he's got his stuff back.

"Soon as the argument ended, Lorenzo came
trotting halfway to home plate. 'TIME!' I screamed
and stepped out to meet him. 'What'sa matter,
Lorenzo?'

" 'How'm I doing so far?'

" 'Great, Lorenzo,' I told him, 'great.'

" 'Yeah, I think I like this umpiring.'

" 'Go back behind first base, Lorenzo.'

"I made it all the way to the top of the second inning without another problem. The Reds' lead-off hitter singled, so I motioned to Lorenzo to move to the middle of the field. The next batter hit a ground ball to Pirates' shortstop Gene Alley. Alley made a great play and threw to Bill Mazeroski covering second base. Mazeroski, the ball, and the runner got to the base at the same time. Then Maz makes a great pivot and throws to first base. The play at first is even closer than the play at second. I looked at Lorenzo to see what he has called. What he has called is nothing. He is just standing there, looking at me.

" 'TIME!' I yelled, throwing both hands in the air and trying to decide what I was going to do with my life now that umpiring hadn't worked out. 'Yo, Lorenzo!' I shouted, but as I did, the runner at second stood up, dusted himself off, and trotted off the field. The hitter was standing at first base and no one said a word. I was standing there with my two hands in the sky.

"Lorenzo said to me, 'What'sa matter?'

" 'How the @$#% do I know?' I snarled and went back to home plate.

"Ken Burkhart finally showed up at the end of the fourth inning. He walked onto the field and introduced himself to me, then said, 'I've just got one question for you.'

" 'What's that?'

" 'Where the @$#%# is Pirate City? I've been driving for three hours!' "

Those umpires who do make it to the major leagues are joining one of the most exclusive clubs in the world. There are only 59 major league umpires. Each of these men is going to be part of baseball history. They will work no-hitters and playoff games and World Series games with eighty million people watching, they will witness incredible fielding plays, unbelievably dramatic moments, they will have the opportunity to work with some of the most gifted athletes ever to play professional sports, they will see players' careers begin and end and watch legends grow inning by inning, game by game, season by season. Lee Weyer and Doug Harvey, for example, were both major league umpires when Pete Rose was a rookie and have watched him play for each of his twenty-one seasons. But nothing matches the thrill of running onto a big league baseball diamond during the regular season for the first time. Davey Phillips was speaking for every man who ever worked a major league game when he said, "I stood at third base during the national anthem, thinking, if they fire me tomorrow, I can always say I made it to the big leagues."

Eric Gregg's first game was in Cincinnati. He was working with a very strong crew. Lee Weyer, the crew chief, was working home plate, Dick Stello was at first, and Satch Davidson was at second. At the conclusion of the fifth inning Weyer motioned for Gregg to come in to the plate. As Eric was trotting in, he was wondering, "What's he going to ask me? This is my first game. I don't know anything."

Weyer took off his mask and asked, "Eric, how'd I look on that last pitch?"

"I didn't know what to tell him," Eric remembers. "He's a fifteen-year veteran and he's asking me how he looked on a pitch? The ball bounced and he called it a strike, I'm going to tell him he made a bad call? 'Lee,' I finally said, 'whatever you called, it was good enough for me.' Then I turned around and ran back to third.

"At the end of the next inning Satch Davidson signaled me to come over to second base. I trotted over there, wondering what he wanted. He hadn't even had a play. When I got to second, he asked me how I was feeling. 'I'll tell you, Satch,' I said, 'right now I'm just so happy, I just feel like screaming.'

" 'Well, go ahead,' he told me.

"So I did. I opened my mouth and started screaming, 'Aaaaaahhhh . . .'

"Joe Morgan looked at me like I was crazy. He yelled over to Satch, 'What's the matter with him?'

" 'Nothing,' Satch yelled back, 'he's just happy.'

"Meanwhile, I'm still screaming, '. . . aaa-hhhhhh . . .'

" 'Oh,' Morgan said, as if he understood, and walked away from me. The next inning I got into my first major league argument. Joe Morgan, who already thought I was walking around with loose change up there, got caught in a rundown. and, trying to evade being tagged, ran about six feet into the outfield. I called him out for running out of the baseline. He started screaming at me, telling me that no one had ever called him out on that before.

"He was like every other ballplayer. He knew I was a rookie, he knew I didn't know the first thing about baseball, he knew that I had gotten off a ship that very afternoon and happened to be walking by the stadium and they stuck me at third base. I said, 'Joe, I'm here for a reason. I don't have anything to do with the fact that nobody's called you out on that before, but if you do it again, I'm gonna call you out again.'

"He just looked at me and said, 'Yeah? Well, let's see who's gonna be here the longest!' The longest? This is my first game. It's only the fifth inning. I was just hoping to finish this one game and he was telling me I might not even make that. I thought, 'This is some way to break into the big leagues.' "

My first game was opening day in Washington, D.C. I started my career in a big way—I lost my umpire's uniform. I had to wear my only dark suit and work the left-field foul line. If anybody died during the game, I was dressed for it. I remember thinking how much better everything was in the big leagues. Except the Washington Senators, of course. But the seats seemed wider, the foul lines seemed neater, even the hot dogs were tastier. I was so nervous I didn't start talking to the fans till the third inning.

I have nerves of aluminum foil. I remember standing out there in left field my first day in the big leagues and making one wish: Let everything be hit to right field. People believed I talked to fans during the game because I was trying to have fun and make the game enjoyable for everyone. In fact, I spoke to fans during the game for two reasons: to help relieve my nervousness and to get them on my side so they wouldn't come down too hard on me when I made the big mistake in the later innings. It sort of worked. Fans never shouted at me, "Luciano, you're blind!" or "Luciano, you're a bum!" Instead, they yelled at me on a first-name basis. "Ron, you're a bum!"

Nervousness, more than anything else, causes an umpire problems on the field. When an umpire starts listening to the dugout, or the crowd, or starts second-guessing himself, he is going to get into trouble. No one has a better temperament on the field than Doug Harvey. He is so cool that you get the feeling when he was born he was the first person to congratulate the doctor. "I am a very calm man," he says calmly. "I learned to be patient driving a tractor. I would start out on a one-hundred-eighty-eight-acre field at five-thirty in the morning and know that by seven-thirty that night I had to get across that field from corner to corner. I didn't stop for lunch. I had nothing to do but watch for big rocks so the front wheels wouldn't slide and cut up the lettuce. Hour after hour, seven days a week for three years, for one hundred dollars a week."

Doug's first game in the National League was Opening Day at Dodger Stadium, April 10, 1962. Just before the game started, just before he was to make his major league debut, Al Barlick walked over to him and asked, "Whattya think of this place, kid?"

He looked around that beautiful ball park and said coolly, "It'd take me about six and a half hours to plow the field. And we could probably get more hay in here than we could turn out of Imperial Valley in a year." Now, do you think a man like that is going to get rattled on the field?

Some people have an easier major league start than others. Some people get cleanly played three-hit shutouts or routs in which no single call is important. Jim McKean opened up in Chicago in April. Wilbur Wood was pitching for the White Sox, and Bill Singer was on the mound for California. It was a typical beautiful spring day in Chicago—a raging blizzard. The game went into extra innings and, in the bottom of the tenth, McKean called out what would have been the winning run at the plate. At the end of the next inning the game was suspended on account of the snowstorm. Later the entire game was replayed, so McKean has never really completed his first major league game.

Rocky Roe was introduced to the fields of major league baseball by the well-known firm of Haller, Neudecker, and Luciano. As we did with all young umpires, we tried to bring him along slowly, keep him out of jams, allow him to get the feel of being a major leaguer. Then, once we did that, we blamed everything that went wrong on him. Managers would come out to argue. "Blame Rocky, he's the rookie." Players would scream at a bad call. "I'd have gotten it right if I wasn't worrying about Rocky." Dead pigeons fell on George Scott. "Blame Rocky, it never happened before he got here."

We did attempt to make things comfortable for him, though. As he was walking out to work his first big league game behind the plate, Jerry Neudecker tried to help him relax. "Now, Rock," he explained, "an umpire is always worried about doing a perfect job the first time he works the plate. A lot of guys end up tightening their strike zone. Now, we play with a plate seventeen inches wide. Use it all, don't squeeze it on them. Get them to swing the bats and you'll see how easy everything goes."

"So I stepped behind the plate," Rocky explains, "thinking, 'Don't squeeze the plate. Don't squeeze the plate.' Jerry Koosman was pitching for the Chicago White Sox. The Mariners' Ruppert Jones was the batter. Koosman's first pitch, the first major league pitch I've ever called, was eighteen inches to two feet outside. 'Striiiikee . . .' Jerry Neudecker was at second base and out of the corner of my eye I saw him jump two feet straight up in the air. Then he takes his hands and looks like he's playing an imaginary accordion, indicating I should narrow my strike zone. I knew he was thinking, 'Oooohh, what have they sent us this time?'

"Ruppert Jones stepped out of the batter's box and asked, in an understanding, calm voice, 'Hey, big guy, was that a good pitch?' Could I lie? Of course. 'Yeah, Rupe,' I said, 'just nipped the corner.' It did not take me long to earn a reputation as a pitcher's umpire."

Admittedly, breaking in with Haller and me was not easy for any young umpire. One night during a game in Minnesota I walked over to Rocky and asked him if I could borrow a dollar. Without saying a word, he pulled out his wallet and gave it to me.

"I did give it to him," Rocky admits, "but then I began to wonder, 'What is he going to do with a dollar bill on a baseball diamond?' In the minor leagues there was nothing you could buy on the field during a game. But I didn't know. I thought, 'This is the big leagues, the big time, things are different.' Well, as it turned out, only some of the umpires are different.

"At the end of the inning I went over to Haller and told him that I thought Ronnie was losing his mind because he had just borrowed a dollar. 'Watch this,' Haller said, pointing to Luciano. He was easing over toward the stands, and there was a soda vendor walking down the steps. Ronnie bought a soft drink, then sat on the fence drinking it and talking to the fans. I thought, 'So this is how it is in the major leagues.' "

Not exactly. No umpire has really become a major leaguer until he rings up his first ejection. Till he throws the bum out. Any bum, doesn't matter. My first ejection was Frank Howard, which shows you how tough I was when I first came up. And stupid, very stupid. But Howard was so big he counted for three. The first player Kenny Kaiser dumped was Texas Ranger infielder Dave Nelson. He was easy, Kenny remembers, he was sitting on the top step of the dugout holding a sign reading, "Kill the Umpire."

Rocky Roe went a few weeks before he chalked up Number One. Fittingly, it was Earl Weaver. A lot of young umpires' first ejection was Earl Weaver, as well as their second, and their third . . . Rocky was working the plate in Baltimore. The Red Sox' Rick Burleson hit Mike Flanagan's first pitch for a single. His second pitch was topped in front of the plate. Oriole catcher Rick Dempsey jumped out in front of Roe to play the ball, completely blocking Rocky's view. The last time he saw the ball it was foul. Dempsey picked it up and whipped it to second, starting what would have been an easy double play. "I was calling, 'foul, foul, foul,' Rocky explains, "and then 'oh, oh, oh,' because Earl was charging out of the dugout. This was my first confrontation with a major league manager. He went right into his rooster act, bouncing all around me in circles. There was only one of him, but he was coming at me from all sides. Finally he threw his hands up in the air and left in disgust. I hadn't ejected him. I looked out at Ronnie in the infield and he looked so disappointed.

"After that, Earl was on me on every pitch. 'Where was it? Looked good to me! That's a major league strike!' In the fifth inning, with two balls and two strikes on Carlton Fisk, Flanagan just missed the inside corner with a curve ball. It was a tough pitch to call and an impossible pitch to hit, but it was inside. Earl just jumped all over me. Fisk hit Flanagan's next pitch into the seats, giving Boston a 5–0 lead. Earl strolled out to the pitcher's mound. I gave him plenty of time to call in a relief pitcher, which he did, but I knew what he really wanted was for me to go out there so he could give me his latest opinions. He felt that Fisk's home run was my fault and wanted to make sure I knew that he knew. Four years earlier I'd been sitting home watching him perform on television and had not yet umpired my first professional game. Now we were about to have our first major league dance. Time certainly does pass quickly, I thought, as I walked out to the mound.

"He was busy kicking the resin bag around. 'Earl,' I told him, 'don't try to show me up on the pitcher's mound. If you've got something to say, let's have it out right here.'

"Turns out he did have something to say. He got about four words into his dissertation when he hit the right combination. That got him into the showers before Flanagan used up all the hot water. Then Earl really went into his act. It was an Olympian performance. He kicked dirt on home plate, on me, he threw his hat, he stomped on his hat. Forty thousand fans were roaring in appreciation. It seemed like it lasted an hour; it probably didn't take much more than forty-five minutes.

"The next day a Boston sportswriter reported that I had had a tough game, writing, "Rocky Roe would have been better off being a flavor at Baskin-Robbins ice cream stores than a big league umpire last night. . . .""

Managers and players will test a rookie umpire at the first opportunity. If the umpire backs off, or blinks, or shows he can be intimidated, he is in for a difficult and probably brief major league career.

Boston's Dick Williams was the first manager to try to test me. He came out screaming over a nothing play at second base. This was so routine even Weaver wouldn't have raised his voice. But Williams was all over me—well, not exactly all over me, I outweighed him by a hundred pounds, so he was all over part of me. Ballplayers were closing in to see how I would handle this. Haller came over from first base, he wanted to see how I was going to react. I listened, but Williams wasn't going to intimidate me. I had already thrown Frank Howard out of a game. After Howard, Williams was going to bother me? After Howard the Dallas Cowboys wouldn't have bothered me. I stood there listening to everything he had to say, I kept my temper, and finally, when he had finished, I said, "That's it? That's what you're out here arguing about?"

"You're @$#%$¢ right I'm arguing over that," he said.

"Oh, that's nothing," I told him, dismissing his complaint with a wave of my hand. "Stick around, I'll give you something to argue about." Well, I thought George Scott was going to die trying to keep from laughing out loud, but Williams didn't get the joke. Eventually I had to ask him to leave the premises. He immediately appealed to Haller, claiming I couldn't throw him out for that.

Haller smiled and walked away. I'd passed.

A few weeks after Doug Harvey came up he called the Milwaukee Braves' Joe Torre out on a tag play at second base. Torre came up screaming, calling Harvey a @$#%¢*. Doug booted him. Braves manager Birdie Tebbetts ran out to discuss the situation. "Now, Doug," he patiently explained, "up here you've got to learn to take a little of that. These players are giving it all they've got and sometimes they . . ."

Harvey listened to this instruction, then informed Tebbetts, "Let me tell you something. He ain't gonna call me a @$#%¢*, you're not gonna call me a @$#%¢*, and no @$#%¢* is gonna call me a @$#%¢*!''

Durwood Merrill believes it takes five major league seasons before managers and players even begin to take an umpire seriously. I agree with him. Of course, I was there eleven years and some people never took me seriously. The first year of working in the major leagues is like a long visit to the best carnival ever to come to town. The cities are all new and exciting, the players are all so talented, a small crowd is twelve thousand to fifteen thousand as opposed to eighteen hundred, and suddenly your friends are seeing you on television. I was in a daze for half a season. (Managers and players can fill in their own punch line here.) I felt so fortunate to be in the major leagues.

But after the second swing around the league, after the first few arguments, after living in an airplane seat, after eating the first hundred luke-warm hot dogs on semi-soggy buns, the initial excitement fades and you discover that there is little difference between the minor league dirt and the major league dirt a manager kicks on your pants and shoes.

I always tried to enjoy myself as much as possible on the field. Because I occasionally did things a bit out of the ordinary, like letting fans umpire in spring training, eating on the field, or reading paper airplane notes during a game, some major league umpires thought I was being heard *and* seen too often, and they made it clear that they didn't like it. I became controversial. I could barely spell it, but I was it.

Once a veteran umpire was temporarily assigned to work with Haller and me. The day he arrived he told me plainly, "I have to work with you, but I don't have to like what you do on the field. Off the field you just leave me alone and we'll get along fine."

After a game a few weeks later, he invited me

for dinner. "I thought you didn't want anything to do with me," I said.

"I did," he told me, "but watching you on the field has reminded me how much fun this can be. I'm enjoying myself more than I have in the last five years."

I'm not saying everything I did was right. William Haller was my best friend on and off the field for almost a decade. I love the man and respect him. In my opinion there has never been a more professional, conscientious umpire in major league baseball. And I *know* I made him crazy. I would do something as innocent as standing in center field talking to Mickey Stanley during a game, and I would look over at him and his eyes would be closed and he would be shaking his head as if to clear Lucianos from his mind. I know he would have preferred me to be quiet. But I was also aware that he knew I took my work seriously and did a good job. I never let my enjoyment interfere with my work.

After eleven years in the major leagues I did lose some enthusiasm for the job. I knew I wasn't hustling as much as I had during my first few seasons. Consequently I was not always in the best position to make a call. Unless, of course, I was calling a cab.

But until my last game, the last inning of the last game, I never lost the thrill of standing on a major league baseball diamond. It was every bit as good as the fantasy of it. An entire world exists between the foul lines, and I was a big part of it. And, as the years passed, and I gained more weight, I became an even bigger part of it. I knew the players and their capabilities. I was able to anticipate plays. I loved passing along gossip, finding out who the players believed had "it" and who was losing "it." I savored the ordinary moments, those things that make memories, not news. All umpires do.

Doug Harvey and the New York Mets came to the National League the same year. The great Charles Dillon Stengel was their manager that first season. The Mets had been built to last—meaning their roster was a collection of older players finishing their careers and younger players who would never have much of a career—last was where they were going to finish. They couldn't even beat the heat. One blistering day in August they were losing, as usual, when a Dodger runner tried to steal second base. The catcher's throw actually beat the runner, but Mets second baseman Charley Neal didn't get his glove down in time and Harvey called the runner safe. Casey was in his seventies then and ambled out slowly to discuss this call. "Young man," Casey said, "I don't know what's taking place out here, but it would certainly appear to me that my man had the ball in plenty of time."

"Casey," Doug replied, "he did have the ball in plenty of time, but he's got a slow glove."

Stengel looked at Doug for a moment, then said softly, "You know, young fella, that seems to be the story of my life this year, slow gloves, slow bats, slow runners. . . ." Then he turned around and started walking back to his dugout, still talking to himself, ". . . slow infielders, slow grass growing, slow ushers . . ."

To me, the best part of being on the field was getting to know the players. I liked to talk to them, and they liked to listen to me. Some of them, at least. There were some people who just wanted to be left alone to concentrate on baseball. George Brett liked to talk on the field. I remember being at third base one night when he sidled up to me and said softly, "Ronnie, please don't tell the other guys, but you're my favorite umpire."

Well! That certainly made me feel good. That made me feel like I was finally gaining the respect of the players. Naturally, I could hardly wait for the game to end to tell Haller what Brett had said. But in the dressing room after the game, before I could open my mouth, Davey Phillips said somewhat shyly, "You know what Brett told me tonight? He said I was his favorite umpire!"

Haller laughed. "Don't you know he tells that to every umpire?" Bill said.

"Yeah, Davey," I added, somewhat weakly, "don't you know that?"

George would simply go around the bases telling every umpire he was his favorite. Even after we all knew what he was doing, he continued doing it. And there is one thing of which I'm certain: Everybody he told believed him. Even after they knew he was telling everybody the same thing, they still believed him. At least I did.

If I had to rate players' sense of humor by position, I would have to say that third basemen are the wittiest. I believe it has something to do with being fatalistic. I know that when I was working third base and a right-handed power hitter like Frank Robinson or Jim Rice came up, I'd back up the third-base line as far as I could without being embarrassed. Third basemen have to stay there. Playing third base is like being a moving target in a shooting gallery during a power failure.

Graig Nettles always made me laugh. "When I was growing up," the Yankee third baseman once said, "I always wanted to be a baseball player or be in the circus. That's why I'm so lucky to be with the Yankees. I got to do both." I was working third base the day Carl Yastrzemski finally got his three-thousandth hit, a sharp single. It was a wonderful moment. The game was halted and people rushed onto the field to congratulate him. The governor of Massachusetts was there. Billy Martin had tears in his eyes. The fans gave him a tremendous standing ovation. A mob of photographers was taking every possible picture. Red Sox officials gave him the ball, then they took up the base and gave that to him. This went on for twenty minutes and was still going strong. Finally, Nettles walked over to me, shaking his head. "What's the matter?" I asked.

"Jeez," he said, "it was only a single."

Graig's teammate Lou Piniella is one of the most aggressive base runners in baseball. Unfortunately, he's so slow he couldn't even beat me to a free meal. He was on first base one night when a Yankee batter hit a long single. Piniella put his head down and ran right past third-base coach Don Zimmer, who was signaling for him to stop at third, and scored what turned out to be the winning run. After the game, when reporters asked Piniella why he had run through Zimmer's stop sign, he explained, "I don't use a third-base coach."

The very next night Piniella tried to stretch a routine single into a double and was thrown out at second by forty feet. "I guess," Nettles said, watching this, "Lou doesn't use a first-base coach, either."

Part of the joy of being on the field for any umpire is watching the games within the game that fans don't usually see, including the confrontations between future Hall of Famers such as Palmer and Jackson, Carlton and Rose, Ryan and Brett. Players of this caliber enjoy these challenges as much as everyone else and always reach back for just a little extra. Pete Rose, for example, led off a game in San Diego against Gaylord Perry. Perry's first pitch split the plate in half, but the umpire called it a ball. Perry took four steps in toward the plate and screamed, "If that wasn't Pete Rose up there that would have been a strike!"

Two pitches later Gaylord threw a breaking pitch maybe six inches outside. The umpire called that a strike. Rose stepped out of the box and yelled loudly enough for Perry to hear him, "And if that weren't Gaylord Perry out there that *wouldn't* have been a strike."

During Reggie Jackson's first year in Anaheim, Jim Palmer started a 7:30 P.M. game against the Angels. Reggie batted fourth and lined a single.

Palmer called Weaver out to the mound and told him he had a stiff neck and could not pitch. As Palmer was leaving the game, Reggie yelled into the Orioles' dugout, "Hey, before the game Palmer told me he was going to pitch until he was forty-five! What happened?"

Kenny Singleton supplied the answer: "Reggie," he yelled back, "he meant seven forty-five!"

One of the strictest unwritten rules concerning an umpire's behavior on the field was that he will not leave the field during a game for any reason. I have no idea who it was who didn't write this rule, but when I came up it was followed dutifully. In all the time I worked with Haller, I never saw him walk off the field before the final out was made. During my first five big league seasons I didn't either, except once when I fainted on top of first base and had to be derricked off and taken to the hospital because of a bleeding ulcer. I noticed then that nobody made a big deal about the fact that this was the first time I'd left the field during a game. So from then on, when I desperately needed to towel off, or get a drink, or mail a letter, or walk the dog, I would do it. The important thing I learned was to always use the home team's dugout.

On a bitterly cold April day in Yankee Stadium, for example, the heaters in the Yankee dugout would be blowing out so much hot air the players would be sweating, while in the visitors' dugout two ushers would be standing at either end lighting matches. And on a blistering, hot day the Yankee dugout would be reasonably cool, while in the visitors' dugout they would finally have gotten the heaters working. Obviously this was true in just about every city. The only times I made an exception to my home team dugout rule was when I had made an important call against the home team, and always when I was in Baltimore.

The second worst thing that can happen to an

umpire on the field is blowing a play. Just murdering a call. There are times I found myself standing there with my hands spread out calling a player safe when I just felt like flapping them and taking off. Every umpire occasionally blows a play, and you just hope it doesn't lead to a run, which leads to a victory or loss, which leads to a pennant being won or lost, which leads to twenty thousand to thirty thousand dollars per player in World Series shares. Rocky Roe had a play one night in Cleveland that he just missed, maybe because it was the day after a time zone change, maybe it was because he wasn't feeling well, maybe it was because he'd been hanging around with me too long, but he blew it. "I can't even claim it was a close play," Rocky explains. "A Tiger runner was out easily and I found myself standing there with my arms outstretched, calling him safe. I was standing there thinking, 'Why am I doing this?' Indians manager Dave Garcia came out to ask me the same question.

"I knew there was no possible way in the world I was ever going to convince Garcia that he was wrong and I was right. When he got out to me he said, 'Rocky, you gotta be kidding me on that call. There's no way in the world he can be safe.'

" 'You're right,' I told him. 'He can't be, but he is.'

" 'What?' he said. I could hear the beginning of confusion in his voice, and I tried to nurture that.

" 'I'm telling you, Dave, you're right. Unfortunately, I can't give that call mouth-to-mouth resuscitation and bring it back to life. He's gotta be safe.'

"Now I knew I had him. He didn't know what to do. 'Well,' he asked sadly, 'what am I gonna argue about then?'

" 'Gees,' I said, 'I don't know. I really don't see any purpose in us arguing about it. There's nothing either of us can do.'

"He had never raised his voice. 'You know,

Rocky,' he told me, 'I feel really foolish just standing here.'

" 'I'll tell you what,' I suggested, 'why don't you just yell at me and I'll yell back at you and we'll make it look good for the ball club and the fans.' So we did, we really went at it for about a minute, and Garcia trotted off the field to a sitting ovation."

Blowing a call is only the second worst thing that can happen to an umpire on the field; the worst is getting booed for blowing a call. The day you find yourself standing in the middle of a baseball field listening to thirty thousand people booing and screaming at you is the day you finally realize there is no place to hide on a baseball diamond. You just have to stand there and take it. Once I made a questionable call against the Red Sox in Fenway Park, where the fans sit very close to the field, and they were expressing their opinion of my work. I decided to get some consolation from Bill Haller, my best friend Bill Haller, my partner Bill Haller, the man I would walk through an Oriole dugout for Bill Haller. As soon as he saw me coming he turned away and walked over to talk to Davey Phillips.

There is absolutely no way to prepare yourself for the experience of being booed by forty thousand or fifty thousand people. You can't sit home listening to a booing record. It's like being caught in a shower of nails. But what happens is you build up to it. I was booed for the first time in baseball in the minor leagues. Luckily, I had been a bad football player, so I had some experience with it. But there weren't fifty thousand people in the minor leagues, there were only two hundred. So I figured, two hundred people, what could they possibly know? A few years later, it was two thousand people. I figured two thousand people, what could they possibly know? By the time I got to the big leagues I was ready to be booed by major league crowds.

To survive in the major leagues, an umpire has to learn to shut out the crowd. When you make a call, you have to believe, deep down in your heart, that it is the right call, and just because fifty thousand people are screaming at you, a manager is throwing his hat on the ground and jumping on it, six ballplayers are in tears, and the players in the bullpen are throwing baseballs at you, it still is the right call. What always bothered me was that I knew I was right, but there was no way I could convince the fifty thousand people in the stands. It would have taken much too long to explain my side of the play to each person individually. So I just tried to shut out that terrible sound.

When an umpire has a problem on the field he really believes that everybody in the entire world knows about it. Cabdrivers, hotel clerks, airplane pilots, everybody knows that you screwed up, but they are too embarrassed to mention it to you. If you had a bad game on a Saturday night, when you walk into church on Sunday morning you expect the entire congregation to turn around and start booing.

The first time my elderly mother heard fans booing me she got very upset. "What kind of job is this," she wanted to know, "where you have to stand out in the middle of a field and let people scream at you?" I tried to tell her that they weren't really booing me, that it was really a gesture of affection. When Lou Piniella came to bat in New York, I explained, the fans would cheer, "Louuuuuuuuuu . . ." In Baltimore, when Boog Powell batted, the entire ball park would scream "Boooggggggggg . . . ," and when I did something they liked they were cheering, "Rooonnnnnnnn . . ."

She didn't buy it. "I'm just old," she told me, "not stupid."

Conversely, the best part of being on the field is listening to the cheers. Of course, the cheers are never for you, but it doesn't matter; if they're cheering someone else, they can't be booing you.

Jerry Dale was working the sixth game of the 1977 World Series when Reggie Jackson hit three long home runs. "The people in New York went berserk," Jerry remembers. "I had goose bumps. Three home runs, each one farther than the last, and each one on the first pitch. The last one, off knuckle-baller Charlie Hough, went about nine miles. Standing there, on the field at Yankee Stadium that night, was the highlight of my career. It was a feeling I know I will never again experience in my lifetime."

"I remember when Hough was coming in," Reggie says. "I couldn't believe they were bringing in a knuckle-ball pitcher because I had ten lifetime home runs against knuckle-baller Wilbur Wood. I just hoped he would throw me a strike. I knew, whatever happened, I couldn't lose. The fans had given me a standing ovation while I was in the on-deck circle."

"It was just a regulation home run until the wind got it," Charlie Hough says seriously. "*Sure* it was. He just crushed that ball. I threw him a good pitch and he just ripped it. I didn't even look at the ball, I watched him standing at home plate, not moving, just posing, and I remember thinking, 'What a year that guy has had tonight.' "

In baseball there are three sides to every play on the field: the home team, the visitors, and the umpires. In the fourth game of the 1978 World Series Joe Brinkman experienced an umpire's ulti- mate nightmare—having to make a call that turns the Series around. Again, Reggie was in the middle of the moment. Brinkman was at second base at Yankee Stadium. The Dodgers had won two of the first three games. Thurman Munson was on second, Jackson was on first, and Lou Piniella was the bat- ter with one out in the sixth inning. "Piniella hit a sinking line drive to the left of Dodger shortstop Bill Russell," Brinkman explains, "and Russell dropped the ball. I had to make a determination:

Did he intentionally drop the ball or not? I had about one-third of a second to make up my mind; the only difference it made was maybe the outcome of the World Series, and only about eighty million people were watching. If I ruled that he had intentionally dropped it, the batter would have been out, the ball would be dead, and all runners would return to their bases. Otherwise, the ball is in play and everyone runs at his own risk. From my angle it was not intentional. Russell had been having a terrible Series in the field, and this looked like another misplay. So I started signaling safe, meaning the ball was in play.

"Russell picked it up, stepped on second base to force Reggie and fired to first base to try to double-up Piniella. If the Dodgers had completed the double play Billy Martin and the Yankees would have been all over me about that call. We would have had to call out the riot squad.

"But things really got complicated. Russell's throw hit Jackson on the hip and bounced into the outfield. By the time the Dodgers retrieved the ball, Munson had scored and the whole ball game and World Series had been turned around. I never actually saw the ball hit Jackson, although I was looking directly at first base, because I was still thinking about Russell's play. All I knew was that the ball ricocheted off Reggie.

"So it was Tommy Lasorda and the Dodgers who came charging out of the dugout. Yankee Stadium was absolute bedlam, you could barely hear Lasorda screaming at the top of his lungs. He was face to face with first-base umpire Frank Pulli, and when he got no satisfaction there, he came to me. 'There's no way that can't be interference!' he was yelling, and pleading, 'You can't do this, you have to call him out!'

"The argument raged for about ten minutes. Pulli came over to me and asked me what I had called. 'Nothing,' I told him. I hadn't made a call, which was the correct call as far as I was concerned. The ball was in play. Finally we resumed play and finished that inning. I had a difficult time concentrating on the game. I kept wondering, did Reggie intentionally interfere or not?

"So at the end of the half inning I walked over to Bill Haller, who was at third base, and asked him what he thought. He didn't even hesitate before telling me, 'I think Russell dropped the ball on purpose!' "

"There was nothing I could say. If that's what Haller thought, that must be what everybody watching the game, eighty million people, were thinking. I had blown the most important call of my life, I had turned the World Series around. I was going to be remembered in baseball history as the umpire who cost the Dodgers the World Series. But as it turned out, nobody even remembered that part of the play. All the reporters and fans wanted to talk about was Reggie getting hit by Russell's throw. That was fine with me; that was wonderful with me."

"I can tell the story now," Reggie recalls. "Munson was on second base when Piniella hit the line drive at Russell. Russell purposely dropped the ball, that's my feeling. I was standing in the base line when Russell threw the ball to first base, so I didn't have to move to get in the way of his throw; I instinctively said to myself, you're already out at second, but you don't have to move out of the way. I was about thirty feet off first base. Russell threw the ball right at me and I moved just enough to protect myself from getting hit on the bone. I kind of twisted and let it hit muscle. The umpire said, 'Hey, he's in the base line, the guy threw it, it's an error on the fielder. Jackson did not fabricate his position.' The most difficult thing I had to do was stand my ground."

"It was total obstruction on his part," the Dodgers' third baseman in that game, Ron Cey, states flatly. "It was so obvious. From my angle at third base I could see him do something that totally obstructed the ball going to first base. He got in the way of it. It should have been called a double play. As a result of it being allowed to stand, they ended up scoring the run that made the difference in the ball game."

These are the special moments on the field that make an umpire wonder about his pension scale.

There are two things that every umpire on the field thoroughly dislikes (two and a half, counting Weaver): organists, and fans who run on the field and interrupt play. Umpires hate organists. Every time we walk onto the field, what do they play? "Three Blind Mice." It's always "Three Blind Mice." There are four of us, but does that matter? "Three Blind Mice." One organist tried a little variation, but that didn't help at all. As I walked onto the field he played "Send in the Clowns."

No one likes baseball fans more than I do; but the people who run onto the field during a game aren't really fans, they're problems. And they're frightening. Most of the time they are just out there to win a bet or get on television, but there have been numerous occasions when they have attacked an umpire.

During the 1980 American League playoffs, for example, a man came out of the stands and tackled third-base umpire Mike Reilly. Graig Nettles grabbed the man, who was struggling to get loose, screaming, "Lemme go, I'll get that Kaiser." Reilly was stunned. He didn't know what was worse, being blind-sided by a fan or mistaken for Kenny Kaiser.

In the late 1960s, Doug Harvey was working third base in St. Louis's old Sportsman's Park. Lou Brock tried to score from first on a single and was thrown out easily at home plate. The Cardinals' third-base coach ran in to the plate to argue with umpire Shag Crawford. Meanwhile, Brock was still lying on the ground a few feet from the plate. The fact that he still hadn't touched it was not enough to prevent a major argument.

"The Cardinals' manager came running out of the dugout to join the third-base coach," Doug explains, "and then Brock got up and they all converged on my man Shag. I started walking toward the plate to handle the overflow. As I got there, I saw a man dressed in a white T-shirt, red slacks, and red-and-white tennis shoes approaching Shag from behind. I thought, 'What in blazes is the Cardinals' trainer doing out here?' I started to tell him he didn't belong on the field when he doubled up his fist and got ready to slug Crawford from behind. I thought, 'Isn't that something, the Cardinals' trainer is going to hit Shag. Why would the trainer do that?' It then occurred to me that this might not be the Cardinals' trainer. That's when my Caribbean riot training came in handy. I hit this guy with a forearm shiver. The entire argument had to be moved away from home plate so everybody didn't get blood all over their uniforms."

Players are just as afraid as umpires of people running onto the field, even well-meaning fans like the man who presented a bouquet of roses to Reggie in right field at Yankee Stadium. You just never know what someone crazy enough to come out of the stands is capable of doing. People are supposed to find their seats and sit there. That's why they are called stands! Jim Kaat was pitching for the Washington Senators one afternoon in Chicago when a drunken fan came out of the stands and staggered toward the mound. "I was just standing there watching him come toward me," Kaat says, "and I was scared. You never know what these people are going to do, you never know which one has a weapon. As he reached me, I said the first thing that came to mind. 'How do you want to pitch this batter?'

"He looked in toward home plate, furrowed his

brow, thought for a second, then said confidently, 'Curb 'em.' "

Perhaps the only good thing that could be said about ball-park streakers, people who took off all their clothes and ran across the field, was that you could see they weren't carrying any concealed weapons. The worst streaker I ever saw was on Opening Day in Chicago in 1974. It was thirty-three degrees, I didn't even want to take off my overcoat, and we had had people stripping all afternoon. In the seventh inning a man stood up in the outfield seats and took off his shirt and flipped it away. Then he took off his pants, his shoes and socks, and finally his underwear. Everybody in the park was cheering him. Finally he leaped down onto the playing field prepared to streak away—and landed wrong and broke his ankle. He had to lie there on the ground, naked, desperately trying to cover up as much of himself as he could, while security people searched for a stretcher.

Supposedly Yogi Berra saw his first streaker one night in Detroit, and the next day he was telling someone about it. That person asked Yogi if the streaker had been male or female. Yogi shook his head from side to side, then said, "Don't know, they were wearing a bag over their head." Supposedly.

Perhaps the most widely publicized incident concerning fans on the field took place in Los Angeles in 1976, the Bicentennial year. Rick Monday was playing center field for the Chicago Cubs when two fans leaped over the left-field fence and ran onto the field. "Whenever you see that," Rick explains, "you always wonder, is this the guy who sent me the threatening letter? Is this the guy who has a weapon? One of the two men was carrying something under his arm, but I couldn't tell what it was. They stopped in left-center field and all of a sudden unraveled it like a picnic blanket. I realized immediately it was an American flag.

"I don't know why I did, but I just started

running after them. They were kneeling down with their backs to me and I saw one of them take out something shiny and start dousing the flag. Now, I'm an intelligent man, I attended a fine university, so I knew this was not holy water. It was, in fact, a can of lighter fluid. A big can of lighter fluid. They were going to do it right. They struck the first match—but a breeze blew it out. I was still running toward them at full speed when I was struck by a disconcerting thought: 'What am I gonna do when I reach them? If I hit them from behind, I might hurt them, and I don't want to do that. I want to stop them, but I don't want to get violent.'

"As they lit the second match I had a terrific idea: If I have the flag, they can't light it.' So just as they were putting the match to it, I ran by, swooped down, and just pulled it away from them. Now I had the soaking wet flag in my hand, and I had only one thought in my mind: 'Is this thing on fire?' Because if it was, I was going to do some dance.

"It wasn't. The next thing I heard was ssshhhhhhhh, as the can of lighter fluid went whizzing by my ear. I kept running toward the infield, and running right past me going in the other direction was the Dodgers' third-base coach, Tommy Lasorda. But the security people got to these fans before Tommy did. If you had seen the look in his eyes, you would be thankful for that.

"Then the most amazing thing I've ever seen in my career took place. Spontaneously, the fans stood up and started singing 'God Bless America.' A chill went right down my back. This was the year of the Bicentennial tire sales, Bicentennial plate collections, Bicentennial wind-up toys, and Bicentennial everything else you could imagine. And here was this genuine outpouring of true patriotism. It was an absolutely thrilling moment, and I'll never forget the feeling.

"I received tremendous publicity for my part in preventing these people from burning the flag. Reporters called me for days, I made TV appearances. I probably gave more interviews during that period than at any other time in my life.

"Now, Jose Cardenal was playing left field for the Cubs, and Jose, a very funny man, likes to be in the limelight. He likes the media, and he saw the attention that my actions got me. So ten days later we were playing at home. At the end of a half inning Jose and I were trotting in from the outfield when he stopped suddenly and grabbed my arm. 'Monday, look!' he said, pointing with his glove into the stands. 'What are those people doing to that flag?' He was ready to jump right into the seats.

"I looked where he was pointing, and laughed. 'It's okay, Jose,' I told him, 'it's okay.' There was a group of fans—waving a Confederate Flag!"

As Monday explained, one of the reasons ballplayers are fearful of people running onto the field is that they do get threats. Ballplayers, as well as umpires and managers, get letters and phone calls warning them not to appear in a certain city. During one recent World Series an umpire was accompanied by armed guards every time he left his hotel room because of a serious threat. This is not a recent development. In 1950, for example, Yankee shortstop Phil Rizzuto received a letter warning him, Hank Bauer, Yogi Berra, and Johnny Mize that they would be shot if they showed up to play against the Red Sox. Rizzuto turned the letter over to the FBI and told manager Casey Stengel about it. Under the circumstances, Stengel did the most prudent thing: He issued a uniform with another number on the back to Rizzuto and gave Rizzuto's old uniform to Billy Martin.

Not all people who run onto the field are men. Morgana, a buxom entertainer, has made a practice of running onto the field and kissing ballplayers for the publicity. She is hardly the first woman to run on the field. In 1935 the Cincinnati Reds accommodated an overflow crowd by putting them on the field behind ropes. In the eighth inning the great Babe Herman was walking to the plate when a woman snuck under the rope and grabbed his bat. She stood at home plate and dared pitcher Paul Dean to throw. He did, and she smacked a one-hopper back at him. Dean fielded the ball cleanly and tagged her out. It worked out very well—the woman appeared for a month at a Cincinnati nightclub, billed as "Kitty Burke, the only girl who ever batted in the National League."

Personally, I rarely had problems with people running on the field. I had to watch as Morgana ran right by me to George Brett. I watched a little girl run out and kiss Reggie Jackson. I saw numerous fans dash across outfields into the hands of ball-park security. But during the first few years of my career no one ever came out specifically to speak to me. Then one gorgeous Arizona afternoon during spring training, I was working first base in an Oakland A's–Chicago Cubs game. Between innings I looked up to see an attractive woman walking toward me holding a pen and a page from a program. I thought, "Isn't this nice, someone finally wants *my* autograph." It was during a game and I knew I wasn't supposed to do it, but it was only spring training and this was a very attractive woman. "Mr. Luciano," she said sweetly, holding out the pen and paper, "could you do me a favor?"

"Certainly," I said, taking it.

"Could you please get me Reggie Jackson's autograph?"

FIVE

THERE IS NO PLATE LIKE HOME

There is no plate like home. Thank goodness. Working behind home plate is the toughest job for a major league umpire. Besides the normal 290 ball-strike decisions, the plate umpire, or umpire-in-chief, is responsible for rubbing up the 60 baseballs that will be used in the game with special mud, filling up the pitcher's resin bag, supervising the exchange of starting lineup sheets and recording all substitutions, getting the game started on time, keeping home plate clean, calling batted balls fair or foul until they reach the bases and all safes and outs at home plate, all decisions concerning the batter, including batting out of order, properly placing the runners on overthrows, fan interference and obstruction, suspending play, forfeiting a game, and mediating conflicting decisions of the base umpires. About the only thing the plate umpire doesn't do is repair refrigerators.

But just to make things slightly more interesting, home plate is situated between opposing dugouts, so the plate umpire has to do all this while listening to stereophonic managers. The individual who laid out the baseball field so that I would be equidistant between Earl Weaver and Billy Martin is a very troubled human being. Throughout the entire game I would hear, "Pitch was good," in one ear and "Pitch was low," in the other, or "Pitch was high," or "You finally got one right." The only reason managers complain on every pitch is that they have nothing to complain about between pitches.

According to the official rules of baseball, "Home base . . . shall be a five-sided slab . . . a 12-inch square with two corners filled in so that one edge is 17 inches long, two 8½ inches, and two are 12 inches." Why? Who decided that? I can imagine Abner Doubleday and Alexander Cartwright sitting around one afternoon inventing baseball. Abner suddenly snapped his fingers and said, "By George, I've got it. Let's make home base a five-sided slab, a twelve-inch square with two corners filled in so that one edge is seventeen inches long, two are eight and a half inches long, and two are twelve inches! What do you think?"

"Amazing," Cartwright probably replied, "that's just what I was thinking."

There is nothing else that shape in the world. Well, I did go out with this woman once . . . The one thing a plate doesn't look like is a plate. Believe me, if there is one thing that I am familiar with, it is a plate. A plate is round and, at least in my house, has little flowers painted all over it. There are some baseball historians who believe it is home plate's unusual shape that causes all the problems, but if that were true I would have had problems my entire life.

Major league umpires rotate around the bases clockwise, baseball's version of a vicious circle. An umpire will work behind the plate every fourth game, then move to third for a brief vacation, then second where he is within shouting distance of the arguments at first base, and finally first, where there are just enough problems to prepare him for his next plate job.

Every base has special problems. At first base

there are always bang-bang plays on infield ground balls. Second usually has difficult sliding tag plays. And at third base an umpire has to be very careful not to fall asleep because he can easily be hit with a line drive. Umpire's heaven is a place where he works third base every game. Home is where the heartache is.

Every umpire prepares to work the plate in his own way. I was always very calm the day I had the plate, very cool and professional. I tried to get to the locker room earlier than usual and then, about five minutes before I had to go onto the field, I would throw myself onto the floor, kicking my feet and screaming, "I don't wanna go! Don't make me go!"

Actually, I would make sure I got some extra rest during the day and wouldn't eat too much. At some point I would open the newspaper and peek to see who was scheduled to pitch. If someone like Catfish Hunter were starting, someone with great control who didn't argue, I'd be happy for the rest of the day. But if it were Nolan Ryan or Dennis Eckersley or knuckle-baller Wilbur Wood, I'd quickly close the paper and try to persuade myself I was looking at the wrong game.

Eric Gregg will not talk to anybody before he has the plate. Eric Gregg not talking is like Ed McMahon not laughing at Johnny Carson's jokes. "Normally, I like to get to the ball park two hours before game time and visit with people," he says, "but not when I'm working the plate. I go in the locker room and sit by myself, thinking about what I'm going to be doing. If I sat around kidding, pretending it was just another game, I would be putting on a show, because I'm very nervous. It gets just a little easier every year, but if I'm going to give a hundred percent on the field, this is the way I've got to prepare."

There are some umpires who claim they feel no differently about a plate job than any other assignment. Once I remember sitting in a locker room before a game with a veteran umpire who had the plate. He told me he had been doing the job for so long that he no longer got nervous. Then he asked me to toss him a soft drink from the ice chest, and I had to point out that he had two open cans of soda sitting in front of him. But he wasn't nervous.

Jerry Dale is probably the only umpire who warms up his throwing arm in the locker room before working the plate. Jerry is a former pitcher and proud of his ability to throw strikes when tossing a new ball to the pitcher, so he'll throw balls against the wall until his arm is loose.

Doug Harvey says he needs extra rest when he is going to work the plate. "Every time I walk onto the field," Doug says, "it takes a chunk out of me. Every time I have the plate it takes a big chunk. My heart is only so big, my back is only so strong, and at the end of my career, when I walk off the field for the last time, there ain't gonna be any chunks left."

Before every game begins, the umpires and managers gather at home plate to exchange starting lineup cards and go over the ground rules. Chicago's Comiskey Park was built in 1910. I worked there as many as fifteen games a year for eleven years. New walls didn't grow overnight, nobody planted a garden in the outfield, but before every game we discussed exactly the same ground rules. Even then, if a play involving a ground rule occurred during the game, either the White Sox manager would come out to argue my interpretation or the opposing manager would come out to ask for an explanation.

The pregame meeting was good for three things: exchanging gossip, telling jokes, and getting me confused about the lineup cards. I started with four sets of each lineup. I never could figure out who was supposed to get what. I was supposed to end up with one of each; I often ended up with two of one and none of the other, or none at all.

Only rarely are the jokes told during this meeting funny. Don Zimmer was managing the Red Sox during Kenny Kaiser's rookie year. "This was my first time in Fenway Park, and Zimmer was going over the ground rules," Kenny explains. " 'Out in left field,' he says, 'we have the Green Monster.' I looked, and all I saw was this huge green wall. I didn't know it was called the Green Monster. Then he said, 'Now, we have two cockatoos that live on that wall. . . .'

"I looked at him suspiciously. 'Cockatoos?' I said.

" 'Birds,' he told me. 'They come back here every year. We make a ground rule around them.'

"Luciano was standing on one side of me and Haller was on the other. They were nodding their heads, so I nodded my head. 'Really?' I said.

" 'Yeah, really. If a batted ball hits the male cockatoo the hitter gets two bases. . . .'

"I fell right into Zimmer's trap, asking, 'What if it hits the female?'

" 'It's all you can get.' "

Earl Weaver usually sent one of his coaches to the plate with the starting lineup. If Baltimore had won its previous game, it would be the same coach who'd brought the lineup to the umpires for that game. If they'd lost, he would change coaches. If anyone brought the lineup to the plate for five consecutive victories, Earl would buy him a new suit. Umpires used to comment that, based on the way Earl's coaches dressed, the Orioles must have had a lot of four-game winning streaks.

I once asked Weaver if he'd buy me a suit if I called five in a row correctly. He didn't bother answering, although both of us knew he had nothing to worry about: I knew he would never buy me a suit, and he knew I'd never get five in a row right.

On occasion Earl would attend these pregame meetings himself. Stevie Palermo enjoyed the same sort of warm, loving relationship with Weaver as I did, somewhat similar to that of General Custer and Sitting Bull. Because Weaver and Palermo did not get along, Steve was assigned few Baltimore games. In 1981, for instance, he had the Orioles at the beginning of the year, then did not see them again until the final three days of the season. While the umpires waited at home plate before the first game of that season-ending series, coach Cal Ripken started to bring out the lineups. Then the public-address announcer identified Palermo as the plate umpire that night.

"Ripken was halfway to the plate," Steve recalls, "when I heard a whistle from the Orioles' dugout, and here comes Earl. He took the lineup card out of Ripken's hand and came charging toward me. 'How can he be mad at me already?' I wondered. 'They haven't even played the national anthem.'

" 'Where have you been?' he started screaming at me. 'Just where have you been?'

" 'What's wrong with him tonight?' I thought. 'He doesn't like me enough to miss me. Something's gotta be wrong!'

"Finally he reached home plate. He was waving his arms through the air and screaming, 'You're costing me money! You're costing me money!'

"Costing him money? He had it all wrong. The way it usually went was that I would make a call, he would run out and jump up in the air, I would throw him out, and he would get fined by the league office. It was simple. That cost him money. But me?

"Then he explained, 'These commercial companies need your permission to use footage of us arguing, and I'm losing forty thousand dollars a year because they can't make any commercials. How can you do this to me?'

"How could I do that to him? And after all the wonderful things he had done for me. 'Stick around, Earl,' I told him, 'I've got the feeling we're gonna make some money for you tonight.' "

Sometimes a manager will bring up a disputed play or situation that took place during a previous game, and one insult leads to another and he will be ejected even before the game starts. Joe Brinkman and Billy Martin got into a good argument at Yankee Stadium one night and, right at the best part, where Billy calls Joe a $%#%#% and Joe gets to throw him out of the game, the national anthem started playing. The two of them paused, stood next to each other with their hats over their hearts, then the moment the anthem ended started screaming at each other again.

One thing I've always wondered about the national anthem is whether recordings of it come already scratched, or do ball clubs simply buy them used? In my entire football career, in fifteen years of baseball, I have never heard "The Star-Spangled Banner" played in a ball park without the record being badly scratched. In fact, even when somebody's sister is singing it live, it still comes out scratched. I remember when the Oakland–Alameda County Coliseum opened. That ball park cost fourteen million dollars. Of course, they forgot to provide a dressing room for the officials, but what can you expect for fourteen million dollars these days? Everything was brand new, the field was new, the seats were new, the ticket booths were new, everything was new except the recording of the national anthem. I understand that. They'd already spent fourteen million, they didn't want to waste another three bucks on a new record. It was just going to get scratched.

In addition to being scratched, the records either skip or get caught in a groove. I was working in Pittsfield, Massachusetts, I believe, when the record didn't even get past the first sentence. I created enough problems of my own without needing any help, so I was less than thrilled to be standing at home plate listening to a broken record repeating, "Uh-oh, say can you see . . . Uh-oh, say can you see . . ." Sure enough, after the fourth or fifth repetition, one fan shouted loudly, "Well, I guess they know who's umpiring tonight!"

Frank Funk pitched in the International League in 1959, when it truly was an international league. "I was playing for Toronto," he says, "and before every game they would have to play the Canadian national anthem, the United States national anthem and, because the Havana Sugar Kings were in the league, the Cuban national anthem. It was like listening to *Your Hit Parade*. They would be playing music for a week. We'd warm up, they'd play these songs, rigor mortis would set in, and we'd have to warm up all over again."

After the anthem, or anthems, have been played, the plate umpire is supposed to clean off home plate—being careful to keep his back to the pitcher, who thus far has no reason to be mad at him—shout "Play ball!" and start the game. The first thing umpire school students are taught is to shout "Play ball!" Every time they move behind the plate they have to yell it out. Minor league umpires and major league umpires always shout those same two words. Except sometimes.

During a pennant race or before a playoff or World Series game, the plate umpire will do exactly what he is supposed to, jumping out in front of the plate and whisking it spotless, then jumping back behind the plate and proclaiming, "Play ball!" But if it's September and Cleveland is playing Seattle, some umpires might lean over the catcher's shoulder, blow the dirt off the plate, sigh, and say something like, "Let's go," or "Let's get it over with." A few years ago, when Baltimore had beaten Minnesota approximately three seasons in a row, plate umpires would say, "Here we go again."

I always gave 'em the big "Play ball!" I figured, it took me two weeks to learn my line, I wasn't about to improvise.

                    *   *   *

Calling balls and strikes causes the most problems for the plate umpire. If a pitched baseball crosses over the plate between the batter's armpits and knees, or if he swings and misses, or hits it outside the foul lines, it is a strike. Anything else is a ball. Theoretically, it's very simple. But in reality, the batter crouches over the plate so that his elbows are resting on his knees, compressing the space between his knees and armpits to three inches, then the pitcher throws a rising fast ball ninety-three miles per hour that shoots up as it crosses the plate. The umpire has about one-twentieth of a second to determine if the bottom part of the baseball brushed the top of the batter's strike zone as it crossed home plate. If the umpire calls a strike, the batter will step out of the box, turn around, and glare at him. If he calls it a ball, the catcher will want to know if he is having problems with his vision.

Then, if the game is on television, they'll show the pitch in slow-motion instant replay, and the announcers will wonder how anyone could have gotten it wrong.

As an umpire gains experience, he develops his own concept of a strike zone. Players don't mind if an umpire has a wide strike zone, meaning the pitch just has to be near the plate, or a tight strike zone, meaning it must actually cross over the plate, as long as he is consistent, as long as he calls the same pitch the same way every time. Retired American League umpire Ed Runge's strike zone was so wide players would say he gives the pitcher both dugouts. Anything the catcher could reach without leaving his feet was a strike. Runge had the plate in the 1967 All-Star game, which went fifteen innings. He rang up a record-setting thirty strikeouts. But the players knew what to expect from Runge and went up to bat swinging.

Home plate is made out of white rubber, but it has a black border. Usually this black border is covered with dirt. The first thing Lee Weyer does when he has the plate is uncover the black. Then he'll dig little trenches alongside. He wants as wide a plate as possible, because he likes to see batters swinging. In fact, when he's got the plate some hitters start swinging while still in the dugout.

Doug Harvey is just the opposite. "I have a seventeen-inch-wide plate and the ball must touch the plate in my game of baseball for it to be a strike. I decided that's the way it would be the second time I worked home plate in the major leagues. I was in St. Louis, Don Drysdale was pitching for the Dodgers, and Stan Musial was the Cardinals' batter. Musial had been my idol when I was growing up, I even used to imitate his corkscrew stance, so naturally I was very excited.

"The Cardinals were trailing by one run, with two men on base and two out in the bottom of the fourth inning. I had never seen Drysdale pitch before from behind the plate, so I had no idea how much his pitches moved. The count on Musial went to three balls and two strikes. Drysdale threw a fast ball on the outside corner, and Musial fouled it off. Then Drysdale threw another fast ball in precisely the same place. The ball was three feet in front of the plate when I started to raise my right hand to call it strike three—and then it started tailing off . . . and tailing off. It missed the plate by five or six inches. My right hand was in the air and I was hollering, 'Yeah, yeah,' while inside I was thinking, 'No, no.' But there was nothing I could do, the Dodgers were running off the field, the catcher had rolled the ball back to the mound, and twenty-five thousand people had heard me call strike three. There are no do-overs in major league baseball.

"Musial stood at home plate looking at the batboy and told him to go into the dugout and get his glove. As the batboy trotted away, Stan said firmly, still without ever looking at me, 'I don't know what league you were in, but all I want you to remember is that home plate is seventeen inches wide. The ball is supposed to touch it. Now, just calm down and take your time before you call a pitch. Wait for it to cross the plate.' The batboy returned with Musial's glove, and Stan just jogged away. I watched him running out to first base, thinking, 'No wonder they call him "the Man." '

"So, since that day, my belief has been that the batter has as much right to make a living in this game as the pitcher. If baseball wants a wider plate, put a twenty-four-inch plate in there. But right now it's seventeen inches and I don't want anybody asking for just two inches on either side."

This has not made Doug the pitchers' favorite umpire. One day in Chicago, for example, the Cubs' Larry Jackson was pitching against the Phillies. Wes Covington was the batter, and Dick Bertell was catching. The count went to one ball and two strikes on Covington. "As Jackson looked in for the catcher's sign," Doug explains, "I thought, he's going to throw his good hard slider on the inside corner to try to get Covington to go after a bad pitch. Jackson threw—a hard slider maybe an inch inside. I called it a ball. Jackson jumped two feet straight into the air. Bertell asked, 'Why, Doug, why?'

" 'Because it was inside, Dick,' I told him. That made the count two and two. Now, I figured, if I were Jackson, I'd come back with exactly the same pitch. Bertell set his target on the inside of the plate, and I moved over the inside corner. Jackson threw another hard slider in the same spot. 'That's a ball,' I said.

"Jackson jumped four feet straight into the air.

" 'Why, Doug, why?' Bertell asked in a pained voice.

"I leaned over and said softly to him, 'I just wanted to see how high Jackson could jump!' "

When I was working the plate I had a simple philosophy: How do I get out of this? I liked the ball to be over the plate—preferred it, actually—but

I wasn't a fanatic about it. My strike zone was oval rather than square. If a pitch was right across the middle of the plate but a little high, I figured, what the heck, a major leaguer should be able to hit that one. So it was a strike for me. Because I was a little taller than most umpires and used the outside protector, I couldn't get down real low, so I would give pitchers low strikes down the center of the plate. I was also a little wide in the middle of my strike zone because I was a little wide in the middle of my body.

There are more arguments on ball-strike calls than on any other plays in baseball. An umpire is never going to satisfy everybody; I was pleased when I could satisfy somebody. There are just so many close pitches every game that either the batter, catcher, or pitcher is always going to be complaining. Sometimes, in fact, all of them do. Once, for example, Hall of Fame umpire Tommy Connolly called a second strike on Yankee second baseman Aaron Ward. Ward stepped out of the box, took off his hat, and brushed off the plate. Connolly gritted his teeth and said nothing.

White Sox pitcher Red Faber's next pitch was just as close, and Connolly called it a ball. Farber screamed at Connolly and his catcher, Ray Schalk, who then took off his cap and cleaned the plate. Again, Connolly said nothing.

Faber threw again, a fast ball high and inches outside. Ward swung feebly and missed for strike three. Before Ward could move, Connolly took off his hat and cleaned off the plate.

Whenever a batter argued with Frank (Silk) O'Loughlin, one of the five members of the American League's first staff of umpires, O'Loughlin would respond in a booming voice, "I have never missed one in my life and it's too late to start now. The Pope for religion, O'Loughlin for baseball, both infallible." Now, if O'Loughlin only could have conquered his inferiority complex, he would have been a tremendous umpire.

Another old-time umpire, Bill Byron, was known as Lord Byron, the Singing Umpire. When a player argued on a called third strike, Byron would tell him, "Let me tell you something son/Before you get much older/You cannot hit the ball my friend/With your bat upon your shoulder."

Byron once threw the New York Giants' Hall of Fame manager John McGraw out of a game by singing, "To the clubhouse you must go/You must go/You must go/To the clubhouse you must go/My fair manager."

McGraw responded by splitting Byron's lip open with a right uppercut.

Former high school assistant principal and teacher Durwood Merrill once made the mistake of trying to reason with an angry batter. Durwood called a strike on one of the young college stars coming into the league. The batter turned around and demanded, "Where was that pitch at?"

Rather than answering him directly, Durwood called time, took out his whisk broom, and moved around in front of the plate to clean it off. As he brushed away the imaginary dirt, he said, "You're a college graduate, right?"

"Yeah. So, what about it?"

"Well, I'll tell you. Where I went to school, they taught me never to end a sentence with a preposition. At," Durwood explained to me, "is a preposition."

The batter thought about this for a moment, then looked directly at Durwood and demanded, "Okay, then, where was that pitch at . . . jerk?"

Obviously, few plate umpires are going to call 290 pitches correctly every game. I felt I'd done a good job if I didn't call a pitch that was hit foul a ball and missed six pitches or less. And I just hoped that none of my missed calls made a difference in the outcome of the game. There is no worse feeling for a plate umpire than missing a pitch and either ending a rally or giving a batter additional swings, or a walk, which leads directly to runs scoring. Every runner who touches the plate after a missed call is like a stake being pounded just a little deeper into your heart. Early in my career I blew a third strike call to put the Oakland A's Bert Campaneris on first base with two out against the Kansas City Royals. The A's exploded for five runs, and as each one touched the plate, the Royals' catcher said with disgust, "That's another one for you!"

Hey, I had help. I couldn't have done it without the Royals' pitcher. I gave up the walk, but I had nothing to do with the barrage of hits that followed. Knowing that didn't make me feel any better, however.

I never had a game in which I honestly believed I didn't miss a pitch, but I figured a great batter hits safely only three and a half times every ten at-bats, and I knew I was doing better than that.

Players know umpires are going to miss pitches, and umpires will usually allow them some complaint. It's not so much what they say as how they say it that causes ejections. When Bucky Dent first came to the big leagues, he asked Nestor Chylak how he could complain about a call without risking ejection. "If I'm behind the plate and you think you have a legitimate beef," Nestor told him, "you put your head down and air me out. Just don't turn around and look at me, because now you're telling the whole world that I made a mistake. Don't put me in an embarrassing position and you can say almost anything you want."

That's generally the rule most umpires follow and might well be one reason I never had excessive trouble with arguments behind the plate—no one wanted to look at me ever.

Some batters try to be cute; they talk to the catcher rather than the umpire. After a pitch they might say to the catcher in a friendly voice, "Believe that?" Or, "Where was it?" If the catcher is as smart as the batter, he won't answer the question.

Eric Gregg was working a Montreal game and Gary Carter was playing catcher. Hitters kept asking Carter about pitch location. Gregg did not hear Carter answer, which is the correct answer. But between innings, second-base umpire Dick Stello came in and told Eric that Carter was using hand signals to inform batters that pitches were either too high or too low.

Carter, one of the best-liked players in baseball, came to bat the next inning. The first pitch to him almost bounced on the ground. Eric called it a strike. Carter turned around with a look of amazement on his face and asked, "Where was it?"

Eric smiled, then held his hand at about waist height. That was the end of his problems with Gary Carter.

I tried to pay as little attention to players arguing about my calls as players did to my calls. I realized that players react instinctively, that they often say things they don't mean. I remember one day George Scott came to bat in an angry mood. For some reason the Red Sox had dropped him to the seventh spot in the batting order. "Seven!" he was moaning, "I'm no seven, I'm a 'tater man. My momma don't look no further than Number Four in the lineup. She sees this, she's gonna think I'm retired." The first pitch came in and I called it a strike. He stepped out of the box and told me that it was outside, that I was taking the bat out of his hands by calling pitches like that strikes. I let him blow off some steam, then told him to get back into the box.

The next pitch was in the same spot. It was good enough for me. Strike two! Scott stepped out again, picked up some dirt and wiped his hands, and let me have it. He told me I had no idea of the strike zone, that I was killing him, that he was trying so hard and I was preventing him from making his living.

The third pitch was inside. He swung and missed

for strike three. As he started walking away from the plate he paused and asked me quite seriously, "Ronnie, was that a good pitch?" Good pitch! How should I know? If I got the first two wrong, where did my sudden improvement come from? That's the reason I never take batters' complaints seriously.

The key to doing a good job behind the plate is complete concentration, and anything that divides an umpire's concentration can lead to problems. I tried to pay no attention to managers and players shouting at me from the dugouts, but on occasion it was difficult not to listen. Once, I remember, the Yankees' Fritz Peterson was pitching against the Tigers, and just as he went into his windup, somebody on the Detroit bench screamed, "I got one thing to say about you, Luciano. . . ."

Well? That was it, that was all that he said. But instead of paying attention to the next few pitches, I kept waiting to hear the rest of the insult.

A good umpire will keep a bench under control. One of the things an umpire learns early in his career is that if you go over to the bench, you try to give somebody the boot. That usually quiets them down for a few innings. Then, that done, you are able to concentrate on balls and strikes. Usually. When Dale Ford was in the American Association he was working the plate on his birthday. Although he thought he was having a good game, the Wichita bench climbed all over him in the fifth inning. He took it for a while, then called time and marched over there. Wichita manager Mike Roarke really went at it with him, and Dale ended up unloading four or five players.

But he was fuming when he went back to home plate. He was thinking of that argument rather than concentrating on his job behind the plate. He leaned down behind catcher J. C. Martin and ordered the batter, Keith Hernandez, to step in. The first pitch came in and he yanked his right arm into the air and called out, "Str—"

Only then did he notice that home plate was missing.

He walked around Martin and started kicking the dirt. No plate. Meanwhile, everyone on the field began laughing, his partners started laughing, the fans were laughing. He was kicking dirt looking for the plate.

To celebrate Dale's birthday, they had set him up. While he was busy fighting with the entire dugout, the batters' boxes and foul lines had been obscured, and home plate was covered with dirt. Martin and Hernandez took their respective positions about ten feet up the first-base line, and the fielders shifted. Dale was so angry he never noticed.

"Is it still a strike?" Hernandez asked.

"You knew about this, didn't you?" Obviously, he did. "Then you ain't kidding it's a strike. That was right down the middle—if there had been a middle."

Indicating strikes by raising the right hand and balls with the left hand is a baseball tradition begun by Bill Klem. There were no electric scoreboards when Klem was working, so umpires had to shout out the starting lineups and the count on the batter to keep fans informed. At one point an inventor suggested that small, multicolored flags be waved by umpires to indicate strikes, balls, and outs, but Klem made that unnecessary by devising the hand signals still in use today. Tommy Connolly, Klem's counterpart in the rival American League, refused to use Klem's system at first, explaining, "I'm not going to be waving my arms around like a lunatic."

Obviously that never bothered me.

In umpire school, students are taught to stick their right hand straight out to call a strike, but as they gain experience and confidence, they develop an individual style. Steve Palermo, for example, is a proponent of the short jab-punch in the stomach. He calls a strike by shooting his right arm straight out, as if jabbing the air, while at the same time slamming his stomach with his left hand. The National League's Dutch Rennart has the most technically difficult style. When he calls a strike he begins by pointing his right arm toward the first-base dugout if the batter is right-handed, or toward the third-base dugout if he is left-handed, then sweeeeeeeppping it around behind his back, calling "Strrrriiiiiiiieeeeeee," then suddenly taking off and running about six steps in the direction his hand is pointing.

It is such a unique style it took National League players some time to get used to him. "Dutch hollers 'BALL!' right in your ear," Johnny Bench explained, "but he has a call-it-and-run technique for strikes. The second time he worked a Cincinnati game behind the plate he called a third strike on me, and there just wasn't any way it was a strike. I turned around to argue with him, but he wasn't there. He was gone, halfway to the dugout. It would have taken me a half hour to catch up to him with the head start he had, much less run over to him to argue."

For some reason, at some time, every umpire raises his right leg when his right hand goes into the air. It's as if they were connected with a string. Hand goes up—foot goes up. Larry Napp had the most compact, quickest strike call I've ever seen, and his leg would come up just as fast as his arm.

Indicating strikes with the right hand is an accepted convention rather than a rule. But some left-handed people never feel comfortable doing it. When veteran pro basketball official Jake O'Donnell was umpiring in the minor leagues he would occasionally make left-handed calls. Jocko Conlan always called outs with his left hand. And, I must admit, there were occasions when I called strikes by raising my left hand—and I'm not even left-handed.

I would only do it a few times a game, and only in dull meaningless games and only to see if the shock would wake up my partners. Broadcasters, who watch every game, would realize immediately

Umpires have worked very hard to command the kind of respect that Joe Brinkman is receiving here from Manny Trillo (kneeling) and Garry Hancock (genuflecting). For myself, I never required bowing and scraping; a simple "sir" was fine with me.   WIDE WORLD

When the Syracuse University football team arrived
Florida to play in the 1959 Orange Bowl, these beauti
young ladies presented me with an armful of oranges.
I stood there with my arms around them, I could o
think of one thing: I'm *so* grateful we weren't invite
the *Gator Bowl*!

Every baseball argument follows a predictable four-stage pattern:

Objection! Ralph Houk takes exception and states his objection to a Joe Brinkman detection.

WIDE WORLD

Rejection. Steve Palermo explains his rejection of Rod Carew's objection while Jerry Neudecker offers protection.

WIDE WORLD

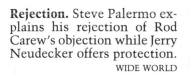

Ejection! Earl Weaver's predilection for making vociferous objections earns another ejection (from Marty Springstead; Durwood Merrill watches the connection).

WIDE WORLD

Dejection. Bill Haller consoles me after my rejection of
an objection led to an ejection. He knew I'd have to file a
report that night. WIDE WORLD

This incident occurred in my second month as an AL
ump. I handled it pretty well, discounting the beanings
and near-riot.

THE AMERICAN LEAGUE OF
PROFESSIONAL BASEBALL CLUBS
280 BOYLSTON STREET
BOSTON, MASSACHUSETTS 02116

UMPIRE REPORT

7/5/69 night   Boston   Ron Luciano
DATE GAME PLAYED   HOME CLUB   Washington

Name of player or players reported on   Managers Ted and
Dick Williams, Humphreys, Siebert

Give detailed description of incident or offence, stating players involved, inning in which incident or offence occurred, and action taken by yourself.

In the top of the 8th inning Siebert
brushed Howard back and hit him on the
arm He then brushed back McMullen In
the bottom of the 8th, Humphreys threw
2 pitches high over Yastrzemski head walking
him. Then he threw at him again. As I
started toward the mound both benches
poured out onto the field Mr Umont
restored order almost immediately
and took both managers aside, telling
them this must stop. Ted Williams
said something about this happening

in another series and Mr Umont
said that he was not interested in
the past. Mr Umont ejected Humphreys
and told Managers Ted and Dick
Williams along with Siebert they would
be reported and ejected if one
more close pitch was thrown No other
Pitch came close.

Time and date this report was written.

7/5/69 Midnight
Mailed from   Boston

R. Luciano
Umpire's Signature

In your opinion was conduct of player under
circumstances judged   ACTION TAKEN BY PRESIDENT

ROUTINE
OFFENSIVE
VERY OFFENSIVE

After failing a tryout with the Washington Senators, no one ever thought Fidel Castro would wind up as the Prime Minister of Cuba. But here he is, winding up. Remember, in Caribbean baseball, umpires can do whatever they want to do. First the dictator tells them what to do, then they do it.

WIDE WORLD

Many umpires have unusual hobbies off the field. Jerry Dale, for example, goes on photographic safaris in Africa. I spent my winters entering Fidel Castro look-alike contests.

Durwood Merrill, right, Billy Martin, left. And that's exactly what happened when Billy objected to Durwood's record-breaking call against Rickey Henderson (right, top). The record? Henderson had just been caught stealing for the 38th time in one season. Just three days later, Durwood calls Henderson safe at second base (middle photo), a record-tying 118th steal. Every umpire likes to share in historic moments, and seconds later, when Henderson successfully stole third, Mike Reilly had the honor of signaling the record-smashing 119th steal (bottom).

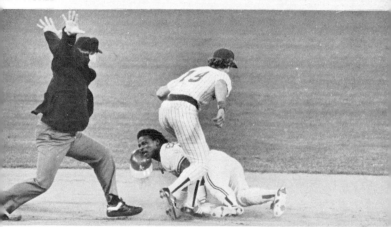

On occasion, managers will argue about the most ridiculous things. Here, for example, Giants manager Frank Robinson tries to convince ump Doug Harvey that the double-knit uniform worn by the Phillies Joe Lefebvre is not as durable as the old flannel uniforms worn during Robinson's Hall of Fame career as an active player.

WIDE WORLD

When Kenny Kaiser wants to eat, he's unstoppable. Here, stalking a hot-dog vendor, Ken is seen as Chet Lemon of the White Sox distracts him and two California Angel players move in to calm him down (top). Actually, Kenny is a sweet, gentle man who enjoys sneaking up behind people and hugging them. Here he is with Rick Dempsey and Jim Rice.

Tommy Lasorda and Eric Gregg both love fine restaurants and often recommend places to each other. Top, Tommy suggests a place Eric should go to, then, lower left, Eric tells Tommy where he should go, and finally Eric tells Tommy to go there *right now*.

Yes, Earl Weaver is short. No, Bill Haller isn't looking for him. Bill had just been run over by a Tiger, Larry Herndon. It could have been worse; he might have been stepped on by a Giant.

WIDE WORLD

Davey Phillips showing Billy Martin the famous Pine Tar Game affidavit. Davey is explaining some of the big words, like "base," "touch," and "home run."

WIDE WORLD

In order to speed up his quest for the all-time strikeout record, Nolan Ryan experimented with a one pitch, three baseball, delivery. Naturally, it didn't work: nearly all batters were able to get a piece of the third ball and foul it off.   WIDE WORLD

Billy Martin and I often entertained each other and the fans by doing impersonations. Here, Billy is doing a crazed manager and I'm doing Winston Churchill ejecting a manager from a baseball game, long a personal favorite of mine.   WIDE WORLD

In umpire school and throughout their careers, umpires are rated in five categories:

☐ hustle

☐ judgment

☐ appearance

☐ positioning

☐ knowledge of the rules

Few persons realize how generous Earl Weaver really is. Throughout his career, without ever being asked, he would come on the ballfield and give umpires a piece of his mind. Here Rocky Roe gets a fine point and Marty Springstead his cap in the bargain.

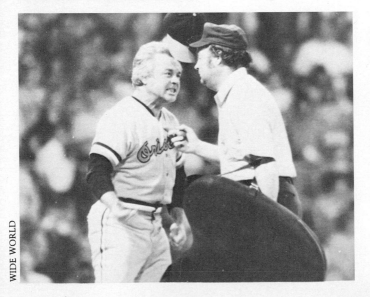

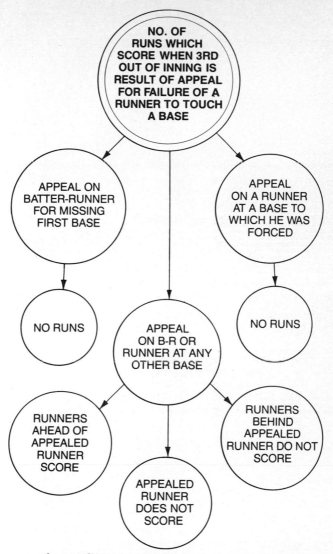

If u cn fllw ths chrt u cn b a mjr lg ump!

This is a page from Nick Bremigan's 'Rules for Idiots' or, as I thought of it, *The Luciano Handbook.* It's part of the manual used by students at Joe Brinkman's Umpire School.

In my first book, *The Umpire Strikes Back*, I asked for help finding my long-lost cousins Nina, Fonda, and Mary. After the book was published and got on the bestseller list, newspapers around the country were printing photographs of me, either in reviews of the book or in advertisements for it. One fine spring day in Denver, Mary noticed her cat wouldn't eat its food. Wouldn't go near the dish. The dish had some newspaper underneath it, and right next to the dish was a photograph. Mary realized the man in the photograph was frightening the cat. She took up the paper and the cat started to eat. Mary looked at the photo and thought this man bore a striking resemblance to her long-lost cousin Ronnie. She immediately called Fonda and Nina. They read the ad closely and decided it *must* be their long-lost cousin Ronnie. The three of them went to the local bookstore to look at the book—*look* at it, not buy it (this should have convinced them we were related then and there)—and when they saw my baby picture inside, the same baby picture that had been on Mary's mantelpiece for years, they were overwhelmed. Furiously turning pages they found the photo of themselves and *almost* bought a copy on the spot.

A reunion in Endicott followed; a terrific time was had by all, and my mother sold them copies at a discount.

I was doing something different, but most of them couldn't tell exactly what it was. It just looked unusual. Ernie Harwell, in Detroit, was the only person who instantly knew what I was doing, and then he assumed I was having problems with my right arm.

American League umpires supervisor Dick Butler also noticed it right away. I had called a few left-handed strikes in Anaheim one evening and found Butler waiting for me in the umpires' room after the game. "Gees, Ronnie," Dick asked, "is your right arm sore?"

"Yeah, Dick," I told him, "I think it's my tennis elbow acting up again." Bill Haller fell off the bench when I said that. The closest I'd ever been to tennis was having a conversation with Oakland catcher Gene Tenace.

"I figured," Dick continued. "I know you didn't realize it, Ronnie, but you called some strikes with your left hand tonight."

"No!" I said. "You're kidding me?" Then I sort of raised my left arm awkwardly into the air. "Like this?" Haller was trying so hard not to laugh I thought he might die.

"Something like that. Listen, I know you must have done it subconsciously, but . . ."

Most umpires really shout out "BALL!" and "STRIKE!" on each pitch, although after a while it becomes "NAAALLLLL" and "YEAKKKIKKE." Lee Weyer teaches students in school to never, ever add the position of the baseball, for example, "inside, ball one," because it gives the batter something specific to complain about. Of course, Lee Weyer often calls out, "BALL'S INSIDE" or "BALL'S LOW." This, I presume, is another application of the six-six rule, meaning anybody over six-six can do just about anything he wants to do.

Jack Sheridan, who umpired in the 1890s, had the most unique way of calling a third strike I've ever heard of. "Strike three!" he would scream, then add, "San Jose, California, the Garden Spot of America." It never occurred to me to sell advertising during my career, but even if I had, I would have had problems. What could I holler, "Endicott, New York, shoe repair capital of western New York State!"?

The thing I had the most difficulty mastering in umpire school was throwing a new baseball out to the pitcher after a foul ball had been hit into the stands, or when the pitcher requested a different ball. Many umpires have played baseball and like to show off their throwing ability. As a former football player, all I have to show off are my scars. So I usually handed new baseballs to the catcher and let him throw them to the pitcher.

Lee Weyer probably has the strongest throwing arm among umpires. During his first few major league years, if he felt a pitcher was complaining too much, he'd just rifle a new ball out to the mound. He stopped doing that the afternoon he drilled pitcher Eli Grba in the stomach. "Tell Weyer ..." Grba said, gasping, "if he ... wants to pitch ... he should come ... out here. ..."

In fact, most umpires have hit a pitcher at some time in their career. Dale Ford actually knocked someone cold in the minors. "We used to talk about throwing arms all the time," he recalls, "and I always thought I had good control, although there were times that pitchers had to make great plays on my throws. One year in Triple-A we had a young pitcher come up and he immediately started giving everybody a tough time. He was griping on every pitch. I wanted to straighten him out right away, so after a foul ball into the stands one night I threw a bullet out to him. Unfortunately, it was a rising fast ball. It sailed over his glove and hit him in the forehead. I didn't just straighten him out, I flattened him out."

Jerry Dale and Dick Stello both occasionally throw knuckle balls back to the pitcher. Dale claims his knuckle ball is so good he could win with it in the National League, and sometimes he tells pitchers as he throws it, "Throw this one next time." Joe Brinkman will toss an occasional spitball—explaining that baseballs get perspiration on them in the umpires' ball bag and sink naturally when he throws them out to the mound.

Now that I've retired, Ken Kaiser has the worst throwing arm in the major leagues. He hits third basemen, first basemen—he'd hit center fielders if he could reach them. His problem is that he is too muscular. One thing I have learned is that if you are going to have a problem, being too muscular is about as good a problem as you can have.

Just as umpires will never allow a player to show them up, they should be very careful never to show up a player. Once, after I'd threatened to eject a player for letting the fans know he thought I'd blown a call, he told me he thought I was showing him up by going through elaborate actions to call him out and laughing when he struck out. I thought about that—and realized he was absolutely right. I was doing exactly what I criticized players for doing, and from that game on I tried to prevent my enthusiasm from overcoming my good judgment. I certainly never did anything as insulting as the umpire who handed pitcher Dick Ruthven a new baseball after Ruthven had given up a long triple, and said, "You'd better take this new one. That kid ruined the other one."

Although ball and strike calls cause the most arguments, the most difficult plays for a plate umpire are safes and outs at home, batters being hit by pitches, and half swings. Making the correct call in each of these situations requires getting the proper angle. Hold the palms of your hands very close together in front of you. Turn them so you're looking directly at the back of one hand. Can you *see* if your two palms are touching? I *know* you can feel it, but this is a visual aid, not a test. You can't really see if your hands are making contact. Now, turn your hands so that your thumbs are facing you. Can you now see if your two palms are touching? Of course, because you have the proper angle.

Once, at a banquet during the off-season, I tried to explain this to a noted major league manager. He watched me put my palms together, and nodded, then asked, "Which one's the base and which one's the runner?"

"Neither one. This has nothing to do with the base and the runner," I explained.

"Then how can you tell if he's safe or out from that?"

"No," I said, "this is an example. It's a means of showing how important it is to have the correct angle in making a call."

"Right," he said, "I understand that, I just don't understand which hand is the base and which hand is the runner."

"Neither one is the runner!"

"Then why are you showing it to me?"

If I could have, I would have thrown him out of the banquet, pre-chicken. The point I was trying to make to him was that it is very difficult for the home-plate umpire to get the right angle on most plays at the plate because the action usually takes place in front of him. He also has problems seeing batters actually hit by the baseball because the batter is usually twisting to avoid the ball, and his body blocks the umpire's vision.

Jerry Dale was working the plate during a Dodgers–Phillies game when a Steve Carlton fast ball ran in on Pedro Guerrero. The ball hit something and rebounded wildly, but Dale really couldn't tell if it had hit Guerrero's arm or the bat handle. "It sounded like it hit wood," he says, "but I wasn't sure. Guerrero immediately dropped his bat and started running toward first base. I decided he was trying to fake me into the call, so I yelled, 'Foul ball!'

"He stopped in his tracks and started screaming, 'The ball hit me, the ball hit me!' Then he pulled up the sleeve of his uniform jersey and pointed to his bicep. 'See?' he said. All I could see was this big muscle. It looked to me like he was carrying a rock in his arm. I didn't see anything that indicated a ball had struck him.

"Tommy Lasorda came trotting out to me and said firmly but calmly, 'The ball hit him, Jerry.' How Tommy could be so sure from the dugout when I couldn't tell from three feet away I didn't know, but I figured if he could call pitches a half inch off the plate from there, this must have been an easy call for him. He wasn't angry and he wasn't yelling, he was just trying to convince me that Guerrero had been hit by the pitch. As he was talking, I looked over at the Phillies dugout and manager Pat Corrales had one foot on the top step, tapping nervously, just waiting for me to change my call and send Guerrero to first base.

"Meanwhile, Tommy was trying to reason with me. 'Listen,' he said, 'this is my Number Four hitter, my cleanup hitter. You know I want him to hit, he wants to hit, but—'

"That was just what I wanted to hear. 'Great, Tommy,' I interrupted, 'then we're all gonna be happy, because he's gonna hit.' That was when Lasorda really got mad."

To make the hit batsman call even more difficult, the batter must make some effort to avoid the pitch to be entitled to first base. This is an umpire's judgment call and, subconsciously, part of that judgment is whether the umpire will be able to leave the ball park in one piece if he doesn't give the batter the base.

Harry Wendlestedt had home plate the night the Dodgers' Don Drysdale was trying to pitch his fifth consecutive shutout, tying the major league record for consecutive scoreless innings pitched. Drysdale had shut out the San Francisco Giants for eight innings but got in a jam in the ninth. The Giants had loaded the bases with no outs and catcher Dick Dietz was the batter.

Drysdale was never reluctant to move a batter away from the plate with an inside fast ball. Once, in fact, a batter started digging into the dirt with his spikes to get a better foothold and the Dodgers' catcher warned him, "Now you've made him angry. If I were you, I'd just keep digging." Dietz had an open stance and leaned over the plate when he batted. With the count two balls and one strike, Drysdale hit Dietz with a soft breaking pitch. But before Dietz took his first step, Wendlestedt was waving his arms and screaming, "No! No! No!" Dietz had moved into the pitch, he said, and refused to award him first base, thus preventing the run that would have ended Drysdale's scoreless streak from scoring. Naturally, the Giants found fault with this judgment and proceeded to verbalize their displeasure at some length.

When everything finally quieted down, Wendlestedt called the pitch a strike. That took more guts than it does to call Andre the Giant a sissy. After that riot ended, Dietz flied out and Drysdale retired the next two batters to tie the record, which he broke a few days later.

Calling half swings correctly requires years of experience behind the plate, keen judgment, a thorough understanding of the strike zone, extremely acute vision, total concentration, and a knowledge of the particular batter's swing. Before making his decision, the umpire has to take all of these aspects into consideration and then he is able to make a good guess.

There is absolutely no way an umpire can really see how far the head of the bat, the thick part, has penetrated into the strike zone. The batter is quicker than the eye. Experience helps, but not as much as a good relationship with the first- and third-base umpires. A base umpire on speaking terms with the plate umpire will rarely contradict his decision. When I was working the plate I would yell either, "Did he go?" if I wasn't sure I'd made the right call and wanted assistance, or "He swung, didn't he?" if I believed I'd made the right call and just wanted it supported.

Lee Weyer had the perfect answer for a half-swing situation. Deron Johnson started to swing at a pitch six inches off the plate but held back. Lee struck him out anyway. Johnson asked disgustedly, "Was it a strike, or did I swing?"

"Both," Lee told him, taking absolutely no chances.

Probably the most heated argument I had during my career took place during the 1978 American League playoffs (with the exception of that silly afternoon when the Orioles made such a big deal over the fact that I called a foul ball a home run), when the Yankees' Lou Piniella tried to score from second on a hit and, although he beat the throw, had his foot in the air when it passed over home plate.

I knew the instant replay was not going to show Piniella's foot in the air, because every camera shot would be from above and couldn't possibly show the few inches between the foot and the plate. Fortunately, I was in the proper position; unfortunately, I was the only person in the entire ball park in that position. To everybody else he looked safe, but I knew he was out. Explaining it was the difficult part.

Close plays on the bases may eventually lead to runs; close plays at the plate lead to runs immediately. The umpire's decision goes right up on the scoreboard and often makes the difference in the ball game. So arguments about those decisions are going to last longer and be more heated than discussions of other plays. I've always suspected this was the real reason plate umpires wear all that extra protection.

There are many places an umpire can position himself when making a safe or an out call at home. He can stay behind the plate to make sure the runner touches it, but then he'll probably be behind the catcher's back and won't be able to see if the catcher juggles the ball when applying the tag. Or the umpire can get in front of the plate to see if the runner reaches the plate or the catcher juggles the ball, but then he has to make sure he doesn't get hit by the fielder's throw, or trampled by the pitcher running in to back up the play, or upended by a second or third base runner trying to score on the same sequence. Or he can move to the side of the plate so he can see if the runner touches the plate and if the catcher tags him without juggling the ball, meanwhile allowing the pitcher and other base runners to get safely past him and not interfering with the throw. Then all he has to do is hope the catcher does not move up the third-base line to make a diving swipe tag, which he will not be able to see, or that an infielder doesn't cut off the outfielder's throw and make a second throw, which will change the entire angle of the play, or that he doesn't trip over the bat the hitter has tossed away, or the catcher's mask the catcher has tossed away.

Actually, there are no good places in which an umpire can position himself when making a safe or an out call at the plate. He should get as close as possible and hope he gets a good look at it.

Sometimes it's easy. In the top of the tenth inning of a game between the Washington Senators and the Baltimore Orioles, a Washington runner slid across the plate, beating the throw so easily the Orioles catcher didn't even bother applying a tag. The runner got up, brushed off his uniform, and started walking away. But then the catcher realized that umpire Emmett Ashford hadn't made any call.

The catcher chased the runner to the Washington dugout and tagged him. *That's* when Emmett finally made a call, jerking his right hand into the air and calling the runner out.

Senators manager Gil Hodges was enraged. He got so close to Ashford that he came between Emmett and his shadow. "There was no play at the plate, Emmett," Gil pleaded. "How could he possibly be out?"

"It's like this, Gil," Emmett said, then paused before delivering one of the truly splendid explanations in umpire-explanation history. "When your runner slid, he bounced over the plate!"

And all I told the Yankees was that Piniella's *leg* was in the air.

There are extraordinary situations in which the basic rules of baseball do not apply. For example, the rules state clearly that for a run to score, a player must touch home plate. Unless, of course, there is no home plate.

In the deciding game of the 1977 American League playoffs, the Yankees' Chris Chambliss hit a home run leading off the bottom of the ninth to win the game and the pennant. As the baseball cleared the right-center-field fence, thousands of fans leaped onto the field to celebrate. Meanwhile, Chambliss was trying to circle the bases. "I got to first base before the fans did," Chris remembers, "but they got to me as I tripped over second base. They were trying to take away my helmet, my shirt, anything for a souvenir. I put my helmet under my arm, bowed my head, and ran toward third base. Third base was gone. So I just rounded the spot where it used to be and went straight into the dugout—I didn't want anybody taking *me* home as a souvenir. When I got into the clubhouse everybody started asking me, 'Did you touch home plate?'

"I noticed that nobody had stayed around to watch me. 'Heck,' I told them, 'I didn't even touch third.' Then I mentioned that there was no home plate.

"Nobody knew what to do, so we got Billy [Martin] and told him. He said that he thought I should go out there and touch the home plate area, as long as he didn't have to go. So we got two policemen and went back onto the field. We went to the spot where home plate used to be and I touched the dirt."

I can make one guarantee: As soon as the mob swarmed onto the field, the umpires decided Chambliss touched all the bases. Once again, Caribbean riot training came in handy.

Now, there are many people who believe umpires are not smart enough to come in out of the rain, and there are just as many people who believe umpires are smart enough to come in out of the rain. This belief is usually based on the score of the ball game when it starts raining.

Only umpires are required to answer this philosophical question: When is enough rain? Once a game has started, the decision to stop play before five innings are completed (or four and a half innings if the home team is ahead), in which case the game is simply replayed from the beginning, or call it after five innings when it is an official game and the team leading at the end of the last completed inning is the winner, is solely that of the home-plate umpire. There is one thing of which that umpire can always be certain: For the team losing, there will never be enough rain to call the game. A monsoon might be taking place, flood waters can be sweeping away the outfield fences, waves can be washing over the bleachers, and the manager of the trailing team will come to the umpires' room and say, "It's not raining at the airport," or "The radio just said it's going to stop in five minutes," or, "It's a good thing this field drains quickly."

The decision to resume play after a long rain

delay is one in which the umpire has to choose between the angry gorilla and the irate lion. If, after a suitable delay, he decides the rain is not going to stop or the field is unplayable, the manager of the losing team will scream, "You just want to get home early!" It can be 2:00 A.M., play might have been halted five times and an old man might be putting pairs of animals in an ark in center field, but the umpire just wants to get home quickly. Or, if the rain stops and play is resumed, the manager of the team in the lead will threaten, "I want to go on record as warning you that if one of my players gets hurt because you're forcing them to play on this field, I'm gonna hold you personally responsible."

After the game has started, the umpires usually will do everything possible to get in at least five (or (four and a half) innings and make it an official game; otherwise it will add another game to the schedule, which umpires love about as much as vampires enjoy a sunny day at the beach. But when it is threatening to rain the manager of the team in the lead will do everything possible to speed up the game, including ordering his players to make outs intentionally, while the manager of the trailing team will try to slow things down to the speed of the Nash Metropolitan that McSherry and I bought in Florida. It is the umpire's job to prevent either of these managers from being successful and to protect the integrity of the game.

Sometimes, though, managers will fool us. Sometimes, in fact, they will fool themselves. When Durwood Merrill was in Triple-A, Shreveport, the visiting team, was leading by one run in the bottom of the fifth inning. If the half inning was completed without the other team scoring the game would be official, Shreveport would win the game. "You could see the storm coming," Durwood remembers, "and I've gotta get three outs to make it official. The home team got the potential tying run to second with one out. Then Shreveport's manager, who later managed briefly in the major leagues, came out and told me he wanted to substitute for his right fielder. I figured he was putting a player with a stronger throwing arm out there, a good move in this situation. The manager went back into the dugout and we got ready to resume play. Suddenly he called 'Time!' and came marching out of the dugout. He told me he wanted to put in a new center fielder. Okay, I told him. I was figuring that he was a real strategist, he was putting in his best throwing arms in the outfield to cut off the tying run at the plate.

"Then he put in a new left fielder and a new first baseman. It began to dawn on me that he was stalling. I couldn't figure out why, he was winning the game, but when he put in a pitcher to play third base I was sure of it. I finally threw him out of the game. I decided that anyone who didn't know that rule didn't deserve to stay around."

Sometimes players will drop small hints to the umpire about weather conditions. Once, for example, when I was working the plate during a heavy drizzle in Detroit, the Tigers' Norm Cash came to bat wearing toy eyeglasses with windshield wipers. And years ago, the New York Giants' great deaf and dumb pitcher, Dummy Hoy, waddled out to the pitcher's mound during a rainstorm wearing the groundskeeper's hip boots, a rain slicker, and a sou'wester.

The only person in baseball who can *cause* a rainstorm is the Atlanta Braves' cheerleader-mascot Chief Noc-A-Homa. During a promotional appearance at nearby Huntsville, Chief Noc-A-Homa, a member of the Ottawa-Chippewa tribe, did a traditional rain dance. It rained within hours, ending a drought, although no precipitation had been predicted. A week later, before a Braves game, the chief did the rain dance on the field. Within seconds, the entire sprinkler system went on, soaking him.

After an umpire has halted play, he must wait at least thirty minutes before calling off the game.

But there is no rule how long he may wait before resuming play. If, in fact, forecasters are predicting the storm will end within a reasonable period of time, umpires may wait hours before deciding.

Catcher Clint "Scraps" Courtney was a feisty player who later became a feisty minor league manager. Although never a great hitter, he was proud of the fact that he was very tough to strike out. Once, when he was with the Orioles, he was at bat with a full count on him in the bottom of the ninth inning. Baltimore was trailing by one run but had the bases loaded. Suddenly, one pitch away from either a tie or a complete game, it started pouring and the game was halted. The umpires waited almost three hours before resuming play. The first pitch to Courtney was a called third strike, ending the game. Manager Jimmy Dykes was livid. "My toughest hitter to strike out," he complained, "and he takes a fast ball for strike three."

"Yeah, sure I struck out," Courtney said when he heard Dykes complain, "but it took 'em three hours to do it."

Weather problems usually are the reason games are called or suspended today, with the occasional exception of a hole in the dome, but until every major league stadium except Chicago's Wrigley Field installed lights, games often were called because of darkness. How dark was too dark? About as much rain is enough! In those days players would do everything from coming to bat with a miner's hat on to carrying a flashlight to the plate to hint to the umpire that it was getting too dark to continue playing. The Yankees' Lefty Gomez came up to bat against Cleveland's Bob Feller in the twilight and struck a match. Umpire Bill Summers was not amused and ordered Gomez to put it out, telling him, "You can see the mound."

"Oh, I can see Feller, all right," Lefty replied. "What I want to make sure is that Feller can see Gomez."

Both the easiest and most difficult thing for an umpire to do is forfeit a baseball game. The rules governing when a game shall be forfeited are quite explicit, but umpires do not want to charge a team with a loss when the game hasn't been contested on the field. Earl Weaver pulled the Orioles off the field in the fifth inning in Toronto during the 1977 pennant race because he wanted some loose boards holding down the rainproof tarpaulin removed. Marty Springstead tried to convince Earl to put his team back on the field, but when he absolutely refused, he had no choice but to award the victory to Toronto.

In 1975, Beer Night in Cleveland got dangerous and Nestor Chylak had to forfeit the game, but that was nothing compared to Bill Veeck's Anti-Disco fiasco at Chicago's Comiskey Park. As a promotion, Veeck offered an admission discount to anyone who brought a disco record with him or her to the ball park. Between games of a White Sox–Detroit Tigers double-header there was to be a huge bonfire to "destroy disco" by burning the records. It turned out that more people disliked disco than even Veeck anticipated, and fifty thousand anti-rock 'n' roll fans showed up.

In the seventh inning of the first game, one fan sailed his record onto the field. Then a second fan did it. Then a third. Then four thousand. From the seventh inning on, a shower of records rained onto the field. Plate umpire Davey Phillips had to halt the game about five times to allow the grounds crew to pick them up. Finally though, the game ended. The anti-disco demonstration began.

Normally, umpires are supposed to allow twenty minutes between games of a double-header, but this varies depending on the quality of the between-games meal served in the umpires' room. If a complete, hot meal is waiting for the umpires after the first game, it may be twenty-five minutes before the second game starts, giving the fans an additional five minutes to spend money at concession stands. But if the umpires are served cold hot dogs on frozen rolls, that second game might start eight or nine minutes after the end of the first game, and the fans have less time to spend their money.

About fifteen minutes after the first game had ended, a security guard came into the umpires' room and told Phillips the second game could not start on time, as approximately twenty-five thousand fans were destroying disco on the field. Apparently they were also destroying the field.

The umpires agreed that one of them had to go out there to see if the field was in playable condition. The problem was *which* one of them. Phillips decided it should be a democratic decision, so he suggested the four of them take a secret ballot. And, by a vote of 7–2, Phillips won.

Durwood Merrill volunteered to go with him. "I'll be right behind you," he said, "maybe forty or fifty yards. Just shout if you need help, but you'd better shout loud." Since going onto the field dressed in an umpire's blues would be akin to going out there wearing an "Elvis Loved Disco" T-shirt, they both put on groundskeeper's coveralls and solemnly shook hands with their partners. Phillips gave Dan Morrison a letter to mail in case something happened out there and, with Durwood whistling the first verse of the "High and the Mighty" walked onto the field at Comiskey Park.

They returned within a few minutes, shaken. Durwood slumped into his folding chair, his head bowed, and said in an astonished whisper, "It's gone."

"Home plate?" Morrison asked.

Durwood looked up at him and said evenly, "Comiskey Park."

Meanwhile, Detroit Manager Sparky Anderson was claiming the field was unplayable and demanding a forfeit, while White Sox' owner Bill Veeck was insisting he could get the fans off the field and the game could be played. "How?" Davey Phillips asked Veeck. "The grass is gone, home plate is

gone, the pitcher's mound . . . gone, the rest rooms
. . . gone . . . center field is smoldering . . ."

"Details," Veeck said.

Supervisor of Umpires Nestor Chylak happened
to be there for the party, and he suggested to Phillips,
"Look, let's start the game, and if one record comes
onto the field we'll call it off."

"One record?" Phillips said. "One record? You've
got 50,000 people there and you're waiting for one
record and then you're going to try to stop the
game? Nestor," Phillips continued, "I've learned a
lot from you. And the thing I remember you telling
me right at the beginning of my career is to never
give myself the worst of it. Let me tell you something, if I go back on that field, I'll be giving myself
the worst of it."

Nestor thought about that for a moment, then
said, "You know, maybe you're right. I wouldn't go
out there either."

In situations like this, when twenty-five thousand dancing fans are setting fire to the field, the
best thing for an owner or general manager to do is
offer the umpires more food. But in this case even
that wouldn't have been enough. Phillips decided
that the field was unusable and suspended the second game.

The next day American League President Lee
MacPhail ruled that the White Sox had failed to
provide adequate playing facilities and awarded the
game to the Tigers, probably the only time in baseball history a game has been forfeited because of a
record-breaking performance by the fans.

Sometimes, though, the plate umpire would be
better off if a game had been called or suspended,
because more than an umpire's pride can be hurt
behind the plate. Foul balls, thrown catchers' masks,
and tossed bats inevitably are drawn to the most
vulnerable spot on an umpire's body. Many umpires have lost teeth, have had toes smashed, and

have twisted ankles and knees while working the plate; and every umpire who has stood back there has been bruised on his shoulders and arms. One man I worked with in the minor leagues even suffered a scalp burn when a foul ball whizzed by his head.

Because a plate umpire needs as much protection as possible, almost everything he wears is different from that of a base umpire. The plate hat, for example, has a much smaller brim than a base hat so that a face mask can be easily taken off and put on. Plate shoes have steel toe plates to deflect foul balls. Beneath the shoes umpires wear long, thin sanitary hose to absorb perspiration, and black socks, never blue, always black and only black—which made it difficult for me to understand how I could end up wearing two different-colored socks. Plate pants have extra-wide legs so that shinguards can be worn beneath them, and an extra-wide waist if the umpire uses the inside chest protector. Plate pants also have canvas pockets so they will last longer. They do, however, have an ordinary zipper in the proper place.

Why, people ask, do umpires wear wide belts even when thin belts are in fashion? Besides holding up their pants, the wide belts are needed to hold canvas ball bags. Right-handed umpires wear their ball bags, which holds five or six new baseballs, on their right side, and left-handed umpires wear them on their left side, making it easy for them to dip into the bag when a new ball is needed and toss it to the pitcher. Except left-handed Kenny Kaiser, naturally, who keeps his ball bag on his right side and, when he needs a new ball, has to reach awkwardly across his body to grab it. When I asked him why he did this, he explained, "I throw left-handed, but I think right-handed."

Plate shirts are larger than base shirts to provide room for the inside chest protector. When I first came up to the majors, the American League insisted that all umpires wear long-sleeve shirts, even though the sleeves were covered by long-sleeve coats. The reason for this was obvious: Umpires have always worn long-sleeve shirts. I tried to point out that at one time umpires also wore silk high hats and sat on a high chair set to the side of home plate, but no one understood what that had to do with long-sleeve shirts.

Eventually, after only a hundred years, umpires were permitted to wear short-sleeve shirts. Imagine, putting in the designated-hitter rule and allowing umpires to wear short-sleeve shirts in the same century. And some people think baseball is conservative.

The most important thing about a shirt was the league patch. In the minor leagues this patch was always worn over the heart to show undying devotion to the Florida State League or the Appalachian League. Although I never actually did it, when I was in the minors I always wanted to sew a bowling league patch to my shirt, and when someone asked me what league I was in I would tell them, "Mixed doubles." Sometimes life in the minor leagues wasn't all that exciting.

Umpires also had to wear their coats behind the plate my first few years in the majors. They were a very attractive burgundy color, which is obviously why we were called the men in blue. The pockets of these coats were large enough to hold eight baseballs. This was not the kind of jacket one would wear to a dinner party, unless it was being held on the pitcher's mound.

The decision to put identifying numerals on the shirt and coat was made while I was still active. I voted against it. I told them I preferred not to be so easy to identify on the field. "Ronnie," Haller pointed out, "you're six-foot-four, you weigh three hundred pounds, and you have a face like a friendly beagle. Who do you think people are going to think you are?"

"Ken Kaiser?" I said hopefully.

Kaiser, in fact, was among the majority who voted to wear numbers on their sleeves. "I want my number on my shirt," he said.

I agreed with that. I told him, "I want your number on my shirt, too."

Black ties always had to be worn with the coat. No exceptions. A lot of people wore clip-on ties. I always wore the real thing. I firmly believed in sartorial elegance, so I would carefully tie a four-in-hand, being very careful that the top knot was even at the collar and that the dimple was in the center of the tie. Then I would take my tie clasp, a rusty safety pin, and pin that thing to my shirt. Other people with All-Star game and World Series souvenir tie clasps had ties popping out all the time, while my rusty safety pin held my tie down. The only exception to the tie rule was veteran Jocko Conlan, who wore a polka-dot bow tie throughout his umpiring career. The bow tie was his trademark, in the same way my shirttail coming out of my pants was my trademark.

In addition, most umpires carry a handkerchief, and plate umpires have either a pen or a pencil with which to mark changes on the lineup cards. Incredibly, I went through my entire career without ever forgetting to carry a ballpoint pen onto the field. At the beginning of my career, when plate umpires were still required to wear coats, I would be sweating so profusely by the end of the game that the lineup cards in my pocket looked like someone had left them in a shirt being laundered. I couldn't even read what had originally been written on them, much less write anything new. It was embarrassing to have a manager come out to me with a lineup change and have to take this rolled-up wad of paper out of my pocket and pretend to be writing on it. Eventually I began carrying a plastic pocket insert, the type used by soda delivery men to carry pens, and stuffed everything in there. It worked out very well: I always had a pen, and the lineup cards stayed dry. I didn't sell too many cases of soda, however.

My pen also came in handy during an argument I had one night in Texas. A Ranger ballplayer called me a "stupid @$#%$¢!" I was so shocked, I pulled out my ballpoint pen and a slip of paper, got ready to write something, and challenged him to repeat it. He stared at the pen and paper for a few seconds, trying to decide what to do, then finally waved his hand at me and said, "Oh, don't gimme that. You're such a #%$@¢$&% #) (¢&¢er, you can't even spell @$#%#$¢."

"Maybe not," I admitted, "but I sure can spell ejection.' "

Two items umpires are advised not to wear on the field are a ring and a wristwatch. That always made sense to me. An umpire never knows when he might meet a mugger behind second base and have to give up his ring, and he doesn't need a watch because he isn't going anywhere until the game is over. Actually, the theory is that the baseball will hit the ring or watch and break them. Plate umpires are supposed to carry a stopwatch with them so they can give a five-minute warning to a player or manager if that becomes necessary. It could be very embarrassing to an umpire, for example, if he warns a manager to get his team back on the field within five minutes and then has to ask the manager if he happens to have the correct time.

Umpires often carry two keys with them, one to the lock on the ball bag in the umpires' room, the other to the umpires' room itself. Baseballs that have been rubbed up but are not used in the game are stored in a locked bag in the umpires' room. Each umpire has a copy of the key that will open the bag in every ball park. Bill Haller still has the original key issued to him. Ken Kaiser has lost eighty-five keys.

One of the most embarrassing things that can happen to an umpiring crew is to be locked out of their dressing room after a game. This has happened. I've often wondered where an umpire can lose his key. He goes from the locker room to the field to the locker room. But keys have been lost, and crews have had to stand outside the door waiting for security to open the door. There is really only one American League rule about umpires' room door keys: Ken Kaiser will not carry them.

The single most important piece of protective equipment worn by an umpire, with the exception of the protective cup, is the face mask. There are two types of masks: the wire cage and the bar mask. The cage has a number of crisscrossing thin wires that distribute the force of a blow from a foul ball, while the bar mask has two thick steel bars set just close enough to prevent a baseball from fitting between them. Vision is better with the cage, but over a period of time enough balls are fouled off the wires to bend them, and a two-inch opening is narrowed to a half inch and the umpire thinks his sight is failing because he can't see the high pitch any longer.

When using either type of mask, it is imperative that the umpire does not flinch and turn his head to try to avoid a foul ball or a pitch that gets by the catcher. The masks will absorb most of the shock, preventing serious injury, but the umpire who turns away is going to get hit on the side of the head or in the ear and really get hurt. In umpire school, whenever a student flinched behind the plate, Iron Mike, the motorized pitching machine, was put on the mound and threw a hundred pitches. The student would have to stand behind the plate with his mask and chest protector and let those pitches bounce off his equipment.

The problem Bill Haller had with the protective mask was unusual. He has very tender skin, and the padding of the mask often would cause a small rash. To avoid this, Bill would put Dr. Scholl's bunion pads on the padding. And every time he worked the plate I'd see all these tiny decals—making the mask look like it had been taken on many vacations.

Recently Dodgers catcher Steve Yeager invented a throat protector that hangs down from the mask, creatively named a "throat protector" or a "Stevie."

On occasion an umpire will forget to wear part of his "bravery suit." One night in Kansas City Johnny Rice forgot his shinguards; naturally, a foul ball hit him on the knee and caused him to miss four games. Davey Phillips also forgot his shinguards once, but he realized it immediately—in the fifth inning. There were times I left my chest protector in the locker room, but I always realized something was missing before the game started and sent the ballboy for it. And I forgot to wear my mask in a game only once.

There are people who believe I don't really need a face mask, that a foul ball couldn't possibly do any more damage than nature did, but I liked to wear the wire mask when I worked behind the plate. Call me a sentimental fool.

I had the plate for an Indians–Oakland A's game in Cleveland. Davey Phillips was at first base. He remembers the night as well as I do. "You have to understand that Ronnie didn't just walk onto the field," Davey explains, "so much as he arrived. He was a natural showman. He'd go into both dugouts to say hello to everybody, then he'd visit the pitcher, the catcher, fans, he'd have everybody in a good mood before the game started. So finally, Ronnie has finished his introductions and we're ready for the first pitch. Bert Campaneris was leading off for the A's. The Indians' pitcher went into his windup and I glanced toward the plate—and realized Ronnie wasn't wearing his mask! 'A joke is a joke,' I thought, 'but this is dangerous! I started running in to the plate and called 'TIME!' "

Naturally, I didn't realize I wasn't wearing a mask. I just got down behind the catcher for the first pitch and thought, "This is going to be the best game I've ever called. I have never seen the ball better in my life." Then, as the pitch started toward the plate, the reason for that suddenly dawned on me.

I ducked down behind the catcher, Ray Fosse. I had no idea where the pitch was, high, low, inside, outside, I didn't know if Campaneris swung at it or not—but I figured, I didn't see it cross the plate, it had to be a ball.

Meanwhile, Davey Phillips was running toward me with his hands in the air. "What happened," Davey says, and he saw it, "was that Campaneris tried to push a bunt down the first-base line. He bunted the ball, but it hit him as he left the batter's box. Cleveland's manager, Ken Aspromonte, saw me running in and assumed I was going to call Campaneris out for running into a batted ball. So Aspromonte came charging out of the dugout screaming, 'You saw it! You saw it!' I told him that I hadn't seen anything. 'Yeah,' he yelled, 'then why were you running toward the plate?' So we started arguing."

Aspromonte and Phillips had a good one, Aspromonte claiming that Phillips was trying to change his call, while Davey was attempting to explain that he was calling time because I didn't have my mask. But by the time he was able to make that point, the ballboy had gone into the locker room and gotten my mask. Aspromonte saw me standing there with my mask in my right hand, smiling, and decided Phillips was trying to give him a tough time.

Eventually we called it no pitch and started the game again. So I did forget my protective mask once. But I never forgot my ballpoint pen.

The National League's Bill Klem invented the inside protector, so naturally the American League used the outside protector. Although "the balloon" was difficult to master, it did provide more protection for the umpire than Klem's device; using the outside protector was like hiding behind an inflatable wall. But it did make it difficult to bend down far enough to see the low pitch. Consequently, the American League strike zone was a bit higher than the National League's. Now, however, many American Leaguers have switched to the inside protector, so the two leagues are becoming more uniform in this regard.

Almost every umpire will insist he is not superstitious about his equipment. Lee Weyer, for example, has used the same chest protector since coming up to the National League in 1962. It is an old, beaten-up white protector, held together by patches. But he insists he continues to use it because it fits his body so well. "If I could find another one just like it, I'd get rid of this one immediately," he claims. I believe him, too. So if anyone has a white chest protector with patches all over it that's more than twenty years old and would fit six-six Lee Weyer, he would like to talk to you.

Durwood Merrill isn't superstitious either; he's worn his shinguards for only twelve years. And Davey Phillips used the shinguards and plate brush given to him by his father, famous minor-league umpire Bob Phillips, until they were so worn they could no longer be repaired. And Eddie Montague has not only worn the same shinguards since 1974, he also has always worn them on the wrong legs—with the buckles on the inside where they can catch on each other and open. But he is not superstitious.

Apparently the only thing umpires are superstitious about is admitting they are superstitious.

About the only optional piece of equipment used by an umpire is his indicator, the little plastic clicker used to keep track of balls, strikes, and outs. Lee Weyer takes no chances at all: He uses an indicator and shouts out the count after every pitch. Steve Palermo, though, is probably the only major league umpire who does not use one regularly. Others have tried, usually only once. Durwood Merrill, for example, decided in 1978 that he was going to work without an indicator. "It was fine as long as the count was one ball, no strikes," he remembers, "but about the fifth inning a base runner attempted to steal second base. There was a long argument and, when everything settled down and I got back behind the plate, I didn't have a clue what the count was. The scoreboard had been cleared, and I knew I couldn't trust it anyway. I thought, if I get out of this one, I'll get my indicator back and never let it out of my hand. I did get out of it too: I just walked the batter on three balls."

Umpires form emotional attachments to this little piece of plastic. I used mine until it was so worn down the wheels just kept spinning rather than stopping. Jerry Dale's indicator was held together by tape, and the numbers had been worn off before he finally retired it after working home plate in the fourth game of the '77 World Series. And Davey Phillips used an indicator to pay a tribute to a friend.

Phillips had worked the 1976 World Series with Lou DeMuro, an American League umpire killed in an accident in 1982. When Davey was assigned the 1982 World Series he dug out an old indicator Lou had given him years earlier and used it when he worked the plate. "I looked at it after the first few pitches," he remembers, "and became very emotional. 'Well, Lou,' I thought, 'we made it back to the Series, didn't we.'"

SIX

ON A CLEAR DAY ...

During my major league career I had my share of
arguments with managers and players. Unfortunately,
I also had Bill Haller's share, Ken Kaiser's share,
Richie Garcia's share . . . I was sort of a shareholder.
Steve Palermo used to say I was the easiest person
to spot on the field—I was the one with the crowd
around me.

Arguments are as much part of baseball in America as painted grass, ball park pizza, men wearing
bird costumes, Haitian baseballs, and Japanese gloves.
In the first organized game ever played, for example,
on June 19, 1846, umpire William R. Wharton en-
sured his place in umpiring history by fining a player
named Davis six cents for swearing. In the 137
years of games played since then, only the rates
have changed.

Hall of Fame member Walter Alston once said,
"There's never been an umpire who beat me, and I
know there's never been an umpire who beat me
intentionally." Apparently this is not a universally
held sentiment. When a situation goes against a
team, there are usually only two people who can be
blamed: the player, who may have struck out,
dropped the ball, missed a tag, or made a poor
throw, or the umpire, who made the call. Obviously it is the umpire who receives the blame.

Most arguments, in fact, are about decisions on specific plays. But managers will also argue to protect a player about to be ejected from the game, to try to arouse a lethargic team or crowd, or to show the fans and management that, right or right, they are willing to fight for the team. Players argue on the firm belief that umpires were put on the field just to torment them, and they will argue out of frustration—sometimes they wake up on the wrong side of a batting average or won-lost record.

There are two points a manager will always make when arguing about a specific play: "How can you be so close and miss it so badly?" or "You were out of position." Since I am six-four and weighed over three hundred pounds when I was working, some part of me was *always* going to be out of position. I remember once, when I was working second base in Seattle's cozy Kingdome, Mariner manager Darrell Johnson complained, "Ronnie, this place is too small for you to be out of position!"

Sometimes, in fact, umpires are not close enough to a play—but that usually happens because the play takes place three hundred feet away in the outfield. When Joe Altobelli was coaching third base for the Orioles, for example, Kenny Singleton smashed a long fly ball that sailed over the left-field foul pole, and umpire Greg Kosc called it foul. Altobelli was enraged, demanding of Kosc, "Why didn't you run out to see the ball?"

Kosc could have explained that the ball had been hit so hard he would've had time to move about twenty feet before it went out, but logic has no place in a baseball argument. "I'll tell you, Joe," Greg said, "I really would have, but if I had started running out there, my eyes would jiggle!" He then turned and walked away, leaving the perplexed Altobelli trying to figure out exactly what he meant.

Balls hit to the deepest parts of the field cause just as many problems as trapped balls or close plays on the bases, because base umpires don't have the time to get close enough to the ball to see if it hits a quarter inch above a painted line, or if a fan was reaching over a railing to catch the ball. There is, for example, a yellow line painted on a section of the center-field fence in Fenway Park. A ball hit above it is a home run. One night Jim Rice's long drive hit on the line, and Russ Goetz called it in play. Red Sox manager Don Zimmer came out yelling, "Where'd it hit? Where'd it hit?" Managers tend to repeat themselves during arguments.

"It hit the yellow line," Goetz told him, and Zimmer eventually left the field.

Two weeks later Goetz was again working second base in Fenway Park and another ball hit in almost the identical spot. Again Russ ruled it in play. This time Zimmer came out of the dugout considerably slower, and he was shaking his head sadly as he walked up to Goetz. "Russ," he said calmly, "I know what you called it, and there really ain't no sense in me being out here arguing. What we're gonna have to do is take that yellow line down, 'cause you must be color-blind!"

Walter Alston had a similar incident when the Dodgers were in San Diego. At one time there was a padded cushion above the outfield fence, and a ball hitting that cushion was a home run. Ron Cey hit a long drive that thumped into the cushion rather than smacking into the hard wooden wall, but the umpire called it in play. The usually mild-mannered Alston was enraged and finally screamed at the umpire, "That ball hit the cushion! If you can't hear that, you've gotta be blind!"

Sometimes it is not so much the play as the situation that causes the argument. Rocky Roe and Durwood Merrill were in Oakland in 1982 when the A's Ricky Henderson was on the verge of breaking the single-season stolen base record. This was the A's' last home game of the year, thus Henderson's last opportunity to break the record in front of his hometown fans.

In the fourth inning of the game, second base umpire Larry Barnett got sick and had to leave the game. Durwood, on vacation at third base, moved to second. It is well known that any time an umpire moves out of his slot, out of his normal position, he is going to have a difficult game. This particular situation almost caused Durwood to have a difficult life.

In the seventh inning Oakland's Fred Stanley was on second and Henderson was on first. Stanley appeared to walk off the base intentionally and was picked off—dramatically setting the stage for Henderson to tie the record by stealing second, then break it by stealing third.

The crowd was on its feet cheering for Henderson to run. A's third-base coach Clete Boyer was hollering to Durwood, "We need this one! We need this one!" Predictably, Henderson took off for second, and the Detroit Tigers pitched out. The play at second was close, but Durwood called Henderson out. Henderson's last chance to break the record at home was gone.

Henderson argued mildly, and the fans were upset, but there was no real trouble until the end of the inning. As the teams changed sides, the A's Dwayne Murphy and the Tigers' Alan Trammell got into an argument. "What did you want us to do," Trammell shouted, "just give it to him?"

"I suppose maybe I should have learned something from that little fight I tried to break up when I was teaching high school," Durwood said and sighed, "but once I got them stickers out I sort of forgot about it. So I went over to break up this fight. Murphy was happy to see me, naturally. 'You made a gutless call,' he said. 'It's nice to see you, too,' I told him, and ejected him. Then Billy Martin came around to visit and said, 'You had a chance to be part of baseball history and you blew it.' Had to throw him out, too. Then A's coach Charlie Metro started with me. He caught me in the middle of a roll, so I got rid of him. I was getting them at fifteen-second intervals, but I was running low on candidates, so I started toward the A's dugout. They were all screaming at me and I was ready to get a mess o' them."

Rocky Roe headed him off and tried to calm him down. "Normally," Rocky explains, "when the bench is yelling at me I yell back, 'It's a malicious rumor and I've been trying to quit for two years,' but at this moment nobody looked like they wanted to laugh. The fans were throwing things on the field, Durwood had already ejected three people and was hunting for more. . . . I was trying to push him away from the dugout when it occurred to me that I had my back to the stands. This crowd was now very upset, and they were not going to care which person in a blue suit they hit. So I managed to turn around so I could see the crowd. I saw enough and pulled Durwood toward home plate."

They finally got everyone settled down and finished the game. In Oakland, umpires must walk about fifty feet next to the stands to reach their dressing room. As the game ended, Durwood eased up next to Rocky and asked, "Partner, are you ready to take the longest walk of your life?"

"Durwood," Rocky replied, "I'll go anywhere with you. But why don't you go first?"

The fans threw anything not bolted down at the umpires—cups, coins, beer, programs, hot dog rolls, hot dog vendors, bolts. Somebody even threw an expensive sports jacket at Rocky—he kept that—and the umpires finally reached the safety of their dressing room.

Usually, after a game, a small group of fans waits by the entrance to the players' parking lot, in which the umpires also park their rented cars, for autographs. This time the group was not small and did not appear overly interested in autographs. The head of stadium security came into the locker room and explained the problem, then asked if the umpires wanted their cars brought into the stadium so they could drive out another exit.

Larry Barnett, who had not been on the field during the melee, said, "Oh, I don't think that's necessary."

Rocky and Durwood shouted in unison, "It's necessary! It's necessary!"

Eventually the American League held a hearing about the situation. The result was that Fred Stanley was fined for allowing himself to be picked off second base.

Not every argument results in an ejection. Sometimes a manager will come out to discuss a play, realize he is wrong, and leave. There is a word umpires use to describe this: "miracle." Steve Palermo once had a manager argue that he had failed to call the infield fly rule—which states that a batter is out if he hits a fly ball playable by an infielder with men on first and second, or first, second, and third, and less than two out. As the manager was screaming, Steve looked around and, as he thought, there were base runners on first and third. He pointed this out to the manager, who paused, looked around, frowned, and then said, "Well, shoot, it's a nice day to be out in the sun anyway."

The Expos' Gene Mauch came out to inform Eric Gregg that he had completely missed a tag play at second base. Gregg explained that Tim Foli, Montreal's shortstop, had indeed tagged the runner with his glove—but the baseball was in his other hand at the time. Mauch frowned. "Nobody told me that," he said. "Well, as long as I'm out here, I might as well talk to you. How's the family? . . ."

And once in the career of every umpire, he makes a mistake, he just blows a call sky-high. The worst possible thing an umpire can do is admit it, because the manager will spend the rest of both their careers reminding him about it and expecting him to even it up. I would guess a manager's estimate of even is 250 calls to one mistake. "When I know I've made a mistake and it results in an argument," Joe Brinkman says, "I might go as far as to say, 'Look, I made the call and there's nothing I can do about it. I can't change it.' Hopefully the manager or player is listening carefully enough to understand what I'm saying. I don't think I've ever simply admitted that I missed one."

I did, twice. During an Angels–Twins game I called a California runner out at second on a force play, even though I was closer to the base than the Minnesota second baseman. My hand was signaling out while my brain was laughing at my hand. But there was nothing I could do about it. My thumb was in midair, embarrassing me. Angels manager Dick Williams came out and pleaded with me, "Just admit you missed it this one time and I won't argue. I'll just walk away."

It was an interesting proposal. "That's all I gotta do?" I asked suspiciously, "And you'll walk away?"

He nodded. "You admit you missed it and I'm gone."

I hesitated, then realized that everybody has to take a chance in life. And this was going to be that chance for me. I *was* wrong and I was going to admit it. "Hoak-kay," I said, "you got it. I can't believe I missed that play so badly."

"Right," Williams said, then screamed, "WHY, YOU @$#%$¢¢$¢¢$er, HOW THE %&&$%$%$(@! can you admit missing a play like that? . . ."

The second time I admitted having made a slight error I did so only to save the lives of my partners. They were laughing at me so hard I was afraid they were going to die. It was that fateful afternoon in Baltimore when I called an obvious foul ball a home run, obvious to everyone except me. After a discussion with Bill Haller, during which Haller spent considerable time pointing at me and laughing, I changed my call to a foul ball.

Eric Gregg suffered through a similar problem

during the 1978 pennant stretch run. The Phillies were leading the Pirates by a half game in the standings with two weeks to play, and they were playing each other in Philadelphia. Eric was working third base in a 1–1 game. "The Phillies' Keith Moreland hit a line drive right down the third-base line," Eric recalls. "I turned to follow the ball and I just lost it in the glare of the lights. The first thing I saw when my eyes cleared was the very pretty ballgirl jumping up and down and screaming 'Home run! Home run!' Well, I figured, if it's good enough for her, it's good enough for me. So I began signaling home run.

"Waves of Pirates came at me. They were coming from everywhere. I felt like Ward Bond on *Wagon Train*. Finally I managed to tear myself away from them and got together with my crew chief, Doug Harvey, and our partners, Frank Pulli and Jerry Crawford. No one was really sure if the ball had been fair or foul, but we decided that, if it had been fair, it would've had to hit the screen located just inside fair territory. Since it did not hit the screen, it had to be foul. That sounded good to me, but I was still fuming at that ballgirl. If she couldn't tell the difference between a fair ball and a foul ball, what was she doing out there?

"Doug Harvey looked at me and asked if I wanted to change the call myself or if I wanted him to do it. I looked up into the stands of that beautiful ball park. This was Philadelphia, my hometown. There were forty thousand people there, cheering wildly. My people. I looked Doug straight in the eyes and said, 'You do it. They'll kill me if I do it!' "

Of course, it wasn't as bad for Eric as it was for me. All he had at stake when he blew his call was the National League pennant. In my case it meant Earl Weaver was right and I was wrong.

I always understood when managers came out to argue about a close play; it was not one of my favorite things, but at least I understood. It was when they argued about the *replay* that I got upset. How could they not argue about the original play, then tell the umpire he got it wrong on videotape? I once ruled that an Angel outfielder had trapped a short pop-up, and no one argued until the replay made it appear as if he had caught the ball cleanly. Then they came at me, screaming, "He caught it on the replay! He caught it on the replay!"

"But he's got to catch it on the field!" I shouted back.

Steve Palermo called an Oakland runner out trying to steal second in Seattle and even A's manager Billy Martin didn't argue—until the replay, seen from another angle, made it look like the runner had not been tagged. That's when Martin came out. "Look up there," he demanded, pointing to the scoreboard screen.

"It happened here," Palermo responded, pointing to second base. Martin really got upset then, and screamed at Palermo, "You . . . you're nothing but a hotheaded Italian!"

Now, Billy Martin calling Steve Palermo a hotheaded Italian is like me calling Victoria Principal chunky. Even Steve was stunned at Martin's remark. "Uh, Billy," he finally replied, "I don't know how to break this to you . . . but what do you think you are?"

Billy did not respond to the question.

Baseball broadcasters often tell listeners that a manager is not really arguing over that particular play, because he knows the umpire will not change his decision, but rather to ensure that his team gets the advantage on the next close call. Wrong! I would have truly enjoyed having an announcer get dirt kicked all over his pants as a manager shouted, "This is for the next one!" Umpires usually have problems with the same manager and the same players throughout a game. Rarely do you see an umpire argue with one team early in the game and the other team late in the game, which would happen if either manager suspected the umpire was trying to even up his calls. In fact, I've never seen a game in which both managers were ejected, although it has always been a secret fantasy of mine.

Some managers, however, will argue over past plays or even past games. One night Jerry Dale made a routine out call on a force play—and Phillies manager Pat Corrales charged him. "I wasn't really surprised," Jerry admits. "This was the third close call that had gone against him, and it was only the third inning. He told me, 'I let you get away with the last one. This one I had to come out on.'

" 'What last one?' I asked.

" 'The steal play.'

"Actually, I hadn't even considered that one of the three close plays. 'Wait a second,' I said to him, 'are you arguing about this play or that play?' I didn't want to be screaming at him about the wrong play.

" 'Both,' he said firmly, 'you missed both of them.' "

Although Jerry should have gotten twice as mad, he did not, and he ejected Corrales only once.

Don Denkinger was surprised to see Yankee coach Gene Michael bringing out the starting lineup card one night in Yankee Stadium. "Billy [Martin] isn't coming out," Michael explained, "because he's still mad about that call you made in the eighth inning last night."

"Well," Don replied, "you don't work for Western Union, so we don't expect you to deliver messages."

"That's the way it is," Michael said, his voice rising.

"No, no," Don corrected as he ejected him, "that's the way it *was!*"

One of a manager's most important responsibilities is keeping his players from being ejected, even if it means being thrown out himself. When a player and an umpire get into a shouting match, the player's manager will inevitably come sprinting out to intervene, sort of like a slice of ham slipping between two different types of hard roll. "I don't mind being the sacrificial lamb," Texas Rangers manager Doug Radar explained, "but I try to let the umpire know when my heart really isn't in it. On a number of occasions, after I've pushed a player away, I've told umpires to pay no attention to what I'm saying, that I'm just doing it for the benefit of my player. Once, in fact, in the minor leagues, I pointed my finger at the umpire and screamed at him, 'Listen very carefully to what I'm saying. You are absolutely the swellest guy I've ever known, and if I lost my brother, you'd be the man I'd want to replace him. . . .' Meanwhile, everybody in the dugout and the stands was thinking, 'Ole Doug is really telling him how it is.' I think the thing that probably confused them a bit was why the umpire was laughing at me. I kept my ballplayer in the game, though."

Earl Weaver never had to request that an umpire pay no attention to what he was saying . . . or explain why he was jumping up and down and kicking dirt on home plate or ripping up the bases and refusing to give them back. Earl had his own means of making an umpire forget his difficulty with an Oriole player. For example, one afternoon Durwood Merrill and Eddie Murray were going at it with real enthusiasm when Earl squeezed between them and informed Durwood, "You cannot throw a player of this caliber out of the game!"

Durwood smiled. "In that case, Earl," he said, "let me try for a manager." Weaver then put to good use his complete set of lessons at the Mr. T. Charm School while attempting to set a new record for total acreage moved from the infield to home plate.

If a team is in a slump, or listless, some managers will provoke an argument with the umpire just to invigorate their players and fans. Tommy Lasorda is probably the best at this. Of course, Tommy always has enough energy to organize a geriatric marathon. Eric Gregg had the plate at Dodger Stadium one Sunday afternoon, and the Dodgers were trailing, 4–0, and sinking. After Eric had called a Dodger out on strikes, Tommy came hustling out of the dugout. Eric braced for the confrontation, which would end with Lasorda being thrown out of the game for arguing on a strike decision.

"Hey, Eric," Tommy said calmly, "that must have been some pitch."

"Yeah, Tommy," Eric replied, "he's gotta swing at that pitch."

Tommy spread out his hands as if he were trying to plead with Gregg, but said, "What am I gonna do? I know he should swing at that pitch and I've told him that."

Eric waited for Lasorda to say the wrong word, poised on the edge of an ejection. Lasorda just smiled. "Uh, Tommy," Eric finally asked, "what are you doing out here?"

Lasorda shook his head as if were disgusted. "Gees," he said, "I've got fifty thousand people in the ball park today and I've gotta say something. Hey, you live in Philly, right?"

"Right. What about it?"

"Well, you've got to stop in Norristown, because my mother has a little pizza place there. . . ." Meanwhile, fifty thousand people are on their feet, urging Lasorda to tell off the umpire. Lasorda accomplished his objective: The entire ball park had come alive. And Eric? He told Tommy he wanted two large pies, with extra cheese and heavy on the pepperoni.

Tony LaRussa went just a bit farther during his first season as the White Sox manager. He came sprinting out of the dugout to argue with Kenny Kaiser about a routine force play. At first Kaiser assumed LaRussa must have gotten lost on the way to the clubhouse, because there was no reason to argue about that play. "It wasn't even close," Kenny told him.

"I know," Tony agreed, "but we're going so bad I've got to do something. Look, do me a favor, throw me out of the game."

Kaiser, who has been known to eject managers for unnecessary breathing, refused.

"You gotta," LaRussa insisted, his tone getting a bit more demanding, "I want you to!"

"Don't tell me what to do!" Kaiser shouted back, moving a step closer.

"Yeah?" LaRussa responded, "what are you gonna do? Eject me?"

"Not if I don't want to."

"Well," LaRussa finally threatened, "if you don't, I'm gonna throw my hat."

Kaiser pointed a warning finger at him. "You throw your hat and you're out of the game."

LaRussa was eventually ejected without having to throw his hat, and the suddenly inspired White Sox went on to lose by six runs. Kaiser considered this a mercy ejection.

The pressure on baseball players to produce is enormous, particularly with fans today constantly dividing at-bats and pitching victories by salary, and players have little outlet for their frustrations. Players will argue on close plays when they believe they are right, but they will argue just as often out of anger at themselves for failing. As a hitter, for example, Jeff Torborg was a fine defensive catcher. He caught three no-hitters in his career, and he often tells people that if there is anything in baseball he knows about, it is not hitting. "I came to bat one day in San Diego," he remembers, "and at that time that was one of the few cities that put a hitter's batting average on the scoreboard. Mine was exactly .200. I hoped nobody I knew was in the ball park, including my teammates.

"I had two strikes on me, I had earned those myself, when umpire Stan Landes called me out on

a pitch I thought was outside. I started calculating
quickly—and realized that the next time I came to
bat my batting average on the board would be below .200. Knowing it myself was bad enough, I
didn't need it advertised. So I figured it was Landes'
fault. I'm not quite sure how I figured that, but at
that moment it seemed logical. I told Landes how I
felt. He didn't throw me out then, he threw me out
after I tossed my bat in the air and broke the hook
off the dugout wall with my helmet.

"But my batting average was never posted on
that scoreboard."

"The maddest I've ever been in a baseball game,"
remembers Texas Rangers catcher Jim Sundberg,
"was in the middle of the 1977 season. The team
was in the middle of an eleven-game losing streak
and I was going bad. Mike Reilly, whom I consider
one of the better umpires in the league, called me
out on a third strike in the first inning of a game
against the Red Sox. I didn't say a word to him, I
didn't yell, I just decided I wasn't going to leave the
batter's box. Ever. 'I'm not leaving,' I told him.

" 'If you don't get outta there,' he told me, 'I'm
gonna throw you out.'

" 'I'm not leaving,' I repeated. 'I'm gonna stay
here all night if I want to.'

" 'That's it, then,' he said, and threw me out of
the game.

"That's when I lost control. The losing streak,
my batting slump, everything just added up and I
exploded. Totally out of character, I went back to
the dugout and heaved three bats onto the field.
Then I picked up a glove and threw that onto the
field. Then I chucked another glove out there. I was
working my way the length of the dugout, throwing
anything I could get my hands on. I threw another
glove, and it sailed right at Reilly. He was holding
his mask in his hand, watching me, and reached
out and caught the glove in the mask. When I saw

that I paused for a moment and thought, 'Gees, I hope I don't hit him.'

"Finally I reached the end of the dugout. All that was left was this big water cooler. I just looked at it for a moment, then started to go for it. I was reaching out for it when I thought, 'What if I try to pick it up and can't do it?' I knew everybody in the ball park was watching me, and if I tried to pick it up and failed, I was going to be very embarrassed. Luckily, though, there was a large jar of salt tablets sitting on top of the water cooler. Just as if I had intended to get these tablets, I picked up the jar and peppered the field with salt tablets.

"The person who was most upset by my tantrum was the head groundskeeper. Those salt tablets killed all the grass around the dugout."

There are many different ways an umpire can handle an argument. In 1896, for example, a National League umpire had the entire Cleveland Spiders ball club arrested and taken to jail. As much as some umpires might like to do that—not to mention any names, Ron Luciano—it is rarely necessary. In fact, arguments don't even have to result in ejections.

As difficult as it was for me to accept, I learned that fans did not come to the ball park just to see me dramatically throw their favorite players out of the game. Once I faced that reality, I tried not to eject anyone unless they forced me to throw them out. Except Earl Weaver, of course, but that was just recreation. The key to keeping managers and players in the game, I discovered, was knowing how to argue.

Just as umpires develop their own style of calling balls and strikes behind the plate, as they gain experience they learn how to handle an argument without it turning into a massacre. Every umpire does it his own way. "I was an athlete," Joe Brinkman explains, "and I always wanted to win. It took me a while to realize I couldn't win an argument. It was tough for me to accept the fact that I could do my job better by not fighting back. Now I try to listen to what the manager has to say. It takes two people to make an argument, so I try not to start fighting with him."

In the past, one way umpires handled arguments was to be so tough that players knew they would be ejected if they opened their mouths and words came out. One of the toughest was Cal Hubbard. Like me, he was an ex-football player, but he was even bigger than I am. Phil Rizzuto was a Yankee second-year player in 1942 and quickly learned about Hubbard. "I had five hits in five at-bats," he remembers, "and I came to bat for the sixth time leading off the ninth inning. Roy Cullenbine was playing third base for the Washington Senators and he knew he was going to be traded the next day. He told me as we changed sides at the end of the eighth, 'If you want to get your sixth hit, lay down a bunt.' Sure enough, I get up to bat and I look at Cullenbine, and he's playing me like he played Joe DiMaggio, way back on the edge of the outfield grass. I was so anxious to lay down that bunt that I fouled off the first two pitches. Cal Hubbard called the next pitch a strike, costing me a chance to go six-for-six and get in the record book. I started yelling at him. 'That can't be a strike!' I screamed. 'That ball was outside!' Hubbard just stood there for a moment, then lowered that big inflatable chest protector he used, reached down, reached *way* down, and grabbed me by the front of my jersey. His fist was about half the size of my chest. Finally he growled, 'What did you say that pitch was?'

" 'Right down the middle,' I told him, and I never meant anything more in my life. After that, I rarely argued with the umpires."

Of course, if any umpire dared grab a player today, the result would be a huge battle—in court, between the Baseball Players' Association and the Umpires' Association.

"I tell young umpires to keep their mouths shut," Doug Harvey says. "If someone comes out to argue and the umpire refuses to argue with him, what is he gonna do? I learned that early in my career, and it has worked for me since.

"I was working third base in Philadelphia and a runner tried to go from first to third on a single. The Phillies' third baseman, Don Hoak, had the ball in plenty of time, but he was getting a little spike-shy and pulled it up too soon. I called the runner safe. That started it. Hoak got two words into his first sentence and he was gone. Gene Mauch came out, he was gone. A coach went with them. This was a nothing play at third base and we almost had a riot.

"By the time I got home that night I felt terrible. I had an awful headache, my throat hurt terribly, and I was depressed. I thought, 'There's gotta be a better way of doing this.' I wondered what would happen if I just refused to holler and argue with them. It didn't take me long to find out.

"I was at second base the very next night, and the Cardinals' Julian Javier tried to steal. The Phillies' second baseman, Cookie Rojas, had the ball in time but didn't get his glove down. I called Javier safe. Mauch exploded. He was screaming at me, waving his arms wildly through the air, sticking his face inches away from mine . . . it was an impressive performance.

"I thought, 'I'm not going to holler at him.' I crossed my arms and stared at him and didn't say a word. I just started counting to myself. By the time I reached twenty, Mauch had started to run down. He was repeating himself, and his hands weren't waving quite so wildly. Finally, when he paused to catch his breath, I said in a normal tone of voice, 'Hold it right there, Gene.'

"It worked. He just shut up. I said, still in a

normal tone, 'I'm not gonna holler at you. If you want to know what happened, then you ask me like a man.' His mouth fell open. I'm sure no umpire had ever spoken to him like that before. Nicely.

"He stuck both hands in his back pocket, jutted out his chin, and said, 'Okay, what happened?'

" 'Rojas got the ball in plenty of time, but he missed the tag.'

"Gene turned to Cookie, who nodded and admitted, 'He's right, Skip, I missed it.' Mauch was on his way back to the dugout by the time I turned around again. We never had another argument.

"That's the way I've handled arguments since that day. I just let them run out of steam before I say a word. I don't even have to count to twenty anymore. I just refuse to argue or get upset. I don't have to scream to eject someone."

Lee Weyer likes to be aggressive during an argument. If he is working the bases and a manager is coming out at him, he usually charges the manager. He'll give him an opportunity to shout whatever is on his mind, then tell him, "Okay, you've had your say. I'm going to turn around and go back to my position. If you follow me, you're gone." Then he turns around and trots back to his position. Lee is six-six. Not too many people follow him.

I used to try the same technique, but I'd turn around and there would be so many people following me I'd feel like the Pied Piper. Sometimes it looked like a demonstration was taking place behind me.

Because umpires work with the same managers and players for years, they eventually learn how to deal with each person as an individual. I never had another problem with Don Zimmer, for example, once I discovered I could change subjects on him in midargument. When Zimmer was managing the Red Sox he had serious problems with the Boston sports press. One night I called a Red Sox player out on a pick-off play at first, and Don came out quickly to protect his player. He pushed his player away from me and screamed with anguish, "Jeez, how could you have missed that one?"

Sometimes, although many people do not believe this, being screamed at by a manager or player standing inches away, and perhaps spitting tobacco juice on you, is not as much fun as it appears to be from a distance. This was one of those nights. I just didn't feel like arguing with Zimmer, then walking away and having him follow me, then throwing him out of the game. I wanted a little peace and a lot of quiet. Is that too much to ask in Boston?

So instead of responding to his question, I asked, "Did you see that article about you in this morning's paper?" A columnist had just ripped him apart.

It was immediately obvious I had hit a responsive chord. "Oh, Ronnie," he said, "they're burying me in this town. I can't even turn on the television set anymore. . . ."

His player was as surprised as I was. "But what about the play?" he demanded.

Zimmer ignored him, and I certainly wasn't going to start. The only problem I had was getting Don to finish his conversation. Evidently he'd been looking for someone friendly to talk with all day. He just happened to find someone on the field in the middle of a game.

From that point on, anytime Zimmer came out, I'd think of some way to change the subject, and we never had a serious problem again.

Jim Honochick taught me how to deal with Ralph Houk. "Houk'll let you know when he wants to get ejected. You just have to listen to him, nod, shake your head, but don't respond to him. Don't say one word. When he wants to get thrown out he'll take off his hat and drop-kick it. Then you throw him out and he leaves and everybody is satisfied."

Generally the best thing for an umpire to do

during an argument is just keep quiet and control his temper. The most an umpire should say is, "It looked good to me," or "He tagged him good enough for me." He should let the manager or player say whatever is on his mind, then turn around and walk away from him. It is when an umpire gets personally involved in an argument, when he loses his temper, that problems really start. Somebody has to remain sane at all times, and it isn't going to be the manager. Once, for example, umpire Bill McGowen got so mad at a pitcher named Ray Scarborough for complaining about ball-strike calls that he threw his indicator at him.

When Eddie Montague came into the National League he had a reputation as a hothead. Finally, league president Chub Feeney told him, "I don't mind you throwing guys out, but is it really necessary to follow them into the dugout?" Since then, Montague has calmed down considerably.

When Larry Napp was umpiring in the American League he ran his games somewhat like Al Capone ran Chicago. He took no abuse at all. Jim McKean worked with Napp his first few weeks in the major leagues. "It was quite an experience. It seemed like we were having a war every day. We were in Baltimore and Weaver came out to argue and Larry stepped on his foot. Then we went to Detroit and had problems with Billy Martin who was managing the Tigers. Finally we came into New York. It was my first time inside Yankee Stadium, and I was tremendously excited. During the game Larry had problems with Yankee coach Gene Michael, who called him all sorts of names, and Thurman Munson. Larry threw both of them out of the game.

"The Yankees lost and blamed it on Napp. Afterward, as I was walking up the runway to the umpires' room, I heard a commotion. I walked around a corner, and there were Napp and Gene Michael rolling on the ground punching each other. Then Munson jumped into the fight.

"I was in shock. This was only my second week in the big leagues. Suddenly Bill Virdon, the Yankee manager, came around the corner and saw this brawl. 'Wait a second,' he said, pointing at the fighters, 'I don't think this should be going on.'

"Shouldn't be going on? I thought they were killing each other. Eventually we all jumped into the pile and separated them. That was the last time my crew got to New York that season."

Players learn how to argue with umpires, too. They know how much each individual will take. They know who has a quick thumb and who will let them blow off steam. The best umpire I ever worked with in controlling a potentially volatile situation was Bill Haller. "We could have a riot going on at first base," Ken Kaiser says, "with managers, players, and coaches piling up, and as soon as Haller got there from third base it would be like the arrival of Moses at the Red Sea. He has just earned that much respect."

In 1983 a *New York Times* poll of players and managers rated Steve Palermo Number One in the American League. Stevie earned that by being tough. For example, the Milwaukee Brewers' bench was getting all over him one night in New York, and he just strolled over to their dugout. "I took off my mask and threw out a net," he says. "I had some great one-liners, but nobody responded. Finally, I asked how come they had gotten so quiet so quickly?"

" 'Because if anybody says anything you'll throw them out!' somebody shouted.

" 'That's the first thing anybody's said tonight that's right,' I told them, 'and you'd better remember it!' "

Jose Cruz is typical of most major league players in this regard. "I try not to get too ticked off because I know it isn't going to change anything," he explains. "No umpire is going to suddenly say, 'Wait a second, Jose, you're right, let's do it again.' When I get really angry, I start yelling in Spanish, except when Richie Garcia is around, and I always try to smile when I'm telling an umpire that I think he made a bad call."

Probably the most intelligent argument I ever had with a player took place in Baltimore. I was working the plate and the pitcher, it may have been Jim Palmer, but I'm not sure, had been complaining all night. That's why I believe it was Palmer. Finally, we disagreed over still another pitch, and he came striding off the mound toward home plate.

I decided to meet him halfway. I ripped off my mask, walked around the catcher, and began stomping toward the mound. He kept coming. I kept going. The gap between us narrowed to a few yards. I could see the anger in his eyes. He kept coming . . . and walked right past me to talk to his catcher. He never said a word to me, he just left me standing alone in the middle of the infield with half an argument in my mouth.

What causes a manager or a player to be ejected from a baseball game? It can be one serious comment or action, or it can be a combination of many things. Umpires have bad days too, days when the car doesn't start, the toothpaste is rotten, and your partner gets invited to Billy Martin's birthday party and you don't, and they will take less abuse than usual on those days. The situation in a ball game may have something to do with it: A manager can get away with much more in the ninth inning of a one-run game than he can in the seventh inning of a 9–2 squeaker. Past performance is considered: Brooks Robinson went twenty-one years without being ejected, while Jim Sundberg was thrown out six times in one season for following manager Martin's directive to question all close pitches. Doug Rader was ejected three times his first week in the National League and claimed it took him another three years before umpires would give him the benefit of any doubt.

Many fans believe a manager or a player will automatically be ejected for cursing at an umpire. Not true. One man's cuss word is another man's adjective. If a manager or a player uses profanity as part of his normal vocabulary, he is not going to be thrown out for using it in the anger of an argument. "An umpire doesn't eject a manager or player," Eric Gregg believes, "they eject themselves. They know exactly what they can say and who they can say it to. So when somebody is thrown out, he has either completely lost control, or he intended to be run."

Most umpires, for example, do have one word or expression about which they are particularly sensitive. Managers and players know this and know that if they use it, they are going to be ejected. One major league umpire has a hairpiece, and anyone who mentions it is finished. Another umpire is very touchy about being short. If a manager even suggests it might be a short game, he's done. Anyone who yells, "Hey! Hey! Hey!" from Bill Cosby's Fat Albert characters at Eric Gregg will have the rest of the game off. A player once described Bill Klem as looking like a catfish, a description Klem despised, and calling him "Catfish" guaranteed ejection. Calling old-time National League umpire George Magerkurth "Meathead" meant automatic ejection, and on occasion a beating—Magerkurth was once taken to court for assaulting a player in the American Association. For Davey Phillips's father, Bob Phillips, the magic word was "jellybelly." Doug Harvey says, "They can call me 'Doug,' or 'Mr. Harvey,' or 'Harv,' or 'Mr. Umpire.' But they can't call me anything else and stay in the game."

As far as Rocky Roe is concerned, a manager or a player will be asked to leave the premises for calling him anything that starts with "You" or "You're" and is followed by a descriptive adjective and a noun. For example, "You're a @#%$¢$#%ing @#@#%#@$%!"

Joe Brinkman summed it up accurately: "They can holler at the uniform all they want," he explained, "but when they start hollering at the man wearing that uniform, they're going to be in trouble."

I rarely had any problem deciding when to eject someone. A manager or a player would say the wrong thing or make the wrong gesture and pow! It was like hitting the jackpot on a giant quiz show in my mind. I knew he was gone. It became instinctive. But on occasion someone would say or do something right on the very edge of being enough, maybe it was and maybe it wasn't, and I'd find myself wondering, "Should I or shouldn't I?" Once they had me thinking, I was in trouble. Dick Williams, for example, was the most sarcastic man with whom I ever worked, and he always caused me problems. One night he paused in the middle of an argument just to let me fully appreciate the sound of an entire stadium booing me. "Hear that?" he finally said. "They're not just booing the call you made. They're booing your entire career!"

I started thinking about that. And listening. I got so depressed I forgot to eject him. And later, when I realized I hadn't thrown him out, I got even more depressed because I *hadn't* ejected him.

There are certain things besides name-calling and snide remarks that will get a manager or a player ejected. For example, when Babe Ruth was pitching for the Red Sox, he objected to umpire Clarence (Brick) Owens's call by punching Owens in the mouth. (His relief pitcher, Ernie Shore, proceeded to pick off first base the runner Ruth had walked, then retired the next twenty-six batters to pitch a perfect game.)

A manager or player who attempts to embarrass or show up an umpire, will be ejected. For example, National League umpire Art Williams once called Bill Madlock out on strikes on a knuckle ball that might have been outside. Madlock took off his helmet and politely handed it and his bat to Williams, then walked away. Good-bye.

When Eddie Kasko was managing the Red Sox, crew chief Johnny Rice came in from his position at second base to call a Boston runner out at home plate for going out of the base line to avoid being tagged. After Kasko heard Rice's explanation of the call, he stretched out his arms and fell over backward in a dead faint. Good-bye.

Philadelphia manager Frank Lucchesi was so enraged at an umpire's decision he tried to rip up second base and carry it away. Unfortunately, the base was tightly secured and he wrenched his back. He couldn't straighten up so he had to hobble, bent over, off the field. Didn't matter. He got all the sympathy he deserved. Good-bye.

When Red Schoendienst was managing the Cardinals, umpire Frank Secory called Mike Shannon out at the plate. Schoendienst argued that the catcher had never tagged Shannon, and to prove his point, went sliding into home plate himself. Like Shannon, he was out.

One night in Philadelphia, Nick Colosi was having a rough time with the Phillies and the Mets. In the fifth inning he warned the Mets dugout that if he heard one more word he was going to clear the entire bench. To make sure Colosi did not hear that word, each Met put a piece of white tape over his mouth. Coach Bobby Valentine was ejected on what Joe Brinkman would term g.p., general principles.

The battle between right and wrong, good and evil, umpires and managers is never-ending. Years ago Eddie Rommel ejected White Sox manager Jimmy Dykes and his star pitcher, Ted Lyons. Dykes appealed to Rommel to allow Lyons to stay in the game, pointing out that a large crowd was in the ball park especially to see him pitch. And just as Dykes had Rommel convinced, Ed looked into the White Sox dugout—and saw a Chicago player with a jacket over his head being led about by Lyons as if he were blind. Good-bye.

But as far as putting on a performance, there has never been the equal of Earl Weaver. To be ejected by me, Earl didn't even have to try to show me up—all he had to do was show up. I like to say that we had a personality conflict—I had one and he didn't. Although we spent most of our careers together, in the minors and the majors, the only times we really got along was when we were in different places at the same time. He was thrown out of so many games for so many reasons he can be used as an example of everything a manager should not do, except manage. For somebody who spent much of his career in the clubhouse, he won a lot of ball games.

Like every manager, he prided himself on knowing the rules inside out. And that was just how he knew them. One night in Cleveland, for example, a balk was called on an Orioles' pitcher, which Earl believed had to be against the rules. After berating the umpire for a considerable period of time, he threatened, "If you're not going to follow the rules I might just as well tear up the rulebook."

With that, he whirled around and raced into the Orioles dugout. Sitting calmly in that dugout, enjoying Weaver's exhibition, was pitching coach Ray Miller. Miller would like to manage sometime, so, for the three seasons he had been with the Orioles, he had been making notations in a rulebook. Anytime there was a rules conflict, he would write down the details and later study the situation and the applicable rule. After three seasons with Weaver, this was one thick rulebook. Actually, it looked more like *The Baseball Encyclopedia* than a rulebook.

Earl charged into the dugout demanding, "Where's the @$#%$¢ rulebook?" Before Miller could react, Weaver had grabbed the rulebook with three years of lessons inside. "Ea—" Ray shouted, but it was too late. He had about as much chance of stopping Weaver as I have of dancing for the Royal Ballet. Weaver was running toward the umpire, triumphantly waving the rulebook over his head.

"At least he isn't going to rip it in half," Miller remembers thinking just before Earl ripped it in half. Then Weaver threw both halves onto the ground. Earl was officially ejected at that moment, so the rest of his argument was just for practice. "I still had a chance to save my book, though," Miller remembers. "I shoved the batboy onto the field, shouting at him, 'Get out there and save those pieces.' Everybody in the dugout was on their feet, rooting for the kid to get there. It looked like he was gonna make it, too. He was just a few feet away, just getting ready to scoop up the pieces, when Earl bent down and picked them up. Just to show the umpire he wasn't kidding, he took those two halves and started ripping them into shreds."

Good-bye rulebook.

There are only four umpires at every regular-season major-league game, and two or three at each game in the minors, and arrayed against them are an army of fifty players, two managers, perhaps as many as ten coaches, a pair of trainers, batboys, ballpersons, and most of the fans in the ball park. We always figured it was just about even as long as we stuck together.

Ken Kaiser once called out Tigers center fielder Ricky Peters on a foul tip. Peters complained briefly, then returned to his dugout. But as he was trotting out to his position at the end of the half inning, he said something about Kaiser to rookie umpire Dan Morrison working third base. When the Tigers came to bat again, Morrison walked in and told Kaiser what Peters had said, then asked how to handle a situation like that.

"I'll show you how to handle it," Kenny said, tearing off his mask and marching toward the Tiger dugout. Peters saw him coming, picked up his glove, and ran into the clubhouse. Kenny followed him through the dugout but didn't catch him. Instead he took out the Tigers' lineup card, went over to Detroit manager Sparky Anderson, and told him, "Your center fielder's a late scratch!"

When Eric Gregg was in the minor leagues, he and his partner, Joe Pascucci, were having problems with a number of players in the Pawtucket dugout but couldn't determine exactly which players were responsible. Rather than clearing the entire bench, Pascucci decided to set an example. "Next time they yell at me," he told Eric, "I'm gonna shout to you, 'Eric, pick one!' You give me a name, and I'll eject him."

"I thought it was a super plan," Eric says, "and I just looked over at that bench, rubbed my hands together, and tried to decide who I was going to nominate. Sure enough, in the next inning, somebody screamed something at my man Joe. He didn't even hesitate. He whipped off his mask and yelled, 'Eric, pick one!'

" 'Bromberg!' I shouted to him, meaning pitcher Mark Bromberg.

" 'You got it!' He looked into the Pawtucket dugout, pointed at Bromberg, and said, 'You, you're done!'

"We didn't hear another complaint from that dugout that day."

Because it is usually so difficult to figure out exactly who in a dugout is shouting, with the exception of the familiar voices—Weaver, Martin, and Mauch—an umpire on occasion will eject the wrong person. Steve Palermo, for example, was at first base and said that the Yankees' Willie Randolph had not checked his swing on a third strike. The usually mild-mannered Randolph said a few nasties to Palermo, then went toward the Yankee dugout. Just as he got there, Graig Nettles yelled at Palermo, who mistakenly threw Randolph out of the game.

"There wasn't anything Willie could do about it either," Nettles explains. "He couldn't say anything to Palermo or we both would've been ejected. He just had to accept it. I told him after the game that in the future he was going to have to watch what I said to umpires."

Doug Harvey had a similar situation in Cincinnati. "Fred Hutchinson had a very guttural voice," Doug remembers, "and never hesitated to tell an umpire he was wrong. Bob Purkey, a knuckle-baller, was pitching for the Reds. Maury Wills was the batter. The first pitch of the game came in and I called it a ball. Then I heard Hutch, his voice was unmistakable, 'Well, you're oh-for-one.' I looked over to him. He was sitting there quietly. Wills fouled off the second pitch. Again I heard him, 'Well, you're one for two.' I was beginning to get angry, and the ball game was only two pitches old.

"I called the next pitch ball two. 'Well, as far as calling them, you're oh-for-two.'

"That was enough for me. I went right to the lip of the Cincinnati dugout. 'Lemme tell you something,' I shouted at Hutchinson, 'you ain't gonna holler at me about my strike zone, and anybody on this bench who says one word for the rest of the game is gone.'

"I figured that would keep them quiet for at least a few innings. But when I called the next pitch a ball, I heard, 'Now you're oh-for—'

"Wham! I spun around and shouted, 'That's it, Hutch, you're finished!' Out he came, the front of his shirt dripping with water, water dripping down his chin, water all over his uniform pants. He was soaked. I thought, 'Boy, he's really sweating, and it's only the top of the first inning!

"We had our usual argument. He threatened to go to the league office and get my job, and I told him that if he, or anybody else, could get my job, I didn't want it. Then he left. For the next few innings, though, every Cincinnati ballplayer would come up to bat, look at me, and grin.

"I wasn't talking to any of them, so I couldn't figure out what was going on. But every one of them came to bat, looked at me, and grinned. Finally, one of the few players on that team I liked, Gordy Coleman, got up. I asked catcher Johnny Roseboro to go out and talk to his pitcher for a moment and then moved around to clean off the plate. I didn't look at Coleman as I spoke, because I didn't want any of his teammates knowing we were talking. 'Gordy, what happened?' I asked. 'Everybody's walking up here grinning.'

" 'It wasn't Hutch, Harv,' he said, and told me that one of the Reds' coaches had been doing a perfect imitation of Fred Hutchinson. Hutch had been at the water fountain, his mouth full of water, when I threw him out. He had been so upset he spit it all over himself.

"So I let Coleman bat, then the next hitter, then I went over to the Reds' bench. I asked the coach, 'Did you do that?' When I said that, just about everybody in the dugout broke out laughing, so he couldn't deny it. He admitted his guilt. 'Well,' I told him, 'you did a good job because you fooled me.' Then I went back behind the plate.

"But just as the Dodger pitcher started to go into his windup, I called time and went back to the dugout. 'You know,' I told the coach, 'the more I think about it, you didn't do a good job, because I caught you. In fact, you're out of the game!' "

It was always fascinating to me to see how a person reacted to being ejected. The most common response was disbelief. I would tell them they were out of the game and they would look at me and ask, "Whattya mean?" It seemed obvious enough to me, but upon request I would explain. "This is an American League baseball stadium," I would explain, "and I am an American League umpire. You are a major league baseball player and under the official major

league rules, I have the authority to eject ..."
Actually, I never really got that far. Usually I got
only a few words into my speech when they would
tell me, "You can't throw me out of the game."

It always came as something of a shock when
they discovered I could and had.

Some people do have memorable reactions to
an ejection. Rick Monday has been thrown out of
only one game in his eighteen-year career. "It was
late in the game and Bruce Froemming apparently
had a plane to catch," Rick explains. "He called a
third strike on me and I turned around and said to
him, 'Bruce, that pitch hasn't been a strike all day.'

" 'It is now,' he said. 'You only get three, and
that's the third one.'

" 'I only wanted to know why it's suddenly a
strike,' I told him, 'I don't need a smart answer.'

" 'Smart answer'? I got one for you: You're out
of the game.' With that he wound up and pointed at
the dugout, the signal that I was ejected from the
game.

" 'No, Bruce,' I said, 'I got news for you: *You're*
out of the game!' Then I really wound up, took
three or four steps and, with a greatly exaggerated
gesture, threw him out of the game. I think the
thing that upset him most was that I used better
form in throwing him out than he did in ejecting
me. The only problem, of course, was that I had to
go and he didn't."

During a ball game in Seattle, Reggie Jackson
demanded that the plate umpire inspect baseballs
being thrown by pitcher Gaylord Perry. Reggie
claimed Perry was covering them with some substance that made them drop suddenly. The umpire
examined them and found them covered with horse-
hide. Reggie continued to complain and eventually
had to be ejected. Reggie went into the clubhouse,
then returned to the field carrying a drinking bucket
full of Gatorade. "Here," he screamed at Perry as he
poured it on the field, "you might as well use this!"

As shortstop Chris Speier walked back to the Expos' dugout after being ejected for arguing a called third strike, he spotted a bucket of used baseballs in a corner. He picked up the entire bucket, containing about a hundred baseballs, and heaved them onto the field toward the umpire. "Here," he shouted, "try to guess which one of these is a strike!"

Larry Bowa didn't know what to do the first time he was thrown out of a ball game. "It had just never happened to me before," he explains, "and I didn't know what I was supposed to do. So I just went into the clubhouse and sat in my uniform in front of my locker until the game was over. I felt like I was sitting in a corner in school."

When Jeff Torborg was catching for the Dodgers, he was so upset at being ejected that he went into the clubhouse, kicked over the garbage pails, then kicked over a table on which cans of tuna fish had been piled for the postgame meal. As the cans rolled all over the clubhouse, he realized what he had done and spent the next three innings crawling on the floor picking up tuna fish cans and stacking them in neat piles.

Roy Smalley got sick the first time he was thrown out of a game. He was so angry at himself that he couldn't sleep all night, his stomach was upset, and he had a terrible headache. Now, that's the kind of response I encourage.

Earl Weaver and Billy Martin do things just a bit differently when they are ejected—they give umpires an upset stomach and a headache. Although players cannot play after being thrown out, managers can manage. They usually stand on the ramp leading from the dugout to the clubhouse and have coaches relay their signals. And, incredibly, being unable to see the field from there doesn't even affect their ability to know when an umpire misses a pitch by a half inch.

Even being suspended doesn't necessarily prevent a manager from running his team. When Martin had the Oakland club, for example, the league gave him a brief vacation for bumping umpire Terry Cooney. But in the fourth inning of a game being played during his suspension, Kenny Kaiser noticed that the A's third-base coach was getting signs from pitcher Marty Keough, who was talking on the dugout telephone. "Now, maybe I'm not a Rhodes scholar," Kaiser admits, "but I figured Keough was getting signs from either Alexander Graham Bell or Billy Martin. Martin, I decided, was watching the game on television and calling in his instructions. Finally, we got to the bottom of the eighth inning of a 2–1 game, and the A's had runners on first and second. Just the opportunity I was waiting for.

"I started walking toward the dugout. Coach Clete Boyer got in front of me, so I walked over the top of him. Keough saw me coming and dropped the phone, leaving it dangling. 'Get over here,' I ordered Keough. 'Get Martin on this phone.'

"He pressed some buttons and the next thing I heard was Billy asking, 'What's going on down there?'

" 'Billy,' I said, 'you've just been disconnected.' Then I ripped the telephone out of the wall and handed it to Keough.

"After the game Billy came into the umpires' room and handed me a bill for one telephone. I gave him another message."

Unlike managers and players, who can forget about being thrown out when the game is over, umpires have to file official reports with the league office after every ejection. Pertinent information to be included on this form includes the date, the teams involved, the manager or players being reported, the situation, and the actions of the umpire and individuals ejected. There are three categories of reports: routine, offensive, and very offensive. Most ejections are routine. For example, I once reported, "In the bottom of the eighth with New York ahead, 9–3, I called Mr. Burroughs out on strikes. He went to the dugout and called me a few choice names, so I ejected him." On another occasion I wrote, "With Oakland leading, 1–0, in the bottom of the third inning, I called ball four on a 3–2 count on the first batter up. Mr. Fosse jumped into the air and turned to protest the call, and I ejected him."

If I liked the person I had thrown out, or realized he had suffered from a mild case of temporary insanity, I would call the ejection routine no matter what really happened. For example, "With the score 0–0 in the top of the sixth inning, I called strike two on Mr. Thurman Munson. We argued for a while, then he swung and missed and struck out. We continued arguing but the on-deck hitter, Mr. John Ellis, calmed him down and he returned to the dugout. From the dugout Mr. Munson yelled in a very loud voice, '@$#%$¢ you!' I immediately signaled his ejection. Mr. Munson raced out of the dugout to confront me but was grabbed and held by Mr. Ellis. Manager Houk came out and slammed his hat down, and I ejected him. Umpire Frank Umont stepped in to keep us all apart. Manager Houk, who was irritated mostly because his only catcher had been ejected, told me several times the same thing Mr. Munson had said. All this time Mr. Munson would have loved to get to me, but Mr. Ellis held him securely in tow."

So perhaps Thurman was upset, so perhaps he would have enjoyed trying to tear me limb from limb, so perhaps calling this ejection "routine" would be like calling World War II a spat. But Thurman was a man who fought hard every minute and had just temporarily lost control. Houk is respected by almost every umpire because he argues only when he believes he has a just cause or to protect his player and never holds a grudge. So as far as I was concerned, this was routine.

On the other hand, no ejection involving Earl Weaver was ever routine. "The score was 5–0, Texas leading Baltimore," I once reported. "In the top of the fourth inning, I called a Texas runner safe at first. Manager Weaver came out yelling that I was deliberately calling plays against his club. I told him it was not true and not for him to think that. He screamed, 'You are @$#%$¢%&ing me.' I told him no. He shoved his face into mine and repeated, 'You're @$#%$¢%&ing me.' I told him he was ejected. He said he did not care. He repeated several times I had stated in California I hated him and was calling plays against him. He piled dirt on first base. He told me I would not work his games anymore. I answered I didn't want to work for him. He told me I would be driving a garbage truck and not umpiring. He told me I was a showboat and cared more about talking to the press than umpiring. He prolonged the argument to the point of becoming ridiculous, during this time making all types of gestures.

"To start the second game manager Weaver came out yelling, 'You've $@#%$¢ed me for the last time.' I told him not to start again. He repeated it and I told him he was gone and he said he knew it. He continued yelling about hating me and shoving it @$# %$¢ @$# %#¢$ $¢% $#¢*&. He then told his catcher, 'Every time he misses a pitch you turn around and shove your mask in his face and tell him.' He then told me I would have to run all three of his catchers. Finally Mr. Haller got him away, as he did in the first game."

Just another beautiful afternoon in the sun. Obviously, this was a "very offensive" ejection. The real problem I had in working Oriole games, besides the headache, the stomachache, and the earache, was that I would get writer's cramp.

The most important thing for an umpire to do in writing one of these reports was to be completely honest. If I called a player a no-good #$@% @%#¢ %(¢* ¢$%@ $@* $¢$&¢@ %@$#*% $% $ @$## (&% ¢%¢(%&*%Y¼¼$@¢ $%$¢%& $¢% %#&$__* &$er #%$% *%($ # $¢__&%__¢$¢$*%) $%(¢)¢@

%¢))__%¢$, which he undoubtedly deserved, I would include that, @#$#@% @$% @&@ for $¢$I* #%#¢$, in my report. So when Lee MacPhail got this report, he knew I was telling him exactly what happened. "In the top of the ninth inning with Oakland leading, 2–1," I wrote, "I called a California player safe at the plate. Mr. Odom was behind me backing up the play. In his anxiety to argue the play he grabbed me. I imagine in order to turn me around, he ended up pushing up against me with his arms partially around me. I threw my arms up, striking Mr. Odom in the cheek. Manager Williams was there instantaneously, along with catcher Duncan, and Mr. Odom and myself were immediately separated. Mr. Odom then called me a 'blind @$#$#@$¢& %#$@!' And after that statement, I ejected him. Mr. Williams sent Mr. Odom away without letting him say another word.

"After the game Mr. Odom made a special trip to the umpires' room just to apologize. I also apologized for striking him."

It was, however, still an "offensive" ejection.

After years of filling out these forms, I learned the best way to report an incident. Usually, I found, the less I wrote, the better. For example, the worst moment I ever had on the playing field was condensed into one paragraph:

"In the top of the third inning with the score tied and men on first and third, I was working third and called an obvious foul ball a home run. I did not see the ball. When everyone charged me I called all three umpires together and they told me the ball was foul. I reversed my decision. Manager Williams said I would have to run him before he would leave the field. So I ejected Mr. Williams."

Reducing this disaster to one paragraph should rate me at least an editor's job at *Reader's Digest*. If I was able to describe this incident, in which Earl Weaver and every Baltimore Oriole past, present, and future, attacked me, followed by the entire

Angel ball club and everyone in the stadium who had an "a" or an "e" in his or her first or last name, I should be able to reduce *Romeo and Juliet* to something like, "*Romiet*, the story of a boy meeting a girl."

The most difficult part of filling out these forms was keeping my emotions out of them. I tried to be clear and explain exactly what happened, but sitting in a hotel room, with adrenaline still running through me and my heart pumping like a rock musician's drumsticks, it was difficult. Perhaps the most unpleasant day I had on the field involved Texas and Milwaukee, when pitchers from both teams were throwing at the heads of the other team's best hitters. "At home plate," I reported to Mr. MacPhail, "Mr. Martin told Mr. Crandall he would retaliate and throw at Mr. Crandall's shortstop, Mr. Yount, four times. In the first inning two pitches came very close to Mr. Yount. In the next few innings pitches came close to people on both teams. Mr. Broberg came in to pitch and I was forced to warn him when another pitch decked Mr. Yount.

"The next half inning a pitch came close to a Texas player and I informed both managers it would end at this point and the next time a pitch came close I would eject the manager. In the bottom of the sixth inning Mr. Scott came to bat. Mr. Scott's last time up he had hit a three-run home run to make the game 9–3. Mr. Broberg's first pitch went directly at Mr. Scott's head. I signaled Mr. Martin's ejection. I told Mr. Broberg that if another pitch came close, he would go. Mr. Martin remained till the end of the inning, then made an obscene arm gesture, getting a crowd reaction, and left.

"In the eighth inning Mr. Broberg came under the chin on Mr. Coluccio on one pitch and right at his head on the next. I ejected Mr. Broberg at this point.

"In the top of the first inning of the second game a pitch was thrown on the inside to a Texas player. Mr. Martin from the dugout said, "Why don't you warn him?' I told him we could do without his comments. He called me an '*¢$@(&%#.' I ejected him and he left after the half inning was over.

"In the third inning I called Mr. Randle out at 3rd. I turned away in calling him out and saw his helmet at the shortstop position. Mr. Neudecker motioned it was thrown by Mr. Randle. I then ejected him. After his team had been retired, Mr. Randle tried to go to his position but was sent back to the dugout by Mr. Frantz. He then reentered the playing field to come to the outfield grass by second base to tell me how '%$¢#&' I was. I called Mr. Lucchesi out to get Mr. Randle away from me before I would hit him. Mr. Lucchesi went crazy with Mr. Neudecker and Mr. Randle left."

As I remember this incident, as I remember the beanballs, the name-calling, the ejections, the fans screaming at the umpires, the threats, the bitter atmosphere, there is one thought that comes to mind: It wasn't funny at the time.

The best thing an umpire can do when a manager or a player is screaming at him is to listen, discuss only the play, and even then only when it is necessary, then walk away. On occasion, though, an umpire just can't resist responding to a remark. And when he does, that response had better be good. The best I've ever heard was made by Dick Stello while he was still working in the Texas League. He was behind the plate one night and called a line drive that landed close to the left-field foul line a fair ball. The manager of Fort Worth, Alex Grammas, came out to argue that the ball was foul. "Alex," Stello told him, "it hit right on the line."

The ball had landed almost 250 feet away. "Are your eyes really that good?" Grammas demanded.

Stello nodded solemnly. "Listen, Alex," he said, "on a clear day I can see the sun, and that sucker is 93 million miles away!"

SEVEN

THE RULES
OF THE GAME

One of the most appealing aspects of baseball is that, even though tens of thousands of professional games have been played, there is always the possibility, every game, every inning, every pitch, that something will happen that has never happened before.

Appealing to the fan, that is. Umpires do not want to see anything new, they do not want to see anything different. Umpires want to see the same old things: routine grounders to infielders, easy popups to outfielders, swinging strikeouts, and long home runs, and they want to see them over and over and over.

Unfortunately, strange things do take place during baseball games. Balls disappear beneath bases, outfielders collide chasing a fly ball and the ball lands on one player's stomach without ever hitting the ground, three runners arrive at the same base at the same time, a line drive bounces off a pitcher's forehead and is caught by the third baseman, two baseballs are simultaneously in play. These are the plays that umpire school does not prepare a man for, that good judgment doesn't help. These are the plays that a major league umpire will watch carefully, then take a deep breath and wonder, "Why does this have to happen to me?"

The really unusual plays are not specifically covered in the official baseball rules, but in most situations there is an applicable rule. For example, the Cleveland Indians once had an outfielder-first baseman named Jay Kirke, who could not hit a curve ball. So pitchers would throw him mostly curve balls. He was standing in the on-deck circle one afternoon when the Indians' batter singled to center field. A runner on second raced for home. The outfielder made a strong throw to the plate. Just as the catcher was about to grab it, Kirke stepped in front of him and smashed a long drive to the outfield.

Then he stood there and smiled triumphantly.

After the game he explained to reporters, "I couldn't help it. It was the first fast ball I'd seen in a month."

The plate umpire got no argument when he ruled Kirke out for interference and did not allow the Indians' run to score.

Sometimes a play occurs in which two totally different rules apply. Then the umpire must decide which rule takes precedence. Davey Phillips had such a play one night during a Minnesota Twins–Boston Red Sox game. Rod Carew was on first base with one out. Twins manager Gene Mauch was coaching at third base. The batter hit a hard shot to left-center field. It looked as if it would drop safely for a double, with Carew scoring easily. Rod rounded second and was halfway to third base when Freddie Lynn in center field made a tremendous diving catch. "Go back!" Mauch started screaming at Carew while waving his arms frantically. "Go back!"

Now, there are certain mysteries of this world that cannot be satisfactorily explained: the creation of the first atomic particle; deep, meaningful love; and the reaction of Rod Carew on this play. Carew is an extremely intelligent man and a splendid base runner, so it is difficult to understand why he reacted as he did.

Carew did exactly as Mauch ordered. He returned to first base by the shortest route possible—across the infield and over the pitcher's mound. "I stood at second base with my mouth open," Davey Phillips recalls. "I just couldn't believe Rod Carew would do something like that. The rules state very clearly that a runner must retrace his steps when returning to base, meaning Carew would be out for not retouching second base.

"Unfortunately, this was only the beginning of the play. Red Sox' shortstop Rick Burleson took the relay from Lynn, turned, saw Carew, and threw hurriedly toward first base ... and over first base, into the dugout. Suddenly an entirely different rule had to be applied. When a ball is thrown from the field into dead territory, the base runner is entitled to advance two bases without jeopardy. So I pointed to Carew and yelled, 'You, third base!' Rod trotted around second and went to third.

"Red Sox manager Don Zimmer waited until the play was completed, then came out and carefully instructed his pitcher how to appeal. When the ball was put into play, the pitcher tossed it to second base. The second baseman touched the base and appealed to me, claiming correctly that Carew had failed to retouch second base. I called Carew out.

"And hhhheeeeeeerrrrrrrrrreeeeeeeeee comes Mauch, and he is angry. He began by arguing that Carew had touched second base when I awarded him two bases. I agreed and explained that that had no bearing on the original play. Mauch then claimed that the dead ball nullified the original play. I disagreed. He was rapidly running out of arguments. Finally he threw up his hands in disgust and made his final argument. 'I've been in baseball twenty-seven years,' he said, 'and I've never seen anything like that!' "

Davey made the correct call on this play, penalizing the team that caused the problem. My feeling in such situations was that if a team made an obvious mistake, they really couldn't argue too long or too vehemently.

Perhaps the most controversial and complicated rules play that has occurred in major league baseball in the past few decades took place at Yankee Stadium in 1983. With two out in the top of the ninth inning, the Yankees were leading the Kansas City Royals, 3–2. Crew chief Joe Brinkman was working second base, and he was only one out, only a minute, away from the end of the game and the beginning of his two-week vacation. He was flying home to St. Petersburg, Florida, immediately after the game and planned to lie on a beach, play some golf, catch some fish. But the Royals' U. L. Washington singled. Then George Brett slammed relief pitcher Goose Gossage's fast ball into the right-field seats for a home run to put the Royals ahead, 4–3. Brinkman figured his vacation was going to be delayed slightly, as now the Yankees would have to come to bat in the bottom of the ninth inning. But compared to what was about to happen, that problem was comparable to running out of ice cubes on the *Titanic*.

Thus began the famous "pine tar incident."

A few weeks earlier, the Yankees and Royals had played in Kansas City. During that series Yankee coach Don Zimmer had noticed that George Brett was using a bat with more pine tar on its handle and barrel than permitted by the rules. Pine tar is a black, sticky substance that hitters use to improve their grip on the bat. Zimmer did nothing about it in Kansas City except mention it to catcher Rick Cerone and manager Billy Martin. But after Brett hit his home run to put the Royals ahead, both Martin and Zimmer screamed to Cerone, "Check the bat! Check the bat!"

Cerone picked it up and examined it. It looked

perfectly normal to him, as he had forgotten what he was supposed to be checking for. Finally Martin came out of the dugout as Brett accepted the congratulations of his teammates.

"I was at second base," Joe Brinkman explains, "just starting to think about two weeks of sunshine, golf course, and fish. At first I didn't know why Billy was coming out. I've worked with him for a long time and I know he is always searching for the smallest loophole—I've thought about asking him to do my taxes—but I couldn't figure out what it was he wanted this time.

"Then I saw him showing the bat to plate umpire Tim McClelland, and I knew he had to be claiming that the bat was illegal for some reason. McClelland called me in to the plate and explained that the Yankees were claiming Brett's bat was illegal because it had more than eighteen inches of pine tar on it, measured from the handle. I took one look at the bat, which was just covered with pine tar, and I knew my vacation wasn't going to be as much fun as I had anticipated.

"My crew happened to be very familiar with this rule because we had had a similar situation in Cleveland two weeks earlier. I guess we were really on a lucky streak. Boston's Jim Rice had doubled, and Indians manager Mike Ferraro asked us to check Rice's bat for too much pine tar. That bat was clean to about two inches below the trademark, so according to the rules, it was legal. Brett's bat was not.

"So here we were, in Yankee Stadium, New York City, in the ninth inning of a game involving two teams fighting for first place in their respective divisions. And we had a play that probably was going to decide the game and maybe figure prominently in two divisional races, and it wasn't specifically covered in the rulebook.

"I sort of wished I had started my vacation a day earlier.

"We had to make a decision; that's the reason

we were out there. I discussed the play with
McClelland, Drew Coble, and Nick Bremigan. The
rules clearly prohibit the use of a bat covered with
pine tar but did not describe any penalty. So we had
to string together the proper rules.

"Rule 6.06(a) says a batter shall be out when he
hits an illegally batted ball. Rule 2.00 states an
illegally batted ball is one hit with a bat that does
not conform to rule 1.10. Rule 1.10(b) reads, 'The
bat handle, for not more than eighteen inches from
the end, may be covered or treated with any material (including pine tar) to improve the grip. Any
such material, including pine tar, which extends
past the eighteen-inch limitation, in the umpire's
judgment, shall cause the bat to be removed from
the game.'

"So according to 1.10(b) Brett's bat did not conform to the rules. Rule 2.00 states that a ball hit
with a bat not conforming to the rules is an illegally batted ball. Rule 6.06(a) says a batter is out
when he hits an illegally batted ball.

"The one thing none of us questioned was
whether the bat was illegal. But just to make sure
everybody else realized it, we laid it down next to
the front of home plate, which is seventeen inches
in width. The pine tar extended past the plate,
greatly exceeding the limitation. We were getting
real close to a decision now.

"I said to Timmy McClelland, 'You want to
call Brett out, or you want me to do it?'

" 'I've got the plate,' he said, 'I'll do it.' As a
group, we walked toward the Royals' dugout. Timmy
raised his right hand into the air and called Brett
out, ending the game. George's reaction was predictable: He went nuts. The next thing I knew, I was
holding him by the neck, trying to keep him away
from McClelland. There goes the vacation, I figured."

The decision of Brinkman's crew created a tremendous controversy, even among umpires. It
seemed sort of picayune to deprive the Royals of a

victory because Brett had too much tar on his bat. To me, the rules are clear enough and the umpires made the right decision. Other umpires felt that Martin should have been allowed to protest, the bat should have been confiscated and sent it to the league office, and the game should have been finished. There was, however, one point on which everyone else was in agreement: They were thrilled it hadn't happened to them.

The Royals protested the game, and American League President Lee MacPhail upheld their protest, explaining that while the umpires were technically correct, their decision was not in keeping with the spirit of the rules. MacPhail based his decision, at least partially, on rule 6.06(d), which states that a batter shall be called out if he uses a bat "altered or tampered with in such a way to improve the distance factor or cause an unusual reaction on the baseball." Pine tar, Lee said, would not improve the distance, and therefore this rule should not apply.

But Brinkman's crew had not applied it.

MacPhail ruled that Brett's home run would count, putting the Royals ahead, 4–3, that Brett and others would be ejected from the game for their actions in arguing with the umpires, and that the game would be resumed from the point where it had ended. Davey Phillips and his crew were scheduled to be in New York City on the next date both teams had an off-day, and they were assigned to work the conclusion of what had become known as the "Pine Tar Game."

Naturally, Phillips's crew was delighted to be selected. Next to being locked in a tiny office with a crazed dentist, this was probably their greatest wish. "I was at second base in the Kingdome when the original game was played," Davey says. "One of the Seattle players told me that Brett had hit a home run and had been called out and ejected from the game. I thought that was pretty funny, so I told my partners about it. We all laughed, and we were all glad we hadn't been involved.

"Of course, at that time we couldn't possibly know we were about to become the first umpires to present an affidavit to a manager during a game.

"Later, after the 'Pine Tar Game' had been completed, reporters asked us how we had been smart enough to anticipate Billy Martin's attempt to lodge another protest. I told them that the week before the game Dick Butler, the American League's supervisor of umpires, and my crew had tried to prepare ourselves for everything that might happen during the game. We had to know all the details, which people had played and been taken out of the game, how many trips to the mound Martin had made in the ninth inning. We had to keep in mind that Jerry Mumphrey had been playing center field for the Yankees and had since been traded to Houston, that Omar Moreno had not been on the Yankee roster when the game was played, that Bert Campaneris had been put on the disabled list since then, that Steve Balboni had been sent to Columbus. I told the reporters we went through the rulebook trying to figure out what Martin might do. That's what I told them.

"What I didn't tell them was that somebody in the Yankee organization told Butler exactly what Billy was planning to do. Butler had been warned that Billy was going to appeal that Brett had missed a base when circling the bases on his home run and, since my crew had been working in Seattle at that game, protest because we couldn't possibly know if Brett had touched the base or not.

"It was a clever idea, but not clever enough. To prevent this, Butler got a signed affidavit from Joe Brinkman's crew attesting to the fact that both U. L. Washington and Brett had touched all the bases and that both runs counted. I had this affidavit in my pocket when Billy Martin came into the umpires' room before the game.

"But I didn't tell him I had it.

" 'I'm not gonna complain anymore,' he told us sincerely. 'We're just gonna play the game. If we win, we win; if we lose, we lose, that's it. I don't agree with MacPhail, but let's just get it finished once and for all.'

"He was so sincere I almost believed him, but I've known him too long for that. Billy and I have always had a decent relationship, so I asked him, 'Billy, have you got anything up your sleeve for us today?'

"He smiled. 'Oh, maybe one little thing,' he admitted, 'but I promise you, I won't do anything to embarrass you.'

" 'No,' I agreed, 'I'm sure you won't.' And I was sure of that too, because I had the folded affidavit in my pocket.

"As soon as the game was resumed, Yankee pitcher George Frazier stepped off the pitcher's rubber and tossed the ball to first baseman Ken Griffey. Tim Welke, working first base, signaled safe. I looked into the Yankee dugout, but Billy wasn't coming out. Instead he was yelling at Frazier to make the protest to second base. Frazier tossed the ball to second. Actually, this is illegal, as the defense is only permitted one such appeal per runner, but by this time the situation was so bizarre Billy could have started doing a polka on the dugout roof and no one would have stopped him. After the second baseman had touched the base, I signaled safe. And that's when Billy finally came out.

"He walked out toward me briskly, like a confident executive on his way to his office. He had been preparing for this moment for a long time, and I could see he was ready to enjoy it. That was fair. I knew I was going to enjoy it more. 'I want to make an appeal,' he said when he had reached me.

" 'On what grounds, Billy?' I asked, as if I didn't know. Oh, boy, that affidavit was just burning a hole in my pocket now.

" 'On missing a base,' he replied.

" 'Who?'

" 'George Brett,' he said firmly. 'We have reason to believe that he missed first base.' The reason Martin appealed to first is because if we had called Brett out for missing first base, Washington's run would not have counted either.

"It was time to spring *our* surprise. 'Billy,' I said, 'I really hate to do this to you, but I've got this piece of paper here . . .' I took it out of my pocket and slowly unfolded it.

"He looked at me as if I had taken away his new little pony. 'What's that?' he demanded.

" 'It's called an affidavit, Billy, and it says here that the umpires who worked that game have sworn that both runners touched all the bases and their runs count.'

" '@$#% $¢$ %#% #%# %$%W¢# $#%__ $ # %$¢%$ ¢%¢$#%¢ *&&¢ &*$__ %$__¢% ¢__-#$$)%¢ %*$¢ %&(&$%@!!,' Billy said.

" 'Well, maybe that's true, but that's the way it's going to be.' I could see how incredibly frustrated he was. He wanted to scream at somebody, but he had no reason to scream at anybody. 'Scream at Gossage,' I thought, 'he threw the ball that got us here in the first place. Or scream at Brett, he hit it. But don't blame my crew and don't blame Joe Brinkman's crew.'

"After the Royals had made the third out of the inning, almost a month after the second out had been made, Billy finally came up with another reason to protest the game. 'I protest because Quisenberry wasn't pitching in the last game and he's pitching now.'

"I tried to explain the rules to him. 'This is the ninth inning,' I said, 'they can bring in anybody they want to pitch.'

" 'How come?'

" 'We'll go real slow,' I told him. 'Gossage was pitching for you in the ninth inning, right?' He agreed. 'Then you brought in Frazier to pitch. What's the difference between your bringing in Frazier, and Howser bringing in Quisenberry to pitch for him?'

"He finally seemed to grasp the mechanics of the situation. 'You mean this is like a real game?' he asked.

"And except for the fact that it took two weeks to prepare for twelve minutes of baseball, and I had to hand an affidavit to a manager, it was just like a real game."

Because I founded my career on the belief that what I didn't call couldn't hurt me, I would call a runner out on an appeal play only if he had obviously left his base before a fly ball had been caught, or obviously missed a base. But I had a very big obvious zone. If there was any question in my mind, I did not allow the appeal.

Umpires generally do not like appeal plays because they might have to change the result of a play that has already been completed, and that is guaranteed to cause an argument. The rules governing how a defensive team shall make an appeal are very specific: The appeal must be made to the umpire *before* any other pitch, play, or attempted play. I know this part of the rule very well. Believe me, I know it well.

I was working a typical Indians–Brewers game in Milwaukee. The Indians had gone ahead by a run in the top of the fifteenth inning, as they do every time these two teams play fifteen-inning games. In the bottom of the fifteenth—my feet hurt just thinking about it—the Brewers' Charlie Moore was on first base with no outs. The batter hit a deep fly ball to left field, Moore tagged up to go to second, and left first base too soon, much, much too soon. Even I saw this one. I knew exactly what was going to happen: The Indians were going to appeal to first base, I was going to call Moore out, and we were going to have a small riot. It was all very simple.

After the ball had been thrown into the infield, Cleveland called a time-out. Manager Jeff Torborg went out to the mound to show his pitcher, Victor Cruz, exactly how he wanted him to appeal the play. Torborg pretended he was standing on the pitcher's rubber, stepped off, and tossed the ball to first base.

I had one slight hope left: "Maybe he's just teaching him for some future game," I hoped.

Torborg patted Cruz on the back and trotted off the field. In just a moment there would be two out, no Moore on base. Cruz took the ball and stepped on the rubber, putting the ball back in play. He stepped off the rubber, just as Torborg had shown him. I took a deep breath, figuring "Here it comes now" and wondering "Why does this have to happen to me?"

But then Cruz glanced at Charlie Moore, leading off second. When he did that, Moore put his head down and pretended to start running toward third base. Instinctively, Cruz picked up his arm as if he were going to throw to second base to pick off Moore.

I thought I heard Torborg falling straight back onto the concrete floor of the dugout, but he might have just been smacking himself in the forehead. Because when Cruz faked a throw to second, he lost the opportunity to appeal.

So we had a different argument from the one I had expected. Torborg was outraged. Bill Haller and I tried to explain that nothing except breathing can come between the play and the appeal, and by faking a throw, Cruz had made a play to force Moore back to second.

"But the wrong team is being penalized," Jeff protested.

"That's right," I agreed, "it's wrong. But that's the rule."

Later I found out that Brewers manager George Bamberger knew about that rule because it had

been invoked against him a few weeks earlier, when
the Tigers' Ron Leflore stole a run by being thrown
out at the plate. Detroit had a runner on second and
Leflore was on first with two outs. The batter singled,
scoring the runner from second and sending Leflore
to third base. But Leflore missed second by a few
feet.

The Brewers put the ball in play and, as their
pitcher turned to throw to second, Leflore took off
for home plate. The startled pitcher quickly spun
around and fired the ball to his catcher, who tagged
the sliding Leflore for the third out.

But Leflore had saved the Tigers' run. If the
Brewers had completed their appeal to second before making another play, Leflore would have been
called out and the run that scored would not have
counted. So Leflore had absolutely nothing to lose
by breaking for the plate. He was already out at
second, so if his break for the plate had been
successful, he would have stolen a second run for
the Tigers.

The next thing someone will claim is that it is
possible to have four legal outs made in an inning.
And that someone is me. It is possible to have four
legal outs made in an inning.

This is a perfect example of players not knowing the rules and having it cost them a run—and
almost the pennant. During the 1980 National
League playoffs between the Phillies and the Astros,
Philadelphia had a runner on third, Mike Schmidt
on first, and one out. Doug Harvey was behind the
plate.

The batter hit a bloop to right field that looked
like it might fall in for a hit. Both runners took off,
but the outfielder made a fine running catch. "I was
standing at the plate," Doug recalls, "and just as
the outfielder released his throw, the runner from
third crossed in front of me. Now, I've seen quick
runners, but there was absolutely no way that man
could have tagged up on third base and gotten to

the plate so quickly, so it was apparent he had left third too soon. It turned out Schmidt had left first base too early, too, and he was desperately trying to get back to the base.

"Houston made a play on him and doubled him off first base for the third out of the inning. But the rules make it clear that a defensive team can appeal until another play is made or until all infielders have crossed the foul lines. The play on Schmidt at first was a continuation of the original play, so the Astros could still legally make an appeal that the runner had left third base too soon. If they did, it would be considered a fourth legal out and the run would not count.

"I just stood at home plate, I didn't say a word, I didn't signal to the official scorer to count the run, I just waited. But instead of clearing the field, the Astros were congratulating their pitcher for working out of a bad jam. I finally strolled toward umpire Eddie Vargo and said, 'You know, Eddie, until they clear the field I can't—'

"That was as far as I got. Another umpire, who had not seen the runner on third leave too soon, came running in shouting, 'Score that run, Harv, you gotta score that run—'

"I just stared at him and said nothing. I couldn't tell him he was wrong because if the Astros heard me I would be guilty of interference, so I continued staring at him. Finally, though, Houston left the field and I indicated the Philadelphia run counted. I don't think the Astros ever realized that they could have prevented that run from scoring. Fortunately, it did not have a bearing on the final score."

Not only does baseball have four outs, the rules also allow for do-overs. Under ordinary circumstances baseball, unlike football, in which penalties can cause downs to be replayed, has no provision for do-overs. Once a play is completed it is in the record books forever. Of course, if all the games were ordinary, Mamie Eisenhower could have been a great umpire.

Usually, do-overs occur when an umpire has called a time-out and the play has continued. Perhaps the strangest example of a do-over-and-over-and-over took place in the ninth inning of a ball game at New York's Shea Stadium. The Mets were beating Houston—poor Houston—4–1. The Astros had two outs, no one on base, and a count of one ball, one strike on Jeff Leonard. Leonard hit a long foul ball into the right-field seats, and the home-plate umpire flipped a new ball to Mets pitcher Pete Falcone. But just as Falcone began his windup, the ball that had been fouled into the seats trickled back onto the field. Mets right fielder Dan Norman trotted over to retrieve it, and shortstop Frank Traveras called for a time-out.

But Falcone pitched, and Leonard hit a routine fly ball to center field. Lee Mazzilli caught it, and the victorious Mets hustled off the field.

"Not so fast," said third-base umpire Doug Harvey. Traveras had called for a time-out, Doug told Mets manager Joe Torre, and the out would have to be replayed.

So the Mets returned to the field. Falcone went back to the mound, and Leonard came up to bat again. Leonard fouled off Falcone's first pitch. Then he lined a single to left. The ball was thrown in to second baseman Doug Flynn, who whirled to throw to first base . . . and only then did anyone realize that the Mets had been playing without first baseman Eddie Kranepool.

Kranepool had gone into the clubhouse as soon as Leonard hit the routine fly to center field and did not return when the game had been resumed. So the Mets had played two pitches with only eight men on the field.

"Not so fast," said Joe Torre. The rules stipulate that the defensive team must have nine players on the field, and the Mets had only eight. Meanwhile, as Torre made his case, Eddie Kranepool was trying to sneak quietly onto the field. The umpires conferred and agreed with Torre. Leonard would have to bat again.

"Not so fast," said Houston manager Bill Virdon, protesting the game. Coincidentally, National League President Chub Feeney was at the ball park.

Falcone went back to the mound, and Leonard came up to bat again. Thus far, Leonard had flied out and singled during this one at-bat, so he was working on a pretty good season. Finally, with all nine Met players in position, Leonard hit another fly ball to the outfield to end the game. The victorious Mets left the field.

"Not so fast," said National League President Chub Feeney. At the conclusion of the game he went directly to the umpires' room and upheld Virdon's protest. The Astros should not be penalized for the Mets' mistake, he said. He ordered the game to be resumed the following day, before the start of the regularly scheduled game. Leonard was to be credited with a single and put at first base and the next batter in the order was to hit.

"Not so fast," said Joe Torre the next day as *he* protested the game. But Mets pitcher Kevin Kobel retired Jose Cruz to end the game, the game, the game, the game.

The man I felt most sorry for in this situation was Eddie Kranepool. Okay, maybe he is a quiet man, but how could nobody notice he was missing? Not the first-base umpire, the Astros' first baseman, the Mets' second baseman, Pete Falcone . . . You'd think someone would have noticed there was a wider than usual gap in the right side of the Mets' infield.

Of course, this situation was so unusual that to find the last time a similar thing happened, baseball historians had to search all the way back to 1969, when Reggie Jackson of the Oakland A's went into the clubhouse to change his ripped pants, and his own roommate, Chuck Dobson, pitched to a batter without a right fielder. Now, people who have not seen Reggie play the outfield as often or as well as I have might comment that Dobson felt this was a defensive improvement, but that would be an exaggeration.

The best thing about the Mets do-over was that it did not affect the outcome of the game. Had it made a difference in the final score, there would have been a tremendous uproar. The worst thing that can happen to an umpire is to be involved in a controversial situation that turns a game around.

Jim McKean, for example, was known during his first four years in the majors as the luckiest umpire in the American League. He rarely had close plays and never got caught in a difficult squeeze. Other umpires loved working with him, hoping whatever lucky charm he was using would also work for them.

His luck changed abruptly. It was the second game of the 1976 season, and the Yankees were leading the Brewers, 9–7, in the bottom of the ninth inning. McKean was at first base. Milwaukee loaded the bases with one out, and Don Money was batting. Just as Yankee pitcher Dave Pagan got ready to pitch, first baseman Chris Chambliss turned to McKean and requested time be called so he could tell Pagan that manager Billy Martin wanted him to pitch from the stretch position. McKean put both hands in the air and screamed, "Hold it!"

Too late. With McKean's hands high in the air, Pagan threw and Money hit the ball approximately nine hundred feet into the bleachers for a grand-slam home run to win the ball game. "Suddenly," McKean recalls, "everybody was running past me, people were scoring runs, the Brewers were jumping up and down celebrating their victory, and I'm thinking, 'Maybe nobody noticed me.'

"I did not have too much time to think about that. Martin was out of the dugout even before

Money had rounded first base. 'You had your hands up!' he was screaming. 'You had your hands up!'

" 'Just wait a minute, Billy,' I told him, 'just give me a minute.' I was stalling for time, hoping I could figure out something to get me out of this situation. Finally I realized I had no choice. I told plate umpire George Maloney that I had called a time-out before Pagan had pitched. I suspected Brewer fans were not going to be happy.

" 'Are you sure?' George asked.

"I nodded. Nick Bremigan said that he had seen me put up my hands before the pitch. We conferred, but we knew we had no choice. The Brewers had left the field, so we had to go into the clubhouse to get them to come back on the field. They were in shock, so they didn't argue as forcefully as they might have. Nobody even threatened my safety.

"When we started playing again, I stood there hoping that Money would hit another home run. I would have been satisfied with a single. Unfortunately, he did not. Then George Scott made the third out, and the game was over."

The Brewers protested the game but, ironically, Lee MacPhail happened to be an expert on that particular play. When he was general manager of the Baltimore Orioles, the White Sox' Ted Kluszewski had hit a home run that umpire Ed Hurley had disallowed because a time-out had been called. MacPhail rejected the Brewers' protest. "I had been in Milwaukee for the opening game the night before," he noted. "Fortunately, I had left that day. That was the best break I got since I had become league president."

Actually, this was not such an unusual occurrence. Dangerous maybe, but not really that unusual. When Milwaukee was still a National League city, Lee Weyer was working third base for a Braves—Pittsburgh Pirates game. The Pirates' Gene Oliver hit a line drive that was just foul. Jojo White, coaching at third, argued, and Weyer threw him out of

the game. Then manager Bobby Bragan demanded
that Weyer go out to left field to look at the chalk
mark where the ball had hit. "I told him," Lee
remembers, "that I knew where it hit. I didn't have
to go look at it.

" 'Well,' he told me, 'I'm going down to look at
it.'

" 'Go ahead,' I told him, 'but just keep walking,
because you're out of the game.' So now I had
gotten two of them and the play really hadn't even
started to get interesting.

"Gene Oliver got ready to hit again and, just as
the pitcher went into his windup, I noticed that the
Pirates hadn't replaced their third-base coach. So I
hollered 'TIME!'

"Oliver hit the pitch out of the park.

"I figured the longer I waited to break the news
to the Pirates the angrier they were going to be. So I
started running in immediately and stopped Oliver
even before he had gotten to first base.

"Oliver actually took it very well. He simply
got back into the batter's box, struck out on the
next pitch, and threw his bat at me.

"That set a personal record for me, three men
ejected in only one at-bat."

Among the many things I learned during my
career that would ensure a longer, happier, health-
ier life were: Never take a waiter's recommenda-
tion after 10 P.M. Never use an accountant who
drives a bigger car than you do. And, most impor-
tantly, never call a balk.

Balks kill. Balks always cause at least one argument and often cause two.

Generally, the balk rule states that a pitcher
must step in the direction in which he throws, or
throw in the direction in which he steps, except to
second base, to which he can fake a throw as long
as he does not fake a throw by turning in two
different directions, or third base, toward which he

can step without throwing the ball, and that he cannot stand on the pitcher's rubber without the ball, or deliver a pitch from the set position without stopping, or drop the ball, or take one hand from the ball after coming to a set position, or . . .

One reason I never called balks is that I never understood the rule. On paper it is very specific; on the field it is almost impossible to apply because umpires are supposed to allow pitchers to use their natural motion. For example, Luis Tiant, in pitching with a man on base, would nod his head maybe a dozen times, bring his hands down to his belt in a herky-jerky fashion, stopping at least six times, wiggle his moustache, and fail to stop at the bottom of his set position before throwing. His windup brought to mind one of those contests that challenged: "Find the twenty-five balks in this pitching motion and win twenty-five dollars!" But because it was his natural delivery, it was considered legal. Yet some other poor pitcher would move his shoulder one-quarter inch and everybody would start screaming at me for not calling a balk.

It seemed so complicated to me that unless a pitcher actually dropped the ball while delivering it, I ignored it. I always tried to be the second umpire on the field to call a balk. As soon as I saw one of my partners throw his hands into the air to make the call, my hands went right up to reinforce his decision. I figured he must know what he is doing.

The only time I can remember calling a balk first was in Minnesota. I don't remember who the pitcher was, but Twins manager Frank Quilici had been screaming at me all game, "He's balking! Watch his knee! He's bending his knee!" So I watched his knee. The pitcher threw over to first, and his motion looked legal to me. But Quilici started yelling, "Didn't you see it?"

"See what?" I shouted at him. "He didn't bend his knee!"

"Not his knee," Quilici shouted with disgust, "he moved his shoulder!"

His shoulder? Nobody said a word about any shoulder. I was so busy watching his knee I didn't even notice his shoulder. Later in that same game, however, I did call my balk. I heard one of my partners scream it loudly, and I immediately threw my hands into the air and called it myself. It took me an instant to realize that it had not been one of my partners who made the original call, but a fan sitting along the third-base line. One thing I did notice, though: As soon as I made my call, all three of my partners threw their hands into the air.

Unless a pitcher dribbles the ball on the mound, or makes an obvious feint toward first base without throwing, or throws to an unoccupied base, that pitcher and his manager, his agent, and his attorney are going to argue with any umpire who calls a balk, claiming that the umpire does not understand the rule. In my case, they were correct—I did not understand the rule. But that never stopped the same manager who told me I didn't know the rule from complaining that I wasn't calling it on the other team's pitcher. I always prided myself on being very fair about it—I didn't know the rule for both teams.

What often compounds the problem is that the pitcher continues his delivery after the balk has been called and the batter hits the pitch. The result is always confusing and usually leads to a second argument. Doug Harvey had this happen to him in Montreal one night. "The pitcher threw after I'd made my call," Doug remembers, "and the Giants' Jackie Clark hit a long fly ball to the fence. The base runner had no idea what to do. He heard me call the balk and saw the ball hit. So he started running, then stopped, then started running again, then stopped again, then started running. . . . He looked like a car trying to get started on a freezing morning. Finally he made his decision and put his head down and took off around second.

"That's when the outfielder made a great catch. He made a quick throw to the infield, and the shortstop threw to first to try to double up the base runner. The base runner then turned around and started racing back to first. He didn't know if he was supposed to be on first, second, or third.

"Because the balk takes precedence, we called time and advanced the runner one base, to second, and put Clark at bat again. Montreal didn't know whether to argue that it was not a balk or that the fly-out should stand or that there should be a double play."

Durwood Merrill found himself in the middle of a far more complicated situation at Yankee Stadium. "Jimmy Wynn, who was finishing his major league career with the Yankees, was on third base," Durwood explains, "Lou Piniella was the batter, and Jesse Jefferson was pitching for the Toronto Blue Jays. Just as Jefferson completed his windup, Davey Phillips at third base called a balk. But Jefferson threw anyway and Piniella hit this little dinky double into right field.

"The only problem was that Wynn had heard Davey screaming 'Balk!' and had stayed put right there on third base. Now, Billy Martin might not be a genius, but he knew something was wrong and he came out to discuss it gentlemanly-like. 'I don't know exactly what happened,' he admitted, 'but I started with a man on third, then I get a balk, then I get a double, and I *still* got a man on third. I know that can't be right.'

"Seemed to me like the man had a point. The balk rule is pretty specific on that subject. When the batter reaches base after a balk has been called, it states, and all runners have advanced at least one base, the play stands. But it doesn't say one single word about what happens if the batter reaches base and the runners don't advance.

"The umpires got together and decided that the balk had to stand. Wynn would score, and Piniella would go to bat again. The problem was that Piniella refused to leave second base. 'He pitched, I hit,' he said. 'I'm staying right here.'

"Even Billy was pushing for us, telling Piniella he had to leave. But Lou just wasn't going to give up a hit so easily. 'I'm not going anywhere,' he repeated.

"So the umpires huddled again. I suggested that this was a fine time to invoke the Bluff Rule. That way we could score Wynn and let Piniella stay at second, but I didn't receive any support.

"Finally we had to eject Piniella for staying at second, score Wynn, and put the pinch-hitter for Piniella up to bat. About the only person who didn't argue was Jesse Jefferson, who committed the balk in the first place."

I couldn't blame Piniella for wanting to stand safely on second base. I've seen Lou running the bases, and if I was him I'd have wanted to stay there too.

Actually, I know exactly how he felt. When I was growing up in Endicott, my friends would play a game called "running bases," in which they would attempt to run back and forth between two bases without being tagged out by either of the two basemen. I played a similar game, "running base." I would just stand on the base. With my speed, I knew I would be tagged out if I tried to run. And since I was just going to try to return to this base anyway, I figured why run in the first place.

But even if I didn't run, I never got lost between the two bases. One of the things that surprised me about major league players was their ability to get confused on the bases. There are only three bases, and they are called first base, second base, and third base, which should serve as a pretty strong hint about the order in which they are supposed to be touched. Yet players still manage to turn running the bases into high adventure.

Rod Carew is hardly the only player to cut

across the diamond to get from one base to another. For example, if any player in baseball knows how to run the bases, it is Oakland's Ricky Henderson. But in a game against the White Sox, Henderson tried to blaze a new trail from first base to third.

Henderson was on first and, as the pitcher went into his windup, took off for second. The batter swung and lifted a lazy fly ball near the left-field foul line. Henderson made his usual diving, head-first slide into second base and looked up to see the left fielder in pursuit of the fly ball. Because it appeared that the fielder was going to catch it, Henderson quickly got up and retreated halfway to first base. This is when things really got interesting.

The ball landed just inside the foul line and bounced into the seats for a ground-rule double. Henderson figured that he had started on first and the batter had doubled, so he was entitled to third base. Getting there turned out to be the problem. Being a prudent man, he set out to get there as quickly as possible—trotting across the infield.

This is one of those moments that cause an umpire to consider other, more stable careers. Any umpire seeing Henderson doing this would realize something had to be wrong, but figuring out exactly what it was would be the problem. Time was out because of the ground-rule double, yet Henderson broke any number of base-running rules. If this had been my play to call, I would simply have doubled over with pain, complained my ulcer was acting up again, and pleaded with Haller, "You'd better take this one." Fortunately, though, the umpire at third base was Nick Bremigan. Nick knows that third must always be preceded by second—and called Henderson out for not retouching second base when advancing when the White Sox appealed in proper fashion a few moments later.

Even an experienced ballplayer such as Sal Bando can make this same mistake once. He was on first base with one man out when the batter hit a routine fly ball to center field. Sal has never been very fast, but this time he just took off around second and chugged into third base—getting there just in time to be told by the third-base coach, "There's only one out." Two actually, considering that the fly ball had been caught, but that still left one more in the inning.

Sal is a graduate of Arizona State University and undoubtedly learned while in college that the shortest distance between two points is a straight line. So he took that straight-line route back to first base.

Ellis Valentine, when he was with the Mets, also tried some inventive base-running. Caught in the middle of a rundown, with infielders closing in on him from two sides, he turned to the umpire . . . and asked to call a time-out.

Although there are three different bases, on occasion they have not been enough to go around. Two runners often have ended up on the same base at the same time. In fact, at least once in major league history *three* runners briefly shared third base. It happened, naturally, in Brooklyn, New York.

The great umpire Beans Reardon was working third base in Ebbets Field, home of the Brooklyn Dodgers. The Dodgers had the bases loaded, Hank DeBerry on third, Dazzy Vance on second, and Chick Fewster on first. The batter, slugger Babe Herman, slashed a line drive off the right-field fence. DeBerry scored. Vance rounded third and headed for home, but as the ball slammed off the wall in right, decided to return to third base. Fewster, assuming Vance would score easily, rounded second and headed for third. Herman just kept running.

Fewster was only a few feet away from third base when he realized Vance was not going to score.

Let us review: Vance was going back to third. Fewster was standing a few feet away from third, waiting to see what Vance was going to do. Herman was chugging as fast as he could run toward third base. Reardon was watching with growing amusement. The fans were cheering: For the Dodgers to get three men as far as third in one inning was a tremendous accomplishment; for them to get three men to third at the same was simply unbelievable.

Herman sped by Fewster without even slowing down and slid into third base. At just about the same time Vance slid into third base coming from the other direction. Fewster, not knowing where he belonged but realizing it couldn't possibly be third base, stood his ground.

When the third baseman finally got the baseball he started tagging everybody. Vance, the lead runner, was legally occupying the bag, so he was safe. Reardon called Herman out for passing Fewster. Fewster, meanwhile, took off for second base . . . and kept running right past second base into the outfield, where he was finally tagged out. Thus Babe Herman went into the record books as the only man who ever doubled into a double play.

Years later, supposedly, a Brooklyn fan was listening to a Dodgers game on the radio when a passerby asked him what was happening. "The Dodgers have three men on base," the fan replied.

"Oh yeah?" came the response. "Which base?"

I have often said if it weren't for baseball players and managers, umpiring would be the perfect profession. But, in fact, some problems that have occurred have been the fault of the umpires. Occasionally, just as two players will occupy the same base, two umpires will make opposite calls on the same play.

For example, when Joe Torre was managing the New York Mets, they had a rally going—one out and a man on first—when the batter hit a soft line drive to right field. The Cincinnati Reds outfielder made a great effort, so great that one umpire ruled it a catch while another umpire ruled he had trapped it. The runner on first, realizing the batter was either safe or out, finally decided to go to second.

The Reds threw to first base. One umpire ruled it a double play; the other umpire had runners on first and second with one out.

The umpires conferred and finally invoked an important subsection of the Bluff Rule, the Compromise Rule. Two out, man on second. There is absolutely no way this rule can be found in the baseball rulebook, but it might be found in the Marine Corps' survival manual. Of course, this is about the only way that play could not have ended up, but since each team got a little something out of it, there was only a little argument.

Two umpires making two different calls on the same play is trivial compared to the ultimate nightmare of umpires—*one* umpire making two different calls on the same play. This happened one otherwise beautiful evening in Pittsburgh. Naturally, the Dodgers were in town.

Tommy Lasorda was coaching at third base. The bases were loaded; Lee Lacey was on third, Jimmy Wynn on second, and a runner on first. Joe Ferguson, the batter, had a count of three balls, two strikes on him, and two men were out. Jerry Reuss was pitching for the Pirates, and Manny Sanguillen was catching. "Reuss pitched," Tommy remembers, "and the plate umpire called it 'strike three.' I heard him say 'strike three.' Lee Lacey heard him say 'strike three' and trotted off third base toward the dugout to get his glove. Manny Sanguillen heard him say 'strike three' and rolled the ball out toward the pitcher's mound.

"And maybe he did say 'strike three,' but evidently he didn't mean it. Because all of a sudden I see the umpire say something to the batter, Joe Ferguson, who then tossed his bat away and started trotting to first base as if the umpire had called ball four. Suddenly, Sanguillen started running after the baseball, which had stopped rolling near the pitcher's mound. And Jimmy Wynn, who had been on sec-

ond and was running on the pitch, raced past me
and slid safely across home plate.

"Lee Lacey hadn't quite reached the dugout yet
and turned around just in time to see Wynn slide
home safely. So he did the logical thing: He started
running for the plate. By this time Sanguillen had
retrieved the ball. I didn't have the slightest idea
what was going on, but I knew I wasn't alone.
There were Pirates coming in from the field, Dodgers going out to the field, Dodgers running the bases,
and Lacey trying to score from the dugout.

"Lacey made a classic hook slide into the plate,
but the umpire called him out to end the inning.
Walter Alston was our manager and he was irate,
but he had trouble arguing because he couldn't figure out exactly what the umpire had done. He
wanted to protest the game, but I told him to just
be thankful for the one run we got out of it. 'No,
dammit,' he said, 'we had a base on balls with the
bases loaded, that's gotta be one run, and we should
still be at bat.'

" 'You're right,' I agreed, 'but somehow I don't
think Lacey is allowed to score from the dugout.' It
didn't even make any sense when I tried to explain
it."

The umpires finally invoked the Compromise
Rule, crediting the Dodgers with one run and ending the inning. Both Alston and Pittsburgh manager
Danny Murtaugh protested the game, but the pro-
tests were denied. It could have been worse, of
course. At least nobody argued the out call on Lacey
at home plate.

The problem in this situation was that the plate
umpire did the one thing umpires are taught never
to do on the field: think. The only way an umpire
can do his job is to react instinctively and then live
with his call. Debates are for politicians; umpires
have to decide. If an umpire pauses to think about a
play, he is going to be tentative on his call and
eventually get buried. But to make the call without

pausing, an umpire must know the rulebook thoroughly and understand it completely.

For example, Eric Gregg was working second base during an Expos–Pirates game in 1979. Montreal had runners on first and third, and the batter hit an infield pop-up. The infield fly rule does not apply in this situation because second base is not occupied, so the ball was in play and the base runners could attempt to advance at their own jeopardy.

Pirates second baseman Phil Garner settled under the ball, glanced at the runners standing on their bases, then stuck out his glove and just tipped the ball with his webbing. The ball bounced once, he picked it up and stepped on second base to force the runner still standing on first, then threw to first base to complete what appeared to be a double play.

Eric reacted instinctively. Without hesitating, he shouted, "No, no, no, you"—he pointed at Garner—"you deliberately dropped the ball the bátter-runner is out the ball is dead and everybody stays right where they are because nobody else can be put out!" It came out as one long sentence.

"The Pirates attacked me," Eric recalls. "They surrounded me and demanded that I explain the call again. I told them, 'I know I got it right, just give me a couple of minutes to think about it, and I'll get it right again.' Of course, once I started to think about it, I wasn't quite as positive as I had been.

"Doug Harvey was my crew chief and he was right there pushing people away, telling them, 'Let the kid breathe, let him think about it.' Finally I explained it again, slowly, adding that the play would have been legal if Garner hadn't touched the ball. Doug was standing right beside me, nodding, and said, 'Makes perfect sense to me.' "

Like every other professional umpire, I have read the rulebook from cover to cover many times. And, like any other book, there were parts of it I

liked better than others. For example, I loved
7.05(a-e), Equipment Thrown at Ball. I laughed at
5.10(e) and 7.04(c), Fielder Falls into the Dugout. I
cheered 3.14, 4.06, 4.07, 4.08, 4.15, 9.01(b) and (d),
and 9.05, Discipline of Team Personnel. But most
of all, I despised 6.07, Batting out of Turn.

Batting out of order is the most complicated
rule in the entire book. It is so complex that it
makes 8.05, Balk, seem like child's play—a child
playing with a computer, but still a child. Other
people would read Agatha Christie novels when
they were looking for a good mystery; I tried to
figure out 6.07.

At the beginning of every game the manager
hands the umpire a card listing his starting players
in the order they are supposed to come to bat. So
far, so good. I always understood that part. And as
long as each hitter comes to bat after the man listed
before him and before the man listed after him,
there is no problem. But sometimes—and there is
always an explanation that seems rational at the
time—a man gets up to bat when someone else is
supposed to be hitting. He is batting out of turn.

There are three things that can happen to this
illegal batter. If either team brings him to the attention of the home plate umpire while he is still at
bat, the player who is supposed to be up takes his
place and assumes his ball-strike count. There is no
penalty, although there probably will be some
embarrassment.

If, however, he has completed his turn at bat
and the defensive team appeals to the umpire before there has been a pitch to the next batter, or a
play, the man who was supposed to have batted is
declared out and the correct hitter is put up to bat.
The correct hitter is the batter who follows the last
legal batter in the line-up. So a man who has never
batted *can* make out. Any base runners who advance because of the actions of the illegal batter are
returned to their original bases. If the illegal batter

has gotten on base in any way, he is taken off the base. For example, if a player batting out of turn is hit by a pitched ball and the defensive team appeals, the player is taken off the base, thus adding insult to injury.

But if the illegal batter has completed his turn at bat and one pitch has been made to the hitter who followed him, the illegal batter becomes a legal batter and there can be no penalty. However, if the batter at the plate is not the player listed after him in the starting lineup, or an announced substitution, then that player is hitting out of order and the sequence begins again.

Perhaps the best way to understand 6.07 is to use players in these examples. So, for the first time, I have selected an all-star team consisting of the best players I saw during my career in the major leagues. In the correct batting order, they are:

Rod Carew	first base
Fred Lynn	center field
George Brett	third base
Jim Rice	second base
Carl Yastrzemski	designated hitter
Reggie Jackson	right field
Cecil Cooper	left field
Greg Luzinski	shortstop
Thurman Munson	catcher

Okay, this might not be the strongest defensive team ever fielded, but with these hitters the other team is rarely going to get up anyway, and I'm not going to worry about a few runs. This team, of course, is an umpire's dream—not a pitcher's.

Carew leads off for my team. Lynn is supposed to bat second, but for some reason Brett comes to bat. It doesn't matter what Brett does, except to his immediate family. *Then* Lynn gets up. As soon as the first pitch is thrown to Lynn, Brett becomes legal and nothing can be done about him. But be-

cause Brett is the Number Three hitter, Rice, the
Number Four hitter, is supposed to follow him, not
Lynn, the Number Two hitter. If the defensive team
appeals to the umpire after at least one pitch has
been thrown to Lynn, Rice, the man who is supposed to follow Brett, replaces Lynn and assumes
his ball-strike count.

This is the easy part.

Now, the next day Carew leads off. He has the
easiest job. The umpire shouts "Play ball! Carew
knows he's supposed to be at bat. Brett, the Number Three hitter, bats second and doubles. Lynn, the
Number Two hitter, bats third and hits a home run.
Theoretically, Brett is supposed to be the batter
because he follows Lynn in the lineup, but the first
pitch to Lynn made Brett legal, so Rice, the Number
Four hitter, is supposed to be up, not the Number
Three hitter, Brett. The defensive team appeals before
the first pitch is made to the next batter, whoever it
is, that Lynn batted out of turn. Therefore Lynn's
home run doesn't count and Brett, who scored from
second base, must return there. Rice, who was supposed to be hitting after Brett, who became legal
when the first pitch was made to Lynn, is called out.
Not by me, at least not to his face, but by some other,
big, umpire. The Number Five hitter, Yastrzemski,
who would have followed Rice had Rice hit after
Brett as he was supposed to, is the legal batter.

And people laughed at me when I had trouble
understanding this. Of course, they also laughed at
me when I put chocolate syrup on my roast beef.
Unfortunately, though, this is *still* the easy part.
Now it begins to get complicated.

Dependable Rod Carew leads off. He never
causes anybody any trouble. Then Reggie Jackson,
upset because he's batting sixth in my order, comes
to bat and singles. This is not a particularly intelligent team so Rice, the Number Four hitter, follows
Reggie, Number Six, and also singles. Then Lynn,
the Number Two hitter, comes up and hits a home

run. Finally, the manager of the defensive team appeals that something is wrong. He claims Lynn has batted out of order. He should only know what's going on in the other dugout.

The first pitch to Lynn made the batter before him, Rice, the Number Four hitter, the last legal batter. Who is supposed to follow Rice? Yastrzemski, the Number Five hitter. So Yaz is called out without ever coming to bat, which he does not like at all, but there is nothing he can do about it, since this is my problem. Lynn's home run does not count and the runners, Reggie Jackson and Jim Rice, must return to their bases. So who is up? Who follows Yastrzemski? Reggie, the Number Six hitter. But he's on second. How can he be on base and bat at the same time? He can't. So he is permitted to stay on base and Cecil Cooper, the Number Seven hitter, comes to bat.

In umpire school they would always tell us, "It's really very simple if you follow it in order." I would say, "If they followed the order, it would be simple."

The next day Carew leads off again. Brett, the Number Three hitter, follows him and makes out. No one notices. Then Lynn, the Number Two hitter, singles. No one notices. Finally Rice comes to bat and takes a strike. Then someone notices.

The manager of the defensive team realizes something is wrong. He runs out of his dugout waving his lineup card and screaming that Rice is batting out of order. But Rice is listed fourth on the lineup card and is batting fourth in the inning. How can he be batting out of turn? He can, that's how. I didn't make these rules; I couldn't even follow them unless I had my Haller with me.

Because the manager appealed while Rice was at bat, nobody is called out, and the proper hitter takes over the ball-strike count. The last legal batter was Lynn, who became legal because they pitched to Rice, who was illegal, and Brett follows Lynn, so

George gets to bat again in the same inning so he's thrilled with this rule.

If the manager had waited until Rice had made out, Brett would have been called out because he was the player supposed to follow Lynn, but didn't, and then Rice would become the legal batter, because he follows Brett, and he would get to bat again. However, if Rice had gotten a hit and was on base, Brett would be declared out, Rice would be taken off the base because he was an illegal batter, and then he would get to hit again.

If you think this is difficult, try eating chocolate-covered roast beef.

My team is playing at night this time, but we still haven't gotten any better at following the batting order. Carew leads off with a single. Lynn also singles. That's two players in succession who have batted in turn, so I am beginning to believe I've finally got this problem licked. Brett then grounds to shortstop and Lynn is forced at second base, so now we've got runners on first and third, one out. Now Yaz bats instead of Rice. No, I don't know where Rice is, I know where he isn't—that's batting in his proper position. While Yaz is at bat, the pitcher throws a wild pitch, scoring Carew and sending George Brett to second. Yaz then flies out, but Brett tags up and goes to third. If the defensive team appeals before the first pitch to the next batter, Rice is declared out because he is supposed to follow Brett, but Carew's run counts and Brett is permitted to take second because they were not advanced by Yastrzemski. But Brett does have to return to second because he got to third on the fly ball hit by Yastrzemski, and Yaz was never really at bat. Who is the legal batter? Reggie Jackson, right?

Wrong. Yastrzemski is the legal batter because Rice, who was supposed to follow the last legal batter, Brett, is called out, and Yaz is the batter after him.

The *Official Baseball Rulebook* gives a number

of illustrations to help make this rule clear to umpires. I've substituted my all-star team and my batting order for the names they use, and this is how they explain the rule:

"Rice (leads off and) walks and Carew comes to bat. Rice is an improper batter and if an appeal is made before a pitch to Carew, Carew is out. Rice is removed from the base and Lynn is the proper batter. There is no appeal, and a pitch is made to Carew. Rice's walk is now legalized, and Yastrzemski thereby becomes the proper batter. Yaz can replace Carew at any time before Carew is put out or becomes a runner. He does not do so. Carew flies out and Lynn comes to bat. Carew was an improper batter and if an appeal is made before the first pitch to Lynn, Yaz is out and the proper batter is Jackson. There is no appeal and a pitch is made to Lynn. Carew's out is now legalized, and the proper batter is Lynn. Lynn walks. Brett is the proper batter, Brett flies out. Now Rice is the proper batter, but Rice is on second base. Who is the proper batter? RULING: The proper batter is Yastrzemski. When the proper batter is on base, he is passed over and the following batter becomes the proper batter."

This, naturally, clarified everything for me.

Of course, understanding this rule and applying it are completely different things. I don't think I ever had a batting-out-of-order situation, but I wouldn't have recognized it anyway, so I can't really be sure if I had one or not. Don Denkinger, who has taught 6.07 in umpire school for a decade, has never had one. John McSherry, who has been trying to learn the rule for a decade, has had a number of them.

"The last one was in 1980," McSherry remembers. "I was working first base for the Dodgers and Phillies. Paul Pryor was behind the plate, Joe West was at second, and crew chief Billy Williams was at third. For some reason, the Dodgers had changed their batting order that night. Usually Ron Cey came up following Dusty Baker, but Lasorda had flipped them so Baker was listed after Cey in the order.

"The Dodgers had runners on first and third when Baker came up to hit. But it was supposed to be Cey. Pete Rose, the Phillies' first baseman, noticed it immediately. 'We got 'em this time,' he told me, 'Cey's supposed to be up.' 'That's nice,' I said, feeling quite happy that it was going to be Paul Pryor's problem and not mine.

"Baker hit a ground ball to shortstop Larry Bowa. Bowa tossed it to second for the force play, while the runner on third was scoring, but the relay throw to first was too late to catch Baker. I called him safe and looked up to see Dallas Green, the Phillies' manager, standing at home plate with his lineup card. 'I told you we had 'em,' Rose said. Actually, I was a bit surprised to see Green—most managers don't know the proper time to make their appeal. I watched the scene with mild interest, thinking, 'It's not my problem, it's not my problem, I'm so happy.'

"Suddenly Paul takes his lineup cards out of his pocket, walks down the first-base line, and hands them to me. 'Green says they're out of order,' he said.

"I said, 'I want to thank you very much, Paul.' We talked it over and, at first, it appeared to be a simple batting-out-of-turn situation. Baker batted. Who was supposed to hit? Cey. Cey is declared out. Who follows Cey in the lineup? Baker. Baker is taken off the base because he was an illegal batter and comes to bat. The lead runner goes back to third because he advanced due to the actions of the illegal batter and the man who was forced at second. . . . I paused. The runner who was out at second is still out at second. It's a double play. 'It's a double play,' I told Paul.

" 'Yeah, all right!' Dallas Green said.

" 'It's what?' Paul asked.

"I heard myself saying it a second time, so I knew I was convinced. 'It's a double play.'

" 'I know it's a double play,' I said, 'but I don't want it to be a double play.' I was standing on the field trying to remember any reference in the rules to what happens to outs made due to the actions of an illegal batter, but I couldn't remember any. If no advance can be made, why should an out be allowed? Somewhere, I knew, there had to be something covering it. Then I did something I teach every student not to do. 'Wait here,' I told Pryor and West, as if they might decide to leave and grab a sandwich, and I went into the locker room and got my rulebook. I thumbed through it very quickly, stuck it in my pocket, and returned to the field. 'There's nothing in the rulebook that says it's a double play,' I told them. 'I'm putting the runner back on first.'

" 'It's got to be a double play,' West insisted.

" 'I know what you're thinking,' I said, 'but I'm not going to allow it to be a double play. Look, the rulebook says that if Baker had been hitting with an illegal bat, or hit the ball illegally, any other outs that occurred by virtue of that illegally batted ball would stand. Right? Right. If Baker had hit with a lead-filled bat, for example, he'd be out for hitting with that bat and the runner would be out at second. That would be a double play. But in this case we're calling the runner at first out for something that happened while Cey wasn't batting. How can he be out for the actions of a hitter who wasn't up?'

" 'It's a great argument,' West said, 'but you're still wrong.'

"I nodded. 'Yeah, that's what I thought, but that's the argument we're going with.' I put the base runner back on first, declared Cey out for batting out of turn, and put Baker up at bat again. Billy Williams backed me all the way, telling me to do whatever I thought was correct and he would take the heat.

"The Phillies protested, claiming it should have been a double play and that Baker should not have been the hitter. I knew I had Baker right, though. As we resumed play I took my position behind first base, put my hands on my knees, and wondered, 'What else can go wrong now?'

"It did not take me long to find out. Baker hit the first pitch out of the ball park for a three-run homer. While he was running around the bases, I went over to West and told him, 'I'll tell you one thing, Joe. If we're wrong, we're wrong big!'

"The Dodgers won the game, so I had to call the league office that night to explain why the Phillies might have a legitimate protest, and then I had to explain why I didn't think their protest was legitimate. 'What's the problem?' they asked.

" 'The problem is that there is no rule in the book covering what happens to a runner put out by the actions of an illegal batter, that's the problem.'

"The league eventually decided that we had made the correct decision. Nick Bremigan polled the American League umpires and they agreed that the runner had been properly returned to first base. That rule was later inserted in the book."

With all the problems I had understanding the batting-out-of-order rule, I was not surprised that managers didn't understand it either. Once, for example, the Mets' Bud Harrelson was batting out of turn. San Diego manager John McNamara appealed while Harrelson was still at bat, so the Mets were permitted to substitute the legal batter. McNamara argued that that wasn't fair, that there should be some penalty for batting out of turn. The umpires explained the proper enforcement of the rule and McNamara went quietly, but unhappily, back to his dugout.

He needn't have worried. The Mets then substituted the wrong batter for Harrelson. McNamara waited until that batter had completed his turn at

bat and then appealed, and this time the legal batter
was declared out.

The most dangerous type of manager for an
umpire is one who believes he knows the rules,
because then he will try to foil the rules with trick
plays. I hated trick plays. To me, a trick is a horse
figuring out my weight at a carnival, or a magician
sawing a woman in half and then selling the two
halves separately. But I disliked hidden-ball tricks
and plays that involved narrow interpretation of the
rulebook.

Usually, if a manager, or a player, intends to
try something unique, he will warn the umpire
about it in advance to make sure that umpire is
ready for it. I always had a problem with this because it involved keeping a secret. I have never had
any problem keeping a secret, as long as I could
share it with other people. If I was told, for example,
that someone was going to attempt to trick a player
I really liked, I would desperately want to say something to that player like, "The moon rises at six-oh-
five tonight, beware of first basemen bearing empty
gloves." I never did, though, I never did.

Dale Ford also does not like trick plays, and
one night in the minor leagues he got even with a
manager who loved them. "Scraps" Courtney was a
good friend of his and came into the umpires' room
before a game one night and told him he had a
special play. "I @$#%# 'em every time," he said,
"I get 'em every time. Never fails." Then he explained that the rules state a pitcher can only throw
to an occupied base to make a play; otherwise it is
a balk. But the rulebook does not define what
constitutes a play. In certain situations, a runner on
second base will be trying to steal third. So Courtney
instructed his pitcher in those situations to go into
a stretch position, then throw to third. The runner
on second would be so surprised, he would freeze,
allowing the third baseman to make a play on him.

"I handled that play the best way I could,"

Dale explains. "I told the manager of the other team, Billy Gardner, all about it.

"That night, in a later inning, Gardner's team had runners on first and second, two outs, and a three-ball, two-strike count on the batter. This was precisely the situation Courtney wanted, because everybody in the ball park knew the base runners would be running as soon as the pitcher released the ball.

"Just before the pitch I looked into Courtney's dugout and 'Scraps' is in there rubbing up his hands and I know he's thinking, 'Oh, I'm gonna get 'em on this play.' Then I look into the other dugout and Gardner is sitting there with his arms crossed, just smiling.

"Finally, Courtney's pitcher went into his windup, then paused, whirled, and threw to third base. Gardner's runner didn't move three feet off second base. 'Balk!' I started screaming. 'That's a balk! That's a balk!'

"Courtney was all over me, screaming, 'You told him, I know you told him, that play always works 'less someone tells him. . . .' I never admitted it, but then again, I didn't stop laughing either."

The rules of baseball, I learned during my fifteen years in the game, were indeed made to be broken, and broken, and broken. Bill Klem once said, "The rules of baseball were written by gentlemen for gentlemen, rather than by lawyers for lawyers."

I've considered that statement. Oh, he is so wrong.

EIGHT

AND THANK YOU, REGGIE JACKSON

Like most baseball fans, I enjoyed watching an unusual or complex play—as long as I was watching it on television. In a city far away. In the National League. And never, ever when I was on the field.

But there were certain aspects of the game I did enjoy watching from the field. After working as an umpire for fifteen years, I learned to appreciate the subtleties of baseball, the little things that, put together, make a large difference in the outcome of the game, those things that only the most experienced, knowledgeable, intelligent, good-looking fans and umpires notice: pitching, hitting, and catching. To be even more specific than that: offense and defense.

Among the most important things I realized while working as a color commentator on the backup *Game of the Week* was that "the best offense is a good defense," or "the best defense is a good offense," depending on which team was winning, and that "pitching is the name of the game" because "good pitching beats good hitting" and that "pitching holds the key to success" in that good pitching will "lock the door on the opposition" while bad pitching will "open the floodgates." And I could always be sure that pitchers would "show me what they were made of" because they were "real professionals" who had "come to play."

Pitchers are very strange people. Their job is to throw things at other people. The only other people who have this job are knife-throwers, and they work in the circus.

Trying to hurl a hard, round ball through an imaginary rectangle approximately 3½ feet high and 17 inches wide in such a way that a man wielding a stick cannot strike it is a ridiculous way for a grown man to attempt to make a living. One of the few ways of making a living even more ridiculous than that is standing behind that imaginary rectangle and deciding if the pitcher has been successful or not.

Most successful pitchers throw the fastball. *The* most successful pitchers throw the faster ball. Throughout the history of baseball, the pitchers with the overpowering fastball—Walter Johnson, Bob Feller, Sandy Koufax, Bob Gibson—have attracted the most attention when they played. The fastest pitcher I have ever seen is Nolan Ryan. How fast is Ryan? You get a speck of dust in your eye, you miss two innings. Ryan is so fast he can pitch a nine-inning game in five innings. That's how fast he is. "Baseball is a different game when he's pitching," explains Terry Crowley. "You just don't have enough time to see the pitch. It gets up on you too quick. About the only thing you do have time to decide is if you should swing wildly or just take the pitch and yell at the umpire, because you know he can't see it any better than you can.

"Baseball players usually have two sets of equipment—practice bats, practice spikes, helmets, gloves, things they use before the game starts, and game equipment, those things with which you're more comfortable and you don't want to risk breaking or wearing out in practice. Once, I remember, we were playing a five-thirty game and Ryan was pitching and he was throwing little ones. In that twilight he was just impossible to hit. Merv Rettenmund was up before me and he just took his three swipes without coming close to the ball. As he was walking back to the dugout our paths crossed and I asked him, trying to be cute, 'What's he got?'

"Merv shook his head, then told me. 'Don't take up your game bat!' "

There are many National Leaguers who claim that J. R. Richard, before his tragic heart attack, threw as fast as Ryan. "There was only one word that describes the feeling of standing behind the plate when J.R. was pitching," Eric Gregg says, "fear. I worked with him in the minor leagues, the Dominican Republic, and the National League. I knew he was always going to strike a lot of people out, but I worried about the catcher blocking the ball. When he was pitching I'd wear every piece of protective equipment I could find.

"He was one pitcher I loved to see men get on base against because, with runners on base, the catcher at least had to try to block the ball. With the bases empty you'd see catchers diving out of the way, and I'd have to dive with them.

"I worked his last game in the major leagues. Houston was playing the Braves and it was obvious he was having trouble seeing the catcher's signals. Bruce Benedict—'Eggs' Benedict, I call him—was batting and J.R. kept shaking off his catcher signs. Finally I told the catcher to go put on some white gloves because J.R. couldn't see his fingers.

"When I said that, Benedict shifted nervously in the batter's box.

"The catcher told me he couldn't catch with gloves on. 'Okay,' I said, 'go put some white tape on your fingertips. The man can't see your signals.'

"Benedict was listening to this and I could see his eyes were starting to open real wide. He finally stepped out of the box and started rubbing dirt on his hands. 'Uh, Eric,' he asked, 'what's going on here?'

" 'The word is he's having trouble with his eyes,' I told him. 'Supposedly he can't see.'

" 'Time out,' Benedict said softly and walked slowly back to the Braves' dugout. It was obvious he wasn't thrilled about coming back to bat. When he did come back out he didn't stand too close to the plate.

"Richard struck him out. J.R. could still throw strikes. But I would have to say that Benedict was one of the happiest batters who had just struck out that I have ever seen."

Control, getting the baseball over the plate, over any part of the plate, has always been the most difficult thing for a real fastball pitcher to master. A lot of players can throw fast—but only those who can throw fast *and* get the ball near the plate play major league baseball. One fastball pitcher who never managed to solve his control problems was Orioles farmhand Steve Dalkowski. Dalkowski supposedly could throw a baseball through a brick wall—but he just couldn't hit the wall. "He was the fastest pitcher I've ever seen," Doug Harvey says flatly, "the fastest, but he just never knew where it was going. He was too fast for his catchers. In one season, he broke my bar mask, split my shinguard, hit my chest protector on the shoulder and split the protective roll on the edge of it, then knocked me off my feet.

"The game in which he broke the mask was typical. He punched out the first nine batters he faced in order. Maybe one hitter fouled off a pitch, but that was it. He didn't throw more than four pitches to anyone. I thought, 'Man, we really got it going today. They just aren't going to touch him.' And they didn't.

"By the fourth inning he was leading two to nothing. The first batter that inning got up to bat and Dalkowski's first pitch almost cleared the backstop. It had to be twelve feet high. The catcher didn't even bother straightening up, he just looked up as the ball sailed over his head. 'Uh-oh,' he said, my thought exactly, then asked me for a new baseball. He walked it halfway to the mound and shouted, 'That's okay, Steve, that one slipped! It could happen to anybody!'

"But probably not three times in a row. He started bouncing pitches off the catcher, off the ground, off my mask, off the back fence, he didn't come close to getting another out. When they finally took him out of the game the other team had a 3–2 lead and the bases loaded with nobody out, and they still hadn't gotten a hit.

"In the dressing room after the game I just sort of tossed my mask in my bag and heard something go clunk. I picked up the mask and one of the bars had fallen off. That's when I decided to go to the wire mesh mask."

In fact, the single best piece of protective equipment a plate umpire can have is a good relationship with a catcher. If the catcher and umpire do not get along, it can be a painful experience for the umpire. Fastball pitchers are usually easy to work, because hitters come to bat swinging, and the pitches are either right on the plate or way off it. Fastball pitchers do not nibble at the corners or try to set up a hitter with off-speed pitches an inch outside; they just try to blow it by the batter. But when a hard thrower misses the plate, he really misses it. Pitches bounce all over the place, or sail off the catcher's equipment. If the catcher doesn't make a total effort to catch everything, it is the umpire who is going to get hit, hit, hit.

Even worse, because batters have trouble hitting the real fastball pitchers squarely, they are constantly just getting a piece of the ball and fouling it into an umpire's exposed shoulder, or off his toes, or smack off his mask.

During catcher Jeff Torborg's rookie year with the Dodgers, for example, Don Drysdale, a pitcher who could throw a dollar bill past a congressman, was on the mound and Eddie Vargo was working the plate. "We were playing the Pirates," Jeff recalls, "Bob Bailey was the hitter, and Smoky Burgess was on first base. Either Drysdale or I got confused about the signals—I was the rookie so I've got a pretty good idea who it was—and I expected him to throw a curve ball. As his fastball zoomed in, I moved down and outside to catch it when it curved, and it went right over my shoulder and hit Eddie in the stomach. 'Watch it!' I yelled instinctively.

" 'Uggggggghhhhhhhhhhhh,' Vargo said.

" 'Are you okay?' I asked him.

" 'Uggggggghhhhhhhhhhhh,' he repeated. But he survived that day.

"Almost an entire season later we were playing at Dodger Stadium and again Eddie was behind the plate. Claude Osteen was pitching, but this was before we realized he needed glasses. I was continually getting crossed up on pitches. I'd give him a signal to throw a certain pitch and then he would throw whatever pitch he wanted. I guess it was my fault. When I put down a signal, I just assumed he was going to throw that pitch.

"While Claude was warming up at the beginning of the fourth inning, I said casually to Eddie, 'Hey, remember what happened last year?'

" 'Yeah,' he said, 'it made quite an impression on me.'

" 'Well, you don't have to worry about it happening again, we've got everything under control now.' And just as I finished saying that, Osteen bounced his last warm-up pitch in the dirt about ten feet in front of the plate and I leaped out of the way. It skipped to the backstop. Eddie looked at me as if I were crazy and I told him, 'Oh, don't worry about those. We just get out of the way on them.'

"Three innings later I signaled for a curve ball and Osteen guessed fastball. I never came close to catching it, and it slammed Eddie square in the mask. It sounded like somebody had hit him with a hammer. I immediately went trotting out to Osteen to see if we could straighten out the signals, and as I did I heard Vargo pleading with Walter Alston in our dugout, 'Please, Walt, get this kid out of there before he ruins the career of a fine umpire.' "

Later in Torborg's career he proved how vital an intelligent catcher, a catcher who can detect the batter's weakness, is to a fastball pitcher like Nolan Ryan. Ryan pitched two no-hitters in 1973. I was behind the plate for the second one, against Detroit, the only no-hitter I worked in my career. He was awesome. Mickey Stanley fouled off a fastball and started applauding himself. Norm Cash came to bat carrying an oversized, inflatable bat he'd gotten from a concession stand. Torborg had caught Ryan's first no-hitter that year, as well as having caught a Sandy Koufax no-hitter, but he missed this game with a broken finger. Art Kushner was the catcher and Ryan, I later found out, called most of his own pitches. It wasn't too difficult: fastball, fastball, fastball, fastball, fastball . . .

"When I came back from my injury," Torborg explains, "Ryan had fourteen wins, sixteen losses, two no-hitters, and was on his way to breaking the single-season strikeout record. I couldn't understand why, with his fastball, he had lost two more than he had won. So I suggested to him that we try something new: He would tell me what he wanted to throw rather than me giving him the signals. He agreed to try it.

" 'One thing, though,' I cautioned him, 'whatever you do, don't cross me up.' Earlier that season he had thrown a fastball that I missed, and it hit me on the back of the hand. Poor Nolan moped around the clubhouse for a week because my hand hadn't been broken, and he was afraid he was losing his fastball.

"He won his next seven starts, finishing the season with twenty-one victories and sixteen losses, proving that I was either very dumb or very smart, depending on whether I take credit or blame."

Hitters generally do not get angry when they are struck out by a great fastball pitcher. They simply failed to meet the manly challenge. They put their best against the pitcher's best and—this time—the pitcher won. But they do mind, they really mind, they really hate striking out against a knuckleball pitcher. A fast ball is to a knuckleball what the United States Marine Corps is to the Campfire Girls, or what the Incredible Hulk is to Dondi, or what the shark in *Jaws* is to Charlie the Tuna. Hoyt Wilhelm, for example, threw his knuckleball in the major leagues until he was forty-eight years old, and even then he retired only because his eyes and legs were going.

The knuckleball is a pitch thrown so that the ball does not spin and just sort of drifts pleasantly to home plate. I hated working the plate when a knuckleball pitcher was on the mound. The pitch would start up high so I'd stand up, then it would sink, so I'd drop down, then it would swerve sharply outside, so I'd lean outside, then it would dart inside, so I'd quickly move back inside. Finally, just when I had it tracked, it would rise, drop, move outside, then inside, sail and sputter and plop. The real reason I was never very good at calling knuckleball balls and strikes is that by the time the pitch reached home plate I had motion sickness.

At least I looked better trying to call it than most batters did trying to hit it. Even the most graceful batters looked like lumberjacks trying to swat a mosquito with a telephone pole.

Much as hitters remember their longest home runs, knuckleball pitchers remember their greatest pitches. When Floyd Robinson, a fine hitter, was playing for Cincinnati, for example, he batted against Phil Niekro for the first time. "I threw him two knuckleballs for strikes," Niekro remembers, "and he just looked at them. Didn't even attempt to swing. But I could see he was determined not to let me throw a third knuckleball past him. As I went into my windup he gritted his teeth. As the pitch floated toward the plate his whole body tensed, his grip on the bat tightened, his muscles bulged, but he held back, he waited and waited and waited and waited and finally, just as he began to swing, the ball actually swerved behind his back. That didn't bother him at all, he went right after it. He did a complete one-hundred-eighty-degree turn trying to hit that pitch. When he finished his swing, he was facing backward."

When Niekro toured Japan with a major-league all-star team after the 1981 season, his knuckleball created a sensation there. "The Japanese had never seen one before," he explains, "and they just loved it. At first they thought it was some sort of American joke, but they began taking it seriously when I struck out their greatest player, Sadahuro Oh, on three pitches. After swinging and missing on the third pitch he just sat down in the batter's box and stared at me. That was what I call going Oh for three.

"A few weeks after I got back home I was invited to return to Japan to teach some of their younger pitchers how to throw it. I told them I couldn't even describe a knuckleball in English, much less Japanese, but I did go back there for a week. While I was there I couldn't make a single move without being measured or photographed. They measured each one of my fingers, they measured my fingernails, my knuckles, the distance between my fingers, and when they weren't measuring, they were taking pictures. I would scratch my head and two hours later they'd show me a glossy photograph of me scratching my head and want to know what that had to do with throwing a knuckleball."

And so today, somewhere in Japan, because of Phil Niekro, some poor Japanese batter is flailing at a pitch about to swerve behind his back and screaming, "*$#%$¢& $%#c$# $¢ $%$#)#¢& %$ % ¢$&$* Nieklo %#&–¢$ %%% &%%&$¢#*$#* ¢((-)#$!"

About the best thing a batter will say about the knuckleball is that it is thrown too softly to hurt a player if it hits him. One night, for example, Charlie Hough had struck out Pete Rose twice on beautiful knucklers. When Rose batted for the third time he started to swing at a pitch that suddenly sailed in and hit him squarely on the side of his batting helmet. "He sprinted to first base," Hough remembers. "He didn't even have the decency to fall down. And then, when he got to first base, he actually thanked me for hitting him. He said he knew he wasn't going to be able to hit that thing, so he was pleased to be on base.

"At least he was better than Carmine Franzone, who was playing with Spokane in the Pacific Coast League when I hit him square on the funny bone with a knuckler. Franzone didn't think it was funny. He threw his bat down angrily and jogged to first base. I walked over a few steps and asked him if he was all right and he said he was fine.

"I threw about five pitches to the next batter, when all of a sudden I heard someone screaming for time out. I looked over to first base and Franzone was on his knees, vomiting. My knuckleball had hit him in the elbow and made him sick to his stomach! He was the only player I've ever knocked out of a game."

Hough learned how to throw the knuckleball for an intelligent reason: survival. "I was what might be called a straight-ball pitcher in the minor leagues, although there were some people who referred to it as a bounce ball. I had good control, meaning I could pretty much determine into which section of the outfield seats the batter was going to hit the ball. The day one of my coaches asked me how I felt about law enforcement as a career I knew I had to come up with another pitch.

"Goldy Holt taught me how to throw it. At first, I was a typical knuckleball pitcher. I'd get the side out in order: one, two, three, four, five, six, seven, eight, nine, one . . . I'd strike out the sides, but in between strikeouts I'd walk three guys and give up two hits. Finally I learned how to control it, as much as it can be controlled.

"The knuckleball got me to the Los Angeles Dodgers. In my very first major-league game Walter Alston brought me in to relieve against the Pittsburgh Pirates. There were two outs and two men on base. Naturally, I walked the first man I faced to load the bases for Willie Stargell.

"I wasn't nervous; I was numb. I threw him five straight knuckleballs and ran the count to three balls, two strikes. Then my catcher, Jeff Torborg, signaled for a fastball. 'Yeah,' I thought, 'what a great idea! Stargell's expecting another knuckleball so we'll fool him with smoke!' I got about halfway through my windup when I suddenly remembered I didn't have a fastball. At best, I had a medium ball. And that was the pitch I'd been getting killed with in Double-A, that was the reason I had started throwing knuckleballs in the first place. And here I was, winding up to throw a fastball to Willie Stargell with the bases loaded in the ninth inning.

"It seemed a bit foolish to me.

"I threw it right down the center of the plate and Willie swung at it and missed. Torborg caught the ball and jumped into the air. I just stood on the mound thinking, 'He missed it! I don't believe it! He missed it! I'm safe, he missed it! I don't believe it!' "

There are certain batters, however, who are good knuckleball hitters—and they just happen to be the knuckleball pitchers. Although Phil Niekro claims to have six or seven hits against his brother, knuckleballer Joe Niekro, in the game they both remember best, Phil took a 2–1 lead into the seventh inning. Joe came to bat with a runner on base. "I threw him a good knuckler," Phil says, "and he didn't swing at it. So I hollered at him, 'You can't hit it if you don't swing at it!' Then I threw him another good one that he took for strike two. 'You got to swing if you expect to hit it!' I shouted. My third pitch broke into the dirt. My own brother went down on his knees and swung that bat like it was a nine-iron and just golfed my pitch into the stands for a home run and a 3–2 victory. That was it for him. I immediately took him off my Christmas card list.''

Phil Niekro later returned the favor against Charlie Hough, hitting a home run to beat him.

Although many batters claim the knuckleball is immoral, it is not illegal. But—and I know this will be difficult to believe, and some parents may not want their children to read beyond this part—some major league pitchers do cheat. Yes, there are pitchers who actually break the rules to gain an advantage by throwing illegal pitches! I don't mean they pitch illegally—for example, standing a few inches in front of the pitcher's rubber when they throw, as one former Oriole and Yankee pitcher I know does—I mean they have the audacity to put foreign substances on the ball, things such as saliva, sweat, oil, grease, ear wax, paraffin, Jell-O, chocolate chip ice cream, and they also cut or scratch the cover of the baseball to make it move erratically when thrown.

Naturally, baseball officials know nothing about this scandal, and if they did, they would immediately take steps to control this problem. As far as the commissioner's office and the two league presidents are concerned, the only thing allowed to be put on the baseball is good, clean American mud from the Delaware River, which takes off the high gloss and makes it easier to grip.

A "loaded" pitch, or a pitch thrown with a defaced cover is popularly called a spitball, but spit is one of the last things any sanitary pitcher would use—primarily because it just isn't as effective as most other potions, or cutting, slicing, or dicing a ball. Old-time pitchers used to tape a small piece of metal grater inside their shirts and rub the ball against it to roughen the cover, or even force a BB pellet under the seams. One St. Louis Browns pitcher didn't bother being fancy: He simply slit the ball's stitches with a razor blade.

The past master of the defaced baseball was the Yankees' Whitey Ford. He would use any one of a number of different methods to scrape the cover before throwing it. Unfortunately, Whitey once complained, his catcher, Elston Howard, would then scratch the other side of the same ball with the sharpened tip of his belt buckle and neutralize the effect.

The rulebook clearly explains what a pitcher shall not do, but enforcement is the job of the umpire. The first time an umpire sees a pitch that, in his opinion, has been "loaded" he is to call it a ball and warn the pitcher that he will be ejected from the game if he does it a second time. Of course, if the pitcher is caught with the goods, or, more accurately, the goo, he is to be ejected immediately.

Many major league pitchers have been accused of throwing a "doctored" or fixed baseball. Some of them definitely do. The aptly named Rick Honeycutt, for example, was caught with a thumbtack taped to his finger, which he used to scratch the cover of the ball, and was ejected from the game. And other pitchers are absolutely maybes. Don Sutton supposedly has notes in each pocket of his uniform to assist umpires when they are searching for whatever substance they believe he is putting on the ball. The notes read, "warm," "hot," "hotter," "getting colder," "freezing," and "no trespassing."

But Gaylord Perry is the only pitcher within memory to be ejected by an umpire for throwing a spitball without there being a tack of evidence. Perry denies throwing the spitball, but since he titled his autobiography *Me and the Spitter*, that denial is about as valid as my claiming to be underweight.

"It was August twenty-third, 1982," Davey Phillips remembers, "and I was working the plate in Seattle. Gaylord was pitching against the Red Sox. On a number of occasions in previous years I had warned him about doctoring the baseball, but I had never ejected him. In the fifth inning of this game Reid Nichols came to bat and Gaylord went through his usual preparation, touching his cap, his jersey, his hips, his knee. . . . Finally, when he was ready to pitch, Nichols stepped out of the box and asked me to inspect the baseball. I got Perry to throw it in and ran my finger over it. It was almost normal, except that in one spot where I touched it I could see my fingerprints in the grease. In fact, I could see all my fingerprints. In fact, I could have probably lubricated my car with the grease on that ball.

"I could have ejected Perry at that moment, but, in fact, he hadn't actually thrown that pitch. The grease could conceivably have come from somewhere else. I don't know where else, somewhere else. I decided to stretch the rule a bit and just give him the official warning.

"Naturally, he was shocked at my accusation. He claimed to have no knowledge of the grease. 'Gaylord,' I told him, 'I don't know how or when this grease got on the ball, but if I find any grease on another ball, or if I see a pitch that I believe to be a spitball by the flight of the ball, you'll be ejected from the game.'

"The game was tied going into the seventh inning. Then Gaylord got into trouble. Boston had two men on, I think, with one out and Rick Miller at bat.

"Perry's first pitch to Miller was a fastball just outside. Ball one. His next pitch was the most beautiful spitball I've ever seen. It came straight for fifty-nine and a half feet, one foot short of the plate, then it dropped straight down two feet. It just disappeared. Miller swung at it, but he never had a chance. He turned around to argue, but before he could say anything I was on my way to the mound.

"I had two choices. I could have ignored it, just closed my eyes and pretended I didn't see it, even though every member of my crew, the Red Sox, the Mariners, and the people in the pressbox knew exactly what happened, or I could enforce the rule. 'Let's go, Gaylord,' I told him, 'you're done.'

"Gaylord didn't put up much of an argument, and he never denied his guilt, then he left. 'Hey,' I thought, 'that wasn't so bad. Nothing terrible happened to me. The stadium didn't fall down.' In fact, I was still congratulating myself at the end of that inning when I felt a tap on my shoulder. A Mariners public-relations man was on the field. 'Could you come to a press conference immediately after the game?' he asked.

"A press conference? I had ejected a lot of people in my career and no one had ever held a press conference for me before. But I agreed.

"I figured the usual six or seven writers from the local papers would be there, but when I walked into the pressroom after the game there were at least sixty reporters waiting for me. My telephone didn't stop ringing for three days. Reporters were calling from all over the country. I couldn't really understand it: Catching Gaylord Perry throwing a spitball is about as difficult as buying a hamburger along a highway. Only later did I find out that this was the first time in his career he had been ejected for it, that, in fact, nobody had been ejected for it in almost forty years.

"I had no choice. He had been warned and he was flaunting the rules. I've learned that a man builds his career by his actions under pressure, by standing up when he believes he's doing the right thing, and that's all I did."

I never called a spitball on Gaylord Perry, or anyone else during my career. I saw them—in fact, I used to wear a raincoat when Gaylord was pitching—but I graduated from a different school than Davey Phillips did. In the boys' locker room of my school there was a long banner hung over the doorways, and every time I walked through those doorways I saw it and read it and thought about it. I have always tried to remember those words, and I based my career in professional athletics on them. "When the going gets tough," this banner read, "leave."

I came from a small school.

The pitcher's mound is the kitchen table of baseball life. Everything that takes place in a baseball game begins right there. Every player spends much of his time during every game either standing on the mound or directing his full attention to it. More of baseball's human dramas unfold there than anywhere else on the field. But most of all, more conversations take place there than at an insurance salesmen's convention.

Catchers talk to pitchers, pitchers talk to infielders, pitching coaches talk to pitchers and infielders, who then talk to catchers, managers talk to starting pitchers and relief pitchers, starting pitchers talk to relief pitchers, relief pitchers talk to catchers, I talked to everybody, Steve Carlton talks to nobody, and some pitchers even talk to themselves.

Rudy May, for example, falls into that last category. "If I get confused about the count or the situation or if I make a mistake and throw the wrong pitch," he explains, "I'll say something to myself out loud like, 'Gees, Rudy, how stupid can you get?' Then I'll answer that question, 'A lot stupider than that!' Usually that makes me smile and helps me relax out there."

Another pitcher who speaks to himself on the mound is Al "The Mad Hungarian" Hraboski. Unfortunately, Al doesn't understand Hungarian, so he isn't able to answer.

When a starting pitcher is doing a good job he is left alone, but as soon as he gets into trouble he has more visitors than a cut-rate furrier. The first person out there to offer advice is the catcher. I always wondered how a catcher who was batting .230 could know much about pitching—except that he can't hit it.

When Dennis Leonard first came up to the major leagues with the Kansas City Royals, for example, the only pitch he threw was a sinker. And if a sinker-ball pitcher isn't getting the ball to sink, about all he can do is stay loose enough to avoid the line drives that are going to come back at him. "But I just didn't have any other pitch," Dennis explained. "It was sink or shower. One night I was getting hit pretty hard and John Wathan, my catcher, started walking out toward the mound. I watched him coming toward me, hoping he had some idea of what I might be doing wrong.

"Finally, when he reached the mound, he said firmly, 'Okay, let's start mixing 'em up now,' then turned around and walked back to the plate. Mixing them up? I threw my one pitch. How could I possibly mix up my pitch?"

Sometimes the catcher will go out to the mound just to relax his pitcher in a tense situation. They might discuss what they plan to do after the ball game, an attractive woman in the stands, food, or umpires. Jeff Torborg was one of the best at easing the tension. Once, for example, Don Sutton was really struggling, and Torborg trekked out to the mound. Sutton was in no mood to entertain. "Go back in there and catch," he snapped, "that's your job. I'll take care of the pitching, that's my job."

"Right, I know," Torborg agreed, "and that's why I'm out here. You're not doing a very good job, and I'm afraid I'm going to have to fire you." Sutton looked at him as if he were crazy, then smiled, and finally laughed. *Then* Torborg laughed. Because when D. H. Sutton laughs, everybody laughs.

Perhaps the most honest advice ever given to a pitcher was offered by Gary Carter to Ross Grimsley one night in Montreal. "He was really getting lit up," Gary remembers. "They were hitting everything he threw. I mean, they were fighting in the dugout to get up to the plate. There wasn't much we could do about it, it was just one of those games when he had absolutely nothing. So finally I called time and walked slowly out to the mound. When I got there I just looked at him, shook my head, then turned around without saying a word and walked back to home plate."

Of course, Carter had experience in unusual conversations on the mound, having caught Bill "Spaceman" Lee, a man who was once fined by the commissioner's office for telling a reporter he sprinkled marijuana on his morning pancakes. "Bill was in his own ball games," says Carter. "I'd walk out there in a difficult situation to remind him to keep the runners close to their bases and he would nod, then tell me confidentially, 'You know, the reason I'm a left-hander is because the right side of my brain offsets the left side, and that's why I'm always in the right frame of mind.'

" 'Right,' I'd agree with him, 'you got it. But try to remember to watch the runners.' "

At one time infielders often stopped by the pitcher's mound to slow down a pitcher or help relieve the tension, but because baseball has made an effort to speed up the game, that doesn't happen very often anymore. When Phil Rizzuto came up to the Yankees, though, these visits were part of an infielder's job. Unfortunately Phil was just too timid to do it. "In my rookie year," he remembers, "Lefty Gomez was pitching and the Tigers had the bases loaded with nobody out. Suddenly Lefty turned to me and motioned me to come to the mound. 'Holy cow,' I thought, 'what does he want with me?' There wasn't anything I could tell him.

" 'Look,' he said, rubbing up the baseball as we spoke, 'your mother's in the stands, right?' Lefty knew my mother never missed a game at Yankee Stadium, and I told him that she was in her usual seat that day. 'Well,' he continued, 'don't you think she's proud of you right now? Don't you think she's telling everybody around her that the great Gomez is asking her son for advice?'

"It took me a long time to realize *he* was trying to help *me* relax. Lefty was the calmest man I ever saw on the pitcher's mound. If a slugger like Jimmie Foxx or Hank Greenberg was coming to bat with men on base he would call the infielders to the mound and tell us, 'I don't want to throw this baseball, but I'm going to have to. So let's get all the outfielders playing deep, and all you infielders play deep and we'll all work together to keep him from hitting it out of the ball park."

When a pitcher is beginning to struggle but is not yet in enough difficulty to be taken out of the game, the pitching coach often will jog out to speak to him. "Most of the time we talk about mechanics," Orioles pitching coach Ray Miller explains, "maybe the pitcher is getting tired and dropping his arm, maybe he is overstriding. But sometimes I go out there with nothing to say.

"We had a relief pitcher named Dave Stanhouse who violated every rule of good pitching. He'd come in to pitch and give up a hit and a walk and then he'd get the side out without giving up any runs. He drove Earl Weaver crazy. One night in Chicago, for example, we were beating the White Sox, two to one, in the bottom of the ninth and he came in to pitch with a runner on second and one out. He proceeded to walk the next two batters, loading the bases, then threw two balls to the next hitter. Earl was chewing the bench. Finally, Earl just couldn't stand it anymore. He yelled to me, 'Go out there and tell him to throw strikes!'

"Actually, that seemed pretty obvious to me, and I assumed Stanhouse knew that, but Earl was the boss. I hopped out of the dugout and started walking toward the mound, trying to figure out what sort of intelligent advice I could give Stanhouse.

"He was waiting for me when I reached the mound. He knew Earl as well as I did. 'What are you doing here?' he asked. 'You going to tell me to throw strikes?'

"Obviously he had figured out the problem for himself. So I said, 'Nah, I just came out to tell you that your fly's open.'

"He laughed, then told me to go back and tell Earl not to worry, that he had the White Sox just where he wanted them. So that's what I did. Two pitches later the batter hit into a double play to end the game. Afterward, in the clubhouse, a few reporters asked me what advice I had given Stanhouse. What could I tell them? That I had told him to throw strikes? That I had told him his fly was open? So I said that I had noticed he was dropping his arm slightly when he threw the ball and I'd gone out there to remind him to keep it up. And that's what they wrote."

On occasion the manager himself will come out just to give his pitcher advice. Usually it is very specific, and it is based on the detailed scouting reports each club compiles. For example, when Royals manager Jack McKean brought in rookie Dennis Leonard to relieve during a late September game, he reminded him to be particularly careful with the batter. "Whatever you do," McKean warned, "don't give this guy anything good to hit . . ."

Leonard nodded. He could do that, he knew.

Then McKean continued, ". . . but don't walk him, either."

Leonard nodded. He had no idea what McKean was talking about.

When Jeff Torborg was managing the Cleveland Indians he tried to be very specific when talking to his pitchers. "We were in the ninth inning of a game against the Yankees," he recalls, "and we were leading, one to nothing. They had runners on first and second, and the batter was Lou Piniella. I had my bullpen all warmed up, but my pitcher,

Rick Waits, had an excellent curve ball and I wanted him to pitch to Piniella. I told Rick, 'You keep throwing that curve ball and I see a double play coming.'

"Piniella hit Waits's first pitch—a fastball—into the seats for three runs and the game. When he came off the field I held my temper and asked softly, 'Rick, what happened out there?'

" 'I wanted to get ahead of him in the count,' he said.

" 'I left you in there to throw curve balls,' I told him, 'pitches that don't go straight.'

" 'And I was going to, Skip,' Waits replied, 'but I thought I'd sneak a fastball by him first.'

"The next morning Rick sang the national anthem on the *Today* show. I know he did because I was still awake. I had stayed awake all night plotting ways to kill him."

Amazingly, Casey Stengel always made himself understood when telling his pitchers how he wanted them to pitch to a certain batter. Once, Galen Cisco was pitching for the Mets, and Carl Warwick was the hitter. Casey trudged out to the mound and told Cisco to throw breaking balls, all breaking balls, and only breaking balls. Cisco promptly threw Warwick a fastball, which he hit for a home run.

At the end of the inning Casey called Cisco over to him in the dugout and asked him what pitch Warwick had hit. Cisco admitted it was a fastball. "Didn't we go over it that you were only going to throw him breaking balls?" Casey asked.

"We did," Cisco agreed, "but I got behind on the count and I didn't feel I could afford to throw him another ball."

Two innings later Warwick came to bat again, and again Casey walked out to the pitcher's mound. "How you gonna pitch him this time?" he asked.

"I'm going to go along with your idea," Cisco said firmly. "Everything's a breaking pitch." Cisco then threw Warwick five straight curve balls, and

Warwick hit the fifth one over the left-centerfield fence for his second home run of the game.

At the end of the inning Casey called Cisco over to him in the dugout and asked him what pitch Warwick had hit. "Well, Case," Cisco replied, "this time he hit a curve ball—and I'll tell you, yours went a lot farther than mine!"

Many pitchers know that when the manager comes out himself he intends to bring in a reliever, and they will do almost anything to talk him out of making the change. Jerry Reuss, for example, believes in intimidation. Once, just as Dodger manager Tommy Lasorda reached the mound, Reuss started yelling at him, "Just what do you think you're doing here?"

Lasorda was taken by surprise. "Whattya mean, what am I doing here?"

"You'd better get off of here," Reuss responded. "This is my mound and I don't want to see you coming on my mound again." Lasorda shrugged, turned around, and went back to his dugout.

On another occasion, Lasorda came out to get Charlie Hough after Hough had given up a long home run with two men on base. Hough asked to be left in the game, and Lasorda told him, "I'd like to Charlie, but I can't—you're making me look bad."

There have been situations in which a pitcher simply refused to leave the game. Before Galen Cisco became a Met he pitched for the Boston Red Sox. His teammate, six-eight Gene Conley, had been scheduled to pitch against the Washington Senators, but Conley and infielder Pumpsie Green had jumped off the team bus when it got caught in a tunnel and had disappeared. Eventually, it was learned, they had decided to leave the Red Sox in that tunnel and go to Israel.

Pitching coach Sal Maglie asked Cisco to start in Conley's place, and the Senators just raked him. "The score was nine to two in the fifth inning when Maglie came out to the mound," Cisco remembers. 'Look,' he told me, 'we're gonna have to change pitchers.'

"I said, 'Sal, I've come this far in the game and I'm going to finish it. If you want me out of here you're going to have to carry me out bodily, because I'm not leaving this mound.'

"Maglie could obviously take no for an answer, because he shrugged his shoulders and left me in to finish the game. Conley and Green returned to the team about a week later. Naturally, my effort was forgotten and everyone wanted to know why a six-eight major league pitcher who played pro basketball in the winter would suddenly decide to go to Israel. The bus trip hadn't been that bad.

"It turned out Conley had a very intelligent reason for going. 'It's like this,' he finally admitted to me. 'I really wanted to be the tallest man ever to ride a camel.' "

Stan Williams, another former pitcher who, like Cisco, became a pitching coach after retiring, once simply refused to leave when Leo Durocher came out to get him. "I'm not leaving," Williams said flatly, "and that's it."

"All right," Durocher responded just as relief pitcher Larry Sherry joined them on the pitcher's mound, "then I won't leave either. And here comes Sherry and he's gonna want to stay, so this place is going to be very crowded."

In the Dominican Republic one winter season Tommy Lasorda walked out to the mound to take out his pitcher, Pedro Bourbon. Bourbon was not pleased and heaved the baseball over the left-field fence. Lasorda understood. When *he* was a minor league pitcher he once refused to hand over the baseball to his manager—and the manager had to chase him all over the infield to get it. "Don't take me out!" Lasorda screamed at him. "Take out the third baseman, he's the one who made the two errors!"

Dick Williams once came out to remove his

pitcher after the pitcher had given up a long home run. "Lemme have the baseball," Williams demanded.

The pitcher refused.

"Give me the ball," Williams repeated, a bit more firmly.

"I can't," the pitcher said.

"Yeah? Why not?" Williams asked.

" 'Cause the $#¢$&$&$&$)%& thing is about forty rows deep in the bleachers," the pitcher said with a snarl, then stomped off the mound.

There are some baseball games in which the pitcher just doesn't have his good stuff, and he knows it, his catcher knows it, the umpires know it, the other team certainly knows it and, eventually, his manager realizes it. So nobody, except perhaps the other team, is really unhappy when the manager comes out to make the pitching change.

This was the situation on Opening Day of the 1979 season, John McNamara's first day as manager of the Cincinnati Reds. McNamara had replaced Sparky Anderson as manager of the fabled Big Red Machine, inheriting one of baseball's best teams. On this day Tom Seaver was pitching and Johnny Bench was catching, a future Hall of Fame battery. But the Machine really sputtered, and by the third inning of McNamara's first day on the job, the Reds were trailing, 7–1. As McNamara walked out to the mound to relieve Seaver, he was met by Johnny Bench, who said, "Tell me, John, how are you enjoying your debut so far?"

"I'll tell you," McNamara responded, "time sure goes fast when you're having fun."

The thing a manager tries to do when he reaches the mound is state his thoughts clearly and succinctly —and wherever possible, grammatically. For example, when minor league manager Joe Sparks came out to relieve his pitcher Mike Proly, Proly tried pleading, "But, Joe, I'm throwing good!"

"No," Sparks corrected as he signaled to the bullpen, "you *threw* good!"

Hough had one of his worst days in his major league career when Walt Alston was managing the Dodgers. "He'd brought me in to relieve Tommy John in the second inning with us already behind eight to nothing," Hough remembers. "Four innings later the score was sixteen to one, but I had knocked in our run with our only hit. I figured the reason Walt was letting me stay in was because he was hoping I'd get another chance to bat. But I was really getting clobbered. They were hitting everything I threw. Even the outs were hit hard. I was just glad nobody had been hurt by a line drive. Finally, mercifully, Alston came out of the dugout. 'Well, it's about time,' I thought.

"Catcher Steve Yeager was waiting with me on the pitcher's mound. When Walt got to the mound he put his hand on Yeager's shoulder and said, 'Listen, I'm going to bring in Cannizzaro to catch.' Yeager turned around and trotted into the dugout, deserting me. I waited for Walt to tell me he was bringing in a new pitcher, but he didn't say a word. I really wanted to get out of there, but what could I say? 'Spoken to the boys in the bullpen lately?' Or perhaps, 'I'll bet there's a lot of guys would sure love to get their arms loose tonight.'

"Finally Walt sighed and said, 'I might as well bring in a new pitcher too, long as I'm at it.' That was the only time in my entire career that I wanted to thank a manager for taking me out of a game."

When a relief pitcher is coming in, the manager and the catcher meet him on the mound, then the manager quickly reviews the game situation. When Billy Loes, the only pitcher ever to claim he had lost a ground ball in the sun, came in one afternoon to relieve for the Baltimore Orioles, manager Paul Richards pointed out to him that the bases were loaded. "Just gimme the ball," Loes replied. "I didn't think they were extra infielders."

Relief pitchers invariably look cool and confident when they come into the ball game, but many of them undoubtedly have thoughts similar to those of Ron Perranoski when he made his major league debut in relief of Sandy Koufax. "Bob Skinner of the Pirates was the first hitter I faced," Perranoski remembers, "and the only thing going through my mind was, 'Wow, if Sandy Koufax can't get these guys out with the stuff he's got, what chance do I have against them?'"

While the attention of the fans and players is focused on the new pitcher as he takes his warm-up throws, the pitcher who has been taken out goes through the dugout into the locker room. Most often his teammates just pat him on the back or offer a few words of encouragement—or, if the pitcher has been shelled, stay away from him. One day Earl Weaver brought in relief pitcher Dave Ford to face the Brewers' Robin Yount in a crucial situation. Ford warmed up; then Yount bunted his first pitch for a base hit. Ford fielded the ball but didn't bother trying to make a play on Yount. Weaver immediately came out of the dugout and made another pitching change, bringing in a left-hander to pitch to the next batter, a right-handed hitter. Ford went to the dugout after throwing exactly one pitch.

Instead of going directly to the showers, he sat down next to another pitcher, Mike Flanagan. Flanagan waited until Ford was settled, then asked in a loud voice, "So, uh, tell me, Dave, what kind of stuff did you have today?"

There is really only one thing all pitchers do not like: all hitters. Pitchers find hitters offensive. And most offensive of all are the power hitters, the home-run hitters, game breakers, bombers. If a man pitches long enough he is going to give up some home runs and some HOME RUNS. Some real tape-measure shots. Skyscrapers. Rainmakers.

Every pitcher reacts differently after giving up a

mammoth home run. Some of them go into shock. Take Orioles relief pitcher Tippy Martinez, for example. One night in Detroit he was getting banged around, and he threw a high curve ball that the Tigers' Kirk Gibson hit onto the roof of Tiger Stadium, a distance of about five hundred feet. Weaver relieved Martinez, who went directly to the Orioles clubhouse.

Mike Flanagan followed him in there. "Tippy," he asked, "what happened?"

"Jeez," Tippy said, his eyes wide open.

"What'd you throw him?"

"Jeez."

"You got it up too high, I guess."

"Jeez."

Of course, by the next day Martinez had recovered. Pitching coach Ray Miller asked him what had happened. "God," Martinez replied.

Mike Flanagan has also given up some tremendous shots in his career, but one that stands out is the home run Dave Winfield hit off him in Yankee Stadium, a blast that almost went over the bullpen in left-center field. "I knew it was gone the moment he hit it," Flanagan said, "so I didn't even watch. But when I got back to the dugout I realized it must have been some shot because everybody was either looking at the floor or in another direction, or sitting there with their hands over their mouths so they wouldn't laugh.

"But I really didn't know how far Winfield had hit it until the next day. The Yankees have these memorial plaques on the bullpen wall honoring some of their greatest players. And as I opened the door and walked into the bullpen I looked up at Babe Ruth's plaque—and there was the Babe with his hand over his mouth."

There really isn't too much anyone can say to a pitcher who has surrendered a tape-measure home run. "I always tell our pitchers to be proud of them," Dick Howser says. "I mean, you have to have good stuff to throw one that goes that far. Some of those shots . . . you couldn't tee up a golf ball and hit it that far, so the baseball really has to be moving to the plate for the batter to crunch it.

"Pitchers can't really worry about the bombers," Ray Miller explains, "and the ones that just drop over the fence count just as much as the long ones. I try to kid our people when they give up a blast. When someone in Texas hit a shot off Sammy Stewart, for example, I sat down next to Sammy and asked him in a serious voice, 'Show me how you held that pitch.'

"Sammy looked at me and shook his head. 'I held that one *on* the seams,' he said, then thought about it for a moment, and continued, 'I think maybe next time I'll try holding it *across* the seams.'"

After the shock wears off, pitchers tend to remember the longest home runs they have given up with a mixture of chagrin and pride. Tom "Plowboy" Morgan, for example, had a twelve-year career with five major league teams. "I had just started working on a slider," he remembers, "and one day I got two strikes on Ted Williams and decided to throw him one of these experiments. I didn't get two strikes on Ted Williams too often, so this was a momentous occasion for me. I threw it right past him for strike three. He didn't even move his bat. Well, I figured, it's a cinch now, I've found Ted Williams's weakness. I can get him out anytime I want to.

" 'Bout a month later we were playing in Yankee Stadium and he came to bat. I threw him a sinker for a strike, then I started thinking, 'I sure got him set up for the slider now. I'll throw it inside and he won't have a chance.' So I did.

"I had never actually seen a ball hit the back wall of the mezzanine section in right field before. He hit that pitch on a line and it just shot into the seats. Turned out, Williams was setting *me* up!"

The longest home run Dick Ruthven ever gave up was hit by George Foster. "We were in Cincinnati," Ruthven recalls, "and I decided I was going to fool him. I was going to invent a new pitch, the Ruthven Sidearm Curve ball. I threw it and Foster's eyes lit up. He couldn't wait for it to get to home plate. He practically leaped off the ground to hit it. It was what baseball players call a tanker. Actually, it was an upper tanker. In fact, it was an upper, upper tanker.

Mike Proly was pitching for the White Sox in Comiskey Park when Bobby Bonds hit a slider that slid into the lower deck in left field on a line drive. "I don't know if it was the longest I've ever given up, I've thrown some long home runs, but that was the hardest hit. You should have seen the people sitting in those seats scatter when that ball came at them. The next day our owner, Bill Veeck, told reporters he was going to charge me to repair the three seats Bonds's home run had broken—they were three in a row, and not next to each other."

What goes through a pitcher's mind after he has given up a home run and has to stand there while the batter circles the bases? Ferguson Jenkins probably is the expert on the subject. Fergie has spent most of his career among the league leaders in both victories and home runs given up. "The longest one I've ever given up was probably the one hit by Willie McCovey at Candlestick Park in San Francisco," Fergie remembers. "Hitters say they know a ball is gone the moment they hit it. I knew this one was gone the moment I threw it. It was a low curve ball and as I soon as I released the pitch I thought, 'Well, at least there's nobody on base.' He crushed it. It went over the players' parking lot behind the stadium and halfway into the attendants' parking lot before it bounced. It's probably still floating in the bay somewhere.

"After you've given up a home run it gets very lonely on the pitcher's mound. None of the infielders want to share the spotlight with you. Forget about your catcher, he's trying to pretend he doesn't even know you. You don't really want to look at the man who hit it because he's smiling. Finally, the umpire flips you the new baseball and you think, 'Well, I don't give up back-to-back home runs too often.' "

"Once, after I'd given up another home run," remembers Frank Funk, "I stood out there thinking, 'Now I know why the umpire doesn't give me a new baseball until that hitter crosses home plate—he knows that if he gave it to me too soon I'd nail that hitter with it when he came around third base.' "

"When I was pitching," Tommy Lasorda claims, "there was only one thing I really wanted to do before I retired. When a guy hit a home run off me and trotted slowly around the bases, I wanted to be waiting for him at home plate. And as he touched that plate, I wanted to just deck him!"

Pitchers may not remember every home run they give up, but they certainly remember every one they hit. Usually this requires only a very short memory.

Gaylord Perry's first major league home run was a historic one. He was with Alvin Dark's San Francisco Giants in 1968. "I was taking batting practice one afternoon and I was just hitting line drives, I mean line drives. Harry Jupiter, a sportswriter, was watching me and said to Alvin, 'You know, that guy has some power.'

"Alvin laughed. 'Let me tell you something,' he said. 'There'll be a man on the moon before he hits a home run.'

"So a year later I was pitching against the Dodgers when we got the news that Neil Armstrong had stepped on to the surface the moon. I came to bat about twenty minutes after that, against Claude Osteen—and hit my first major league home run. When Armstrong stepped out on the moon he said, 'That's one small step for a man, one giant leap for all mankind,' and I thought, 'and one home run for Gaylord Perry.' "

"It'd be hard to forget my first major league home run," Tom Morgan says, " 'cause it was supposed to be a sacrifice bunt. There was a man on first and I laid down a beautiful bunt, right back to the pitcher. He threw to second for the force-out there, then the shortstop relayed it to first to try to double me up. The shortstop overestimated my speed, though, and threw the ball away. I whipped around first and took off for second.

"The ball bounced around there a while before the first baseman picked it up, but he believed he had a play on me and threw to second. I went sliding into that base—and the ball went sailing over my head into the outfield. I was starting to get pretty tired right there—this was a considerable amount of action on a sacrifice bunt.

"But I got up and took off for third base. I never did have much speed, but I had a fine sense of direction. The outfielder picked up the ball and made a play at third. I went sliding into third base—and the throw got away from the third baseman. So I got up again, and they made another play on me at home, but I beat that throw easily.

"Now, the official scorer didn't exactly call it a home run, but I figured he could call it anything he wanted to. Far as I was concerned, I started at home and got back to home, and that's a home run. After that, though, I went into a slump for the rest of my career."

Very few pitchers hit tape-measure home runs, but Davey Phillips thinks he remembers one who did. "The three longest balls I've seen were hit by Frank Howard, Thurman Munson, and Yankee pitcher Mel Stottlemyre. In 1971, Stottlemyre hit a rocket into the second deck in left field in Yankee Stadium. The only problem is, nobody else seems to remember it. I was there, I know I saw it, but whenever I mention it people look at me as if I'm making it up. I once asked Bobby Murcer if he remembered it, he looked at me, then told me he didn't even remember Mel Stottlemyre."

Umpires enjoy watching titanic shots as much as players do—as long as they don't tie up the game in a late inning. Eric Gregg was working the plate one night in St. Louis when Willie Stargell tied the game in the top of the ninth inning. "It was some shot," Eric says. "In the upper deck, they have a big beer sign, and it went beyond that and took out the back of a seat. I remember watching him hit that ball and, as he rounded the bases, thinking, 'Miss home plate, please miss home plate.' "

The longest home run Rocky Roe has seen was hit by Ted Simmons—while they were both in high school. "We played sandlot ball in Detroit together," Rocky explains. "He was sixteen and I was fifteen. He hit a ball . . . it was just unbelievable. It went out of the ball park over the four-hundred-foot marker, went across a four-lane highway, up the steps of a Catholic church, and finally bounced off the church door. It hit that door so hard that someone opened it up and looked around, then closed it.

"Sandlot baseball in Detroit is well organized and there were maybe fifteen hundred people watching the game. I remember, when he hit it, the crowd went so silent that we could hear the ball bouncing off the door. The ball probably traveled five hundred fifty to six hundred feet. It was an incredible feat."

"I saw Richie Allen swing at a Johnny Podres change-up that almost hit the ground," Doug Harvey says, "and hit it through the light tower on top of the second deck in left field at Philadelphia's old Connie Mack Stadium. But I think the longest one I ever saw was hit by Willie McCovey, also at Connie Mack Stadium. He hit one over the sixty-foot-high scoreboard in center field. Oh, my, that was a mammoth shot. When he came out to play first base the next inning, I asked, 'Sting your hands, Will?'

"He said, 'Harvey, I'm gonna tell you something. I never hit a bigger ball than that. That's it, you've seen the best I've ever hit.' And he cracked a lot of big ones."

Eddie Montague saw Willie Stargell hit a five-hundred-foot home run in Montreal. "I just couldn't believe any man could hit a ball that went that far that fast," he says. "And it would've kept going if it hadn't hit something. That ball should've had luggage tags."

Every player has his favorite home-run story. Mickey Rivers remembers a home run that Dave Kingman hit off Catfish Hunter in spring training in Fort Lauderdale. "That ball went nine miles up and killed a plane," Mickey claims. "Next time Kingman was s'pposed to be up I went out to the field with the catcher's chest protector, mask, and my helmet. I said that that was armor day."

Of course, Catfish gave up so many home runs during his career that Lou Piniella once suggested that the Yankees play their third outfielder *in* the bleachers when Hunter was pitching for them.

No player in recent baseball history has hit more tape-measure home runs than Reggie Jackson, and no player enjoys watching them more than he does. "It's just unreal to me to hit a ball and see it just go and go," Reggie says. "They just keep going, they go the normal home-run distance, and still keep going. It's like, wow! I dig it, whether I hit it or someone else does. Ballplayers appreciate the long home run just as much as a fan does. It's just a real turn-on.

"My first home run in professional baseball was hit in Lewiston, Idaho, when I was in the Rookie League," Reggie continued. "It went out of the ball park, across the street, and landed on the roof of a house. Then I remember the one I hit off Baltimore's Dennis Martinez at Yankee Stadium. It went out in dead center field and hit the back wall of the bullpen on a fly. It even chipped some paint off the wall. That one had to be five-hundred-plus feet. I remember in 1968 when Hoyt Wilhelm was pitching in his nine-hundred-seventh game to break the all-time record for pitching appearances that had been set by Cy Young. I hit the first pitch he threw me over the grandstand in right field in Milwaukee. Another night out there I hit the scoreboard twice off Jim Colborn and we won the game, two to one, for Catfish's twentieth victory. Then, I remember, I hit a shot . . ." Thank you, Reggie.

Steve Kemp remembers the mammoth home run Richie Zisk hit off Dave Rozema into the distant Comiskey Park bleachers. "I was in left field and I didn't even move," he says. "It was gone from the moment he hit it. No question about it."

"I was hoping I could get a triple out of it," Zisk recalls. "I knew I hit it well, but it was four hundred fifteen feet to the center-field wall and the fence was about seventeen feet high. So as soon as I hit it I thought, that's over their heads, you'd better run because you got a chance to get three bases." Zisk, as ballplayers say, is built for comfort, not speed. "I was sprinting around second base when it finally went into the seats."

". . . and then there's the one that stands out that I hit off Jim Perry in Minnesota. It was four hundred twelve feet to the center-field fence in that ball park, and about another fifty feet behind the fence was the scoreboard. That scoreboard was seventy feet high and on top of it there was a beer sign. I hit that beer sign on a fly. It was estimated at five hundred thirty-seven feet. Then, one night in Kansas City, I hit one off Larry Gura that just missed going out of the ball park by five or six feet when I was playing with the Orioles. Then, believe it or not, one night I hit . . ." Thank you again, Reggie.

Doug DeCinces remembers the shot Reggie hit off Larry Gura. "But the exciting thing about it," he says, "was that Lee May was the next batter. And on Gura's next pitch Lee hit one almost as far as

Reggie did, but to left field. It was incredible, in two pitches Gura had given up over a thousand feet of home-run ball.

"Well, maybe Gura didn't find it all that exciting."

Mickey Mantle hit his home runs farther than anyone else during his major league career. "In 1956," Phil Rizzuto remembers, "Mickey hit one off Pedro Ramos that just missed going out of Yankee Stadium. Everybody in the dugout thought it had gone out, but it hit the edge of the upper-deck façade 370 feet from the plate, 118 feet above the field—and he hit it *against* the wind. It was amazing, Mickey hit that ball as hard as a ball has ever been hit, and everybody was disappointed."

"I was playing third base for the Senators when he hit that one," Eddie Yost remembers, "and it missed clearing the ball park by maybe a foot. But I don't think that one was as long as the one Mickey hit off Chuck Stobbs in Washington in 1953. That one was measured at 565 feet, and that's where the expression 'tape measure' home run came from. You watched that one going out and you sort of wished you could cut it up into singles, because it had enough singles in it to last a whole season."

Brooks Robinson remembers a day in Kansas City when Boog Powell hit two mammoth home runs into the sheep meadow. "Charley Finley used to keep a flock of sheep out there in the outfield and Boog hit his home runs right into the flock. So when he came to bat the next time I looked out there and the sheepherder was desperately pushing all his sheep under the scoreboard for protection."

Some players believe the longest home runs they've seen were hit in the minor leagues. Gaylord Perry, for instance, claims he was playing against Frank Howard when Howard hit a ball out of the state of Texas. "Now, it doesn't sound like that much," Gaylord explains, "till you understand we were playing in the middle of the state."

"One Sunday when I was pitching for Spokane in Triple-A," Charlie Hough remembers, "we were short of pitchers and the manager didn't want to take any chances that his better players might hurt their arms, so he asked me to pitch both games of a double-header against the Portland Beavers. I agreed—I knew I didn't throw hard enough to strain my arm. We were in the seventh inning of the first game, which was all they played in double-headers, and I really was pitching a gem. I was leading, seven to five, a neat twelve-hitter. Then Cotton Nash came to bat. I fell behind in the count, three balls, one strike, and I thought, 'Well, I'll throw this big guy my real good high fast ball, I'll just buzz it right past him.'

"Let me tell you how far he hit that baby. There was a huge scoreboard in right-center field. It went over the scoreboard, over a second wall behind the scoreboard, and then over a clock. It didn't come close to hitting anything. It just kept going and going and going.

"I won the game seven to six. But afterward, my manager suggested, 'Ah, let's forget about you pitching the second game. Maybe we'll let some infielder pitch instead.'"

". . . and then there was the one I hit in Yankee Stadium off Mike Barlow when he was pitching for California. That one went into the upper deck in right-center, about five rows above the exit ramp. Maybe four hundred fifty feet, but it was still traveling when it hit. That was the second home run I hit that night. I did hit four home runs in a row in Arizona in spring training once, two of them off Juan Marichal . . ." Great, Reggie, thanks.

Chuck Cottier is responsible for one of the longest home runs in baseball history. He didn't hit it and he didn't throw the pitch—he reported it. "I was managing an Angels farm club in the California League and I got ejected from the game. I went to our dressing room, which was down the left-field line, and used one of the equipment kids to run signals back to the bench. So I was sitting there and one of my players, Mark Brohard, hit a ball over the trees in the outfield. It really was quite a shot.

"After the game the reporters came to speak to me because I was the only one who could see over the outfield fence to tell how far it went. How far did it go? Far. The reporter commented that Brohard had a lot of power for a young player. I said, 'That's got to be the longest home run I have ever seen.'

" 'How far would you estimate it went?'

" 'Phew,' I told him, making it up as I spoke, 'that ball had to be six hundred feet easy. Why, the kids out there were chasing it for nine blocks.'

"The next morning I turned on the radio and heard broadcaster Paul Harvey tell the entire nation that Mark Brohard, a young minor leaguer, had hit a home run that traveled more than six hundred feet, one of the longest in baseball history.

"I wish I had known it was going to get that kind of publicity. Then Brohard *really* would have hit a long home run!"

Not all players are capable of tape-measure home runs—some of them have to be content with ruler-measures—but players remember the shortest home runs they've hit almost as well as the longest. "I hit a shot against Cincinnati," says Larry Bowa, "that must have gone two hundred forty, two hundred fifty feet easy. Outfielders George Foster and Cesar Geronimo both came running in for it. Unfortunately, they collided, both of them were knocked down, and the ball trickled between them. It went all the way to the wall for another Bowa home run.

"Actually," Larry admits, "I don't hit that many of them. I once hit a grand slam off Joe Hoerner—this one went into the seats. Hoerner was so embarrassed that two weeks later, as soon as he came out of shock, he retired from baseball."

Perhaps the shortest home run that actually reached the seats was hit by ... Frank Howard. "We were playing in the old Los Angeles Coliseum,"

Howard recalls. "It hadn't been built for baseball and they really had to squeeze to get a full-sized playing field in there. It was only two hundred fifty-four feet down the left-field foul line, but to prevent pop-ups from being home runs, they had erected a forty-foot-high wire screen.

"Mike McCormick was pitching for the San Francisco Giants and he threw me a high, inside curve ball that I hit right off the handle of the bat and popped straight into the air. It must have been about two hundred feet straight up. At first, I thought the third baseman would make the play, but he drifted under it into the outfield and I thought, no, the left fielder'll come in and catch it. But the left fielder just drifted back and drifted back until he was at the screen, and then the ball started to come down. I think it must've scraped the back of that screen as it landed in the stands for a three-run homer. I would estimate its distance at two hundred fifty-four feet, six inches. McCormick was just glaring at me as I ran around the bases. I think he thought I should have to throw that one back."

". . . of course, there are people who believe the home run I hit in the 1971 All-Star game in Detroit off Dock Ellis was the longest one I've hit. That one hit the transformer on top of the roof in right field. I got all of that one, I'll tell you that. But then there's the one I hit off Bill Travers at the Stadium. That was an upper-decker down the right-field foul line that I really didn't think I hit that well. I honestly felt like I ran at the ball before I hit it. It was a weird feeling. Maybe the longest one I ever saw was the change-up I hit off Gaylord Perry in Oakland. That hit the back wall, where they serve hot dogs, on one hop. That one had to have gone at least . . ." Reggie, please!

Perhaps the two most memorable home runs in baseball history were chip shots. In 1951 the New York Giants' Bobby Thomson hit a line drive about 315 feet into the left-field stands at the Polo Grounds in the bottom of the ninth inning to beat the Brooklyn Dodgers for the National League pennant, and in 1978 shortstop Bucky Dent's three-run homer over the close-in Green Monster in Boston's Fenway Park enabled the Yankees to beat the Red Sox in a single-game playoff for the American League's Eastern Division championship.

"We were winning, four to two, going into the last of the ninth inning," remembers Dodger utility infielder Wayne Terwilliger. "I was sitting in the corner of the dugout thinking, 'Heavens, five thousand dollars for being in the World Series.' We had Don Newcombe pitching for us and Clem Labine and Ralph Branca in the bullpen.

"The Giants got a man on base and someone in the dugout called the bullpen to see if Labine or Branca were ready to pitch, and they were told that Branca was really bringing it. When the Giants got another runner on base, Branca came in to pitch.

"When Thomson hit the ball I really didn't think it was going out. It was a sinking line drive and I was just hoping our left fielder, Andy Pafko, could catch it, because a base hit would've really put us in trouble. I was sitting on the bat trunk and I leaned forward to watch it, and I fell off the trunk onto the floor—and that's where I was sitting when I saw it go into the stands. At first I didn't realize what it meant. Did that mean we were tied up? Then, when I finally understood, I just fell back on the bench and watched.

"Our owner, Walter O'Malley, was great about it. He came into the clubhouse after the game and told us, 'These things are going to happen.' Losing the pennant on a three-hundred-twenty-five-foot home run in the bottom of the ninth inning of the third game of the playoffs? I certainly hoped it wasn't going to happen too often."

Ironically, it is also 315 feet to straightaway left field in Boston's Fenway Park, but the Green Monster, a 37-foot-high pine and tin wall, prevents many routine fly balls from becoming home runs. But not Dent's. "It was just a little fly ball," says Freddie Lynn, who was in center field, "just a little fly ball. First I thought it was going to be caught, then I thought it was going to hit the wall. I couldn't believe it when it went into the screen for a home run. It just brushed that screen as it came down."

What happens to the baseballs that are hit for home runs? ". . . I've hit some so hard that they hit the façade of the outfield deck and bounced back onto the field all the way to second base and . . ." Reggie, go to your room!

If the home run is significant for the player, he might trade with the fan who caught the ball to get it back. If it is significant in baseball history, the ball club will try to retrieve it and send it to the Hall of Fame. And what happened to Bucky Dent's home-run ball? It nestled into the screen atop the Green Monster, along with many other baseballs that had been hit there in batting practice and, according to Joe Mooney, who runs Fenway Park, "We threw that #$*&#*¢*–#$* ball all the way back to New York!"

Spoken like a true pitcher.

NINE

THE TOP OF
THE NINTH

Years ago, a minor league umpire named Roy Funk-
houser retired from baseball after crashing into a
cow while driving to a game. "If I can't see a cow,"
he explained, "how am I gonna see a little white
ball coming up to a batter?"

I never failed the Umpire Cow Test. In my
entire career, I never even came close to hitting a
cow—oh, maybe I grazed a chicken once, but I
don't care what that chicken claimed, she was in
the wrong lane. Fans often ask me why I retired
from baseball. Fans, not players or managers—players
and managers just thank me. I quit because I realized that baseball is a game of inches, for umpires
as well as for players. And when my waistline got
to be forty-eight inches I knew it was time to retire.
I could no longer move quickly enough to get the
proper angle on plays. I felt I was no longer doing
the best job of which I was capable, and I had too
much respect for the players and fans to give them
less than my best effort—that and the fact that
NBC offered me a chunk of money to work two
days a week as a broadcaster.

Naturally, when I announced my retirement,
many people urged me to reconsider. Earl Weaver,

with whom I had started fifteen years earlier in the Eastern League and with whom I had spent some of my most bitter moments on the field, said graciously, "Ronnie who?" And I'll never forget the kind words of Gene Mauch, who bowed his head and said, "Luciano? Is he still umpiring? I thought he retired four years ago." And even American League President Lee MacPhail tried to convince me to work one more year, arguing, "Hip hip, hooray! Hip hip, hooray!"

At the testimonial dinner given for me by my mother and attended by all my sisters as well as those other relatives willing to cough up the $6.75 a plate, I remember my mother, who had been supportive of me throughout my entire athletic career, looking at me and saying, with love in her voice, "If you think you're just gonna sit around the house all day, you've got another think coming!"

It did not take me long to realize what I would miss about being a major league umpire. There is a fine line that separates players, managers, coaches, and umpires from everyone else at the ball park— the foul line. I knew from the moment I announced my retirement I would miss being inside those lines. But more than that, I've learned, I miss the relationships I formed during my life in baseball.

Among all American sports, baseball is unique in that teams play games almost every day for six months, and when they're not playing, they're usually traveling. An umpire spends most of the season on the road, living and working, day after day, night after night, with the same people. Day after day, night after night, day after day ... Players spend only half that time living out of suitcases in hotels, with the same people day after day, night after night, day after ... And because of this great amount of time people in baseball are forced to spend together and because of the tremendous pressure under which they all work, firm friendships are formed.

Even more than the game itself, I miss being part

of those relationships. I miss the practical jokes. I miss the long conversations during late-night suppers, early-morning breakfasts, in-flight snacks, long lunches, midafternoon dinners, pregame meals . . . I miss that special pride I felt being a member of a select group of professionals who have one of the most exciting jobs in the world. I even miss Kenny Kaiser . . . well, let's not get carried away. . . .

Some baseball friendships began long before the people involved were professionals. Warren Cromartie and Mickey Rivers grew up together, for example. "We always called him 'The Weatherman,'" Cromartie recalls. "It had nothing to do with politics, he was just good at predicting the weather. He would come out to the field and say, 'We'd better hurry because it's gonna rain in the fourth inning.' And in the fourth inning it would start raining. He was much better at predicting the weather than the people getting paid to do it on television."

"I get the urge," Mickey explained. "I come out on the field and they ask me, 'Mick, can we play six innings today?' And I'd feel the breeze and say, 'No, we can only get in three, so it don't make no difference about my hitting today.'

" 'Weatherman,' that was my best nickname until Whitey Herzog gave me another one. He said, 'Look, I gotta give you a name. I know what, I'll call you Chancellor.' I asked him why, and he told me that a chancellor was an important person in the government. So I liked that, I liked being the chancellor.

"Then I found out he had a little hunting dog named Chancellor. He named me after his favorite dog."

Ted Simmons and Rocky Roe grew up nearby each other in Detroit. Simmons, in fact, once knocked out Rocky with a fast ball in a Little League game. But perhaps the high point in their friendship took place when Rocky was pledging for the high

school Varsity Club and Simmons told him to eat a
bar of soap. "I knew this was one of those moments
that would benefit me in later life," Rocky explains,
"because if I could talk my way out of this one, I'd
be in real good shape for anything that happened in
the future. 'Let's be realistic here,' I said. 'What
would be accomplished by making me eat that soap?'
Nobody could really come up with anything beyond
the fact that it would make *them* feel good, so I
didn't have to do it. Naturally, it was an easy jump
from that moment to being a major league umpire."

Because Davey Phillips's father was a minor
league umpire, Davey spent much of his childhood
around young baseball players. And of all the
ballplayers he knew, of all the hundreds of ballplayers
he knew, of all of them, one became his idol, one
was the kind of ballplayer he wanted to be. One out
of hundreds. Oh, this hurts.

Earl Weaver.

"I thought he was the greatest," Davey remembers. "He played second base for the Omaha Cardinals. He was from St. Louis, just like me, and he
was small and feisty. And even then he was having
problems with umpires.

"At that time, of course, I didn't understand
the relationship between players and umpires. Once,
after my father had ejected him from the game, I
went into the umpires' room and said something to
the effect of, 'How could you throw Earl Weaver
out of the game?' Anyway, when I picked myself
up, my father told me to never, ever question anything that takes place on the field between a player
and umpire.

"Weaver was managing Rochester when I was
working in the International League. And when the
American League purchased my contract, Dick Butler asked me about my relationship with him.
'Weaver helped me a lot,' I told him. 'I really believed when I got to the International League that I
was a super ump, but he really taught me how to

handle situations.' Butler asked what I meant and I explained. 'I had so many problems with him, he did so many crazy things, things that a normal person wouldn't do, that I learned how to handle events that I never even dreamed were possible.' Butler understood.

"In my entire career, I never mentioned my father to Earl. I wasn't even sure that he knew my father had been an umpire. Then, the last time I worked a Baltimore game before he retired, I sent a baseball to the Orioles' locker room for him to sign. He wrote, 'Dear Dave, To the only father-and-son team that ever threw me out of a game.' So he knew, the whole time he knew."

Few managers have ever been as tough with their ballplayers as Earl Weaver. Once, for example, when he was managing Elmira, a young outfielder playing for him named Lou Piniella didn't hustle after a long fly ball. So while the play was still in progress, while runners were circling the bases, Weaver came out of his dugout, ran to the outfield, and got into a fight with Piniella. That's like Muhammad Ali vs. Don Knotts—but I wouldn't bet my house against Knotts.

And Earl didn't change when he got to the major leagues—he still encouraged close, warm relationships with his players. "Earl was always threatening to take me out of ball games," says Rick Dempsey, who caught for Weaver for seven years with the Orioles. "So one day in Milwaukee I was having a rough game. The plate umpire got in my way when I went after a foul pop-up and I couldn't reach it. Then the batter singled in the go-ahead run. Later in the game I was on first base and the runner on second got picked off. He got in a rundown and I advanced to second. Then he got out of the rundown and made it back to second. I felt awfully silly standing on that base, so I took off for first and was tagged out.

"Earl was furious. At the beginning of the next

inning, while I was warming up the pitcher, he
came out to home plate with his lineup card and
showed me that he had scratched out my name. So
I came off the field. Now I was furious. He was
standing on the top step of the dugout and as I took
off each piece of my catcher's equipment I threw it
at him. I took off a shinguard and sailed it to his
left. He picked it up and threw it right back at me. I
sailed the other shinguard to his right. He threw it
back. I couldn't get the chest protector to sail, so it
landed at his feet. Meanwhile, he was ripping me
up and down, telling me I couldn't play baseball, I
didn't know what I was doing out there. I took off
the iron mask and started to throw that, but I realized I could really hurt him with it, so I aimed at
his feet. By this time the game had stopped and
everybody was watching us throwing equipment at
each other.

"Personally, I thought Earl was acting incredibly immature. I didn't want to hear him anymore,
so I started to go up the runway to the clubhouse,
tearing off my uniform as I walked. He followed
right behind me, still screaming, 'I'm the manager
and you'll do what I say when I say it or . . .' I
walked into the locker room, he followed me into
the locker room. I just wanted to get away from
him, so I kept right on walking, right into the
showers.

"He followed me right into the showers, still
yelling at me. 'First you turn the wrong way on
a pop-up, then you don't know how to run the
bases . . .'

"He was standing right behind me, screaming
in my ears, his voice echoing in the shower, and I
figured if I turned on the water he would have to go
away. Well, I was wrong there, too. He stood there
with water spraying all over him, and he was *still*
screaming.

"I was running out of escape routes. So I stepped
to the side and turned off the hot water. If that

wouldn't cool him off, I figured, nothing would. I couldn't believe he would stand there in the freezing cold water shouting at me. I mean, he had made his point.

"He didn't even slow down. He just kept yelling and yelling until he didn't have anything left to yell. Finally he shook his head and said, 'You haven't heard a single thing I've said,' then turned around and went back to the ball game."

Having worked with Earl Weaver for almost fifteen years, I can imagine what he would have done if he *didn't* like and respect Dempsey. Of course, Earl would have been even more successful as a manager if he could have somehow overcome his terrible shyness.

But there was a totally different side of Earl Weaver. A side the fans never saw. A side most of his players never saw. A side I certainly never saw. The inside. As tough as he could be, the relationships born on the baseball field were important to him. Pitcher Eddie Watt, for example, had been with Weaver for four years in the minor leagues and then eight more with the Orioles. "Then, one day," Watt remembers, "I got a phone call from the office telling me I had been sold to Philadelphia. It was a tough day for me. I went to the ball park to pick up my equipment and, as I was leaving, ran into Earl. I could see he was as uncomfortable as I was. 'You know,' he said very professionally, 'it was just a move we had to make. I'm really sorry, but Bob Reynolds is almost five years younger than you are—' And then he stopped. He looked at me and smiled and said softly, 'We've been through a lot of things together, haven't we?' He started reminiscing about some of the seasons, the wins and the losses, and as he did a part of his character I hadn't seen in twelve years came through. Then he started crying. He finally had to turn away and leave. It's a good thing he did, too. I was feeling the same way."

I can understand that. I often felt like crying when I saw Earl Weaver.

While Earl ran his teams as a dictatorship, Tommy Lasorda ran his clubs more like a Marx Brothers movie. He let his players know that the door to his office was always open—it had to be, in fact, his players stole it—and used humor to create a breezy, friendly atmosphere on his ballclubs. Of course, that was before they barricaded him in his house or raided his office. "As enthusiastic as he is about the Dodgers and baseball today," Charlie Hough says, "he was much worse in the minor leagues. I signed my first contract with the Dodgers when I was eighteen years old and was assigned to Ogden, Utah. When I got there, I saw this maniac pitching batting practice. He was screaming at everybody, telling them they had to believe in the Great Dodger in the sky. 'You gotta believe that!' he was shouting. 'I'm telling you, you gotta believe that!' I was really shocked when I found out that the maniac was my manager.

"He still owes me a Cadillac from that year. Now, Tommy never won a game as a major-league pitcher, but after listening to him for a season I was convinced he'd at least won the Cy Young Award. One day when he was pitching batting practice he bet me I couldn't hit his famous curve ball out of the ball park. Then he just hung one right out there and I hit it out—but I never did get that Cadillac. Judging from his curve ball, however, I'd guess there is a long line of people ahead of me."

"Tommy was always a great clubhouse orator," Bobby Valentine, who also played for Lasorda in both the minors and the major leagues, remembers. "But he only has one speech. He gives the same speech at a free breakfast for the Holy Name Society as he does to corporate executives. I've heard that speech one hundred and twenty-three times.

"The first time I heard it was at Idaho Falls, Idaho, in the Rookie League. We had one kid on that team who did everything possible to irritate the manager. If Lasorda said wear shoes, The Kid wore sneakers. If Lasorda said be there at one o'clock, The Kid would be there at one-thirty. But he could play ball. And as long as we were winning, Tommy could tolerate him.

"But at the end of July we went into a little slump and Tommy decided it was time to give his speech. He called a team meeting. For most of us, it was our first team meeting in pro ball.

"Tommy was magnificent. He walked up and down the locker-room aisle, his voice rising and falling. 'You people are playing like a team of old ladies,' he said. 'Who do you expect to beat like this? You're all just protecting your batting averages. The only way we're gonna win is to play a team that's weak against infield pop-ups. Garvey, I don't know what you're swinging at half the time. Valentine, when I tell you to steal a base, you've got to steal that base. . . .' He was really getting into this speech, the veins in his neck were sticking out, he was sweating. He held all of us absolutely spellbound.

"Actually, not quite all of us. Not The Kid. The Kid was huddled in the corner reading a newspaper. I saw him, but Lasorda didn't, at least not right away. He continued walking up and down that aisle, pleading with us, imploring us, berating us, inspiring us, reinforcing our confidence. Finally he reached his dramatic conclusion, the most impassioned part of his speech. 'I'm telling you guys,' he screamed, 'and I mean this from the very bottom of my heart—' That was when he turned around and saw The Kid reading the newspaper and paying absolutely no attention to him. Almost any other manager I've known would've exploded; they would have destroyed The Kid. Not Tommy. Without pausing to take a breath, Tommy fell onto his knees, clasped his hands together in supplication, looked toward heaven, and cried, 'Why, Lord? Why me? Why, of all the managers on earth, did you send him to me? Why do I have that dumb @$#%$¢ playing on my team?'

"And then he rested there, on his knees, waiting for an answer. Even The Kid couldn't help laughing at him. Of course, that was the end of our losing streak. Tommy had successfully broken the tension."

". . . Did I mention that Nolan Ryan used to try to challenge me? If he had a big lead, or if he was losing by a large margin in later innings, he'd tell me he was going to throw only fast balls and we would see how far I could hit it—*if* I could hit it.

"Early in 1973 we were playing in Oakland and he had thrown me two straight fast balls. I was looking for another fast ball, so I was really pumped up, and he threw me a curve ball. I got all of it. All of it. The center-field fence in Oakland is three hundred ninety-seven feet, and about a hundred feet beyond that they stored the batting cage used before the game. There was a big metal gate that came down near the cage and I hit that gate on one hop. It was a short hop, though. And I remember . . ." REGGIE, THAT'S ENOUGH! You're in the wrong chapter.

Anyway, baseball relationships may begin on the diamond, but they are nurtured off the field. Players, managers, coaches, and umpires spend a considerable amount of their time searching for things to occupy their time between games. Umpires, for example, love fast games, because the sooner a game is over the more time they have off the field to try to find something to do to kill time before the next game.

Like all mature, sophisticated adults who conduct their personal and business lives out of a suitcase six months a year, baseball people fill their free time by pursuing a number of exciting and intellectually stimulating activities. Among the most popular are museum tours, attending classical art lectures, taking foreign-language correspondence courses, and enjoying chamber music concerts and obscure Italian movies without subtitles. On those rare occasions when none of these diversions are available to them, baseball people may resort to fine dining and social pursuits. But the one quest that fills many off-the-field hours, the single activity second in importance only to the game itself, is the search for the perfect practical joke.

The practical joke is the psychiatry of baseball. It is the means baseball people use to relieve some of the incredible pressure inherent in their work. Naturally, I, myself, was much too mature and sophisticated to participate in these ofttimes juvenile activities. Except once, when I left a huge, dead fish in Ken Kaiser's toilet bowl in Seattle, so that late at night, when he went into the bathroom and turned on the light, this ugly monster was staring right back at him. And except for the other time when I put Jim Honochick's plate shoes into the deep freezer until five minutes before game time, so he had to wear frozen shoes during the game. And except for the time Haller and I soldered closed the straps on Honochick's shinguards. And maybe that one other time when I sewed closed George Maloney's shirts. Or that time when I tied knots in all Maloney's equipment, and then there was the time . . . but that is nothing compared to the terrible things other people would do.

Maloney, for instance. George Maloney, who would offer soft chocolate to some other umpire on the field on the hottest day of the year so that it melted in the hand of this poor, lovable, hungry other umpire. The same George Maloney who would get up early in the morning, take my newspaper from in front of my door and glue some of the pages together, then put it back. One of the true delights in my life is ripping a newspaper apart to try to read it. But perhaps the worst thing George Maloney ever did to another, kind human being was hide a metronome in the air-conditioning duct of my hotel room.

George knew that one of the things that bothers me most in the world are repetitive sounds like water dripping or Weaver complaining about balls and strikes. So one day while we were in Texas, George purchased a battery-operated metronome, a device that musicians use to keep steady time, and hid it inside the duct. For three days and three nights all I heard was tick ... tick ... tick. ... I searched every inch of that room but found nothing. I pounded on the walls ... tick ... tick ... tick. I slept with two pillows over my head ... tick ... tick. ... I got up every five minutes to make sure it wasn't a dripping faucet ... tick ... tick. ... I called in my best friends in the entire world, my partners, my crew ... tick ... the people who cared most about me ... tick ... tick ... and they claimed they couldn't hear anything ... tick ... tick. ... I turned that room upside down ... tick. ... I tried to ... tick ... get another room but the ... tick ... hotel was booked ... tick ... solid. ... The tick clerk, Maloney's friend ... tick ... ticked me. I didn't sleep for tick nights ... tick ... but did they tick? ... tick ... tick. ... All I ticked for three days was that incessant ... tick ... ticking ... until its battery ticked ... tick ... down ... tick. ... But when I found out, was I ticked at George Maloney? ... tick. ... Of course I was, I was furious. I was supposed to be the man who played the jokes, not the one who got the jokes played on him. *That* was Kaiser.

Crew partners get to know each other better than almost anyone else in the world, which is wonderful for working together but not so good for playing practical jokes off the field. Kaiser, for example, was not a great inventor of practical jokes. He would do things like put food in the pockets of my jacket and let it mold there. That never worked well with me, of course, because I always assumed I left the food in my own pockets. Once, though, when I knew he'd put a chicken leg in a pocket about two weeks earlier, I waited until we were walking along together and reached into my pocket and pulled out a dry chicken leg I'd planted about an hour earlier . . . and ate it. Kenny just stared at me; he couldn't believe it. He kept asking me, "How does it taste, how does it taste?" I told him, "Just like my mother makes."

Kenny liked physical jokes. I guess that was why he liked me so much. For instance, he was friendly with infielder Fred Stanley, who would occasionally stuff seven or eight baseball gloves under his shirt and then imitate Kaiser clomping around. To get even, after a game one night Kaiser hid behind Catfish Hunter's van. Catfish would do anything for a good joke—even listen to Kenny. When Stanley walked by on the way to his own car, Kenny picked him up, tossed him into the back of Hunter's van, and locked the door. Hunter then drove home to New Jersey.

Haller and I liked to think we trained some good men. Problems arose, of course, when two of them later worked on the same crew. "It was all his fault," Rocky Roe claimed, referring to Durwood Merrill. "He started the whole thing when we were working with Larry Barnett and Mike Reilly.

"I was in the shower after a game and he snuck in and threw a glass of ice water on me when my back was turned. Then he tried to pin it on Larry Barnett, shouting at him, 'What did you do that to poor Rocky for?' He just didn't expect me to charge out of the shower and catch him standing there holding the smoking gun—or, in this case, the empty glass. Naturally, I had no choice. I had to nail his shoes to the floor and his equipment bag to the bench so that when he picked it up the entire bench came out of the wall. I didn't want to do it, but he left me no choice.

"He tried to retaliate. He put mustard in my undergarments, so that forced me to hide the hamburger in his shoe bag. I can now confirm that after five days in a shoe bag, a hamburger will look remarkably like a hockey puck.

"That was when Durwood made his real mistake. He threatened to get even without having the firepower to back it up. I have always believed that the best defense is a good offense, so I slipped a semichewed half pound of chewing tobacco in his ball bag the next time he worked the plate. Unfortunately, Durwood did not realize it was there until the seventh inning, so it had time to ferment. In the seventh inning I saw him reach into the bottom of the bag for a new baseball—and the expression on his face made it obvious to me that he'd found the tobacco. He just kept his hand in there for the longest time, then started looking around the bases to see which member of the crew was laughing hardest. For weeks his ball bag, his plate pants, everything just reeked of tobacco.

" 'I've been hit with a torpedo!' he screamed after the game, but I hadn't even gotten started. I wanted unconditional surrender. And I had a plan.

"Toward the end of the season we were in Seattle and two hours before game time I had an Eastern Oniongram delivered to him in the umpires' room. A young girl dressed in a cowgirl outfit and riding a toy horse—in honor of his Texas heritage—arrived and chimed, 'Roses are red, violets are blue, Durwood, keep your eyes open, 'cause Rocky's gonna get you.'

"Then we went to Detroit for the final series of the season. I like to remember it as my crowning moment. I had been getting my hair cut in the same place in Detroit for years, and Durwood had also started going to this place. So while we were in Detroit, we both made appointments.

"Durwood was being shampooed and had closed his eyes. Now, anyone with any sense would think that the man had realized by this time that he couldn't trust me. But he thought I was also getting a shampoo. What I was really doing was getting the

cream pie. I tapped the woman giving him the shampoo on her shoulder and she stepped out of the
firing line. Then I said softly, 'Oh, Durwood?'

" 'Yeah, Rock?'

" 'Remember that girl in Seattle who told you
to always keep your eyes open because Rocky was
going to get you?'

"He paused, then replied nervously, 'Yeah?'

" 'I really think you should have listened.' And
with that, I buried this whipped-cream pie in his
face. Right down to the tin. There was whipped
cream all over his face, his hair, his clothing. Of
course, I had a photographer there to record this
humiliation, and he began snapping pictures. That
night, in the locker room, Durwood finally admitted he was beaten, and beaten, and beaten . . .

"I hope that sometime in the future Durwood
and I have an opportunity to work together again,
because I've honed down a few pretty unusual ideas
that I'm anxious to try on him."

Some of the jokes were not as elaborate. One
now retired umpire used to carry a dollar bill to
which a wire had been attached with a paperclip.
On an airplane he'd plant that dollar in the aisle
and, when someone bent down to pick it up, he'd
yank it away. Of course, he never fooled me with
that trick—at least, not after the second time. But
perhaps his most memorable effort took place during a flight to Cleveland. The dollar bill was set out
in the aisle as a distinguished-looking man wearing
a three-piece suit and carrying a copy of *Time* magazine and an attaché case came toward it. As soon as
this businessman spotted it and before the umpire
could pull it away, the man stamped his foot on it.
The umpire yanked—and pulled off the paper clip.
The man picked up the bill, put it in his pocket,
and proceeded to the rear of the plane. "Hey, that's
my dollar," the umpire pleaded, but the man just
kept walking.

Telephones are the prop used most often in

practical jokes. Jim Evans is one of the better practi-
tioners of the art among umpires. He does a wonderful assortment of card tricks, all of which end with
me losing a dollar, and he would occasionally offer
someone a soda before a game and serve it in a
dribble glass. He couldn't trick me there—my shirts
came prestained. But his best work was done with a
battery-operated telephone and ringer that he kept
in his pocket. We'd be in a crowded elevator and
suddenly that telephone would start ringing. Everyone would look around to try to discover where it
was coming from, and finally Jimmy would answer
the phone in his jacket. He'd pretend to listen for a
moment, then hand it to whomever was standing
next to him, telling them, "It's for you."

Now, who would be expecting a telephone call
in an elevator? But inevitably the man or woman
would take the phone from him, look at it a bit
quizzically, then ask, "Hello?" The introduction of
the cordless telephone has made this particular di-
version even more effective than before.

Lee Weyer and Eddie Montague have worked
together for years. Among the many interests they
share is a love of magic—both of them are excellent
performers—and Eddie claims his greatest ambition
is to be in the middle of an argument with a player,
then suddenly say a few words and make him
disappear. One of the men they have worked with
on the field is the great Dutch Rennart. In a recent
poll National League players gave Dutch an excellent rating, which he deserved. He is also a wonderful showman and a nice person—in other words, a
perfect foil for Weyer and Montague. "We were in
an airport in Cincinnati getting ready to catch a
flight to St. Louis," Lee explains, "when Dutch
decided to call his wife at home. Eddie and I were
standing nearby, and Eddie had this wonderful idea.
He took the number of the telephone Dutch was
using and wandered down the corridor to another
booth. As soon as Dutch hung up, Eddie called that

number. 'That's your phone, Dutch,' I said. 'You'd better go back and answer it.'

"When Dutch picked it up, Eddie disguised his voice and said, 'Sir, this is the operator, I'm sorry, but the charges on the call you just made were seven dollars and fifty cents. Please deposit that amount right now. Thank you.'

" 'No,' Dutch replied, 'there must be some mistake. That was a collect call. It's been billed to my home.'

" 'I'm sorry, sir,' Eddie the operator continued, 'but that billing did not go through. You have to deposit seven dollars and fifty cents right now.'

" 'Call my wife back,' Dutch told him. 'She'll tell you it's okay.'

"Eddie pressed a few buttons to create a beeping sound, then waited a moment and said, 'I'm sorry, sir, that party will not accept the charges. Please deposit seven dollars and fifty cents and do it now.'

"Dutch was started to get a big frazzled. 'What do you mean, she won't accept it? Of course she will. Look, there's obviously some mistake here—'

" 'Let's go, Dutch,' I said, tapping my watch crystal, 'we're gonna miss the plane.'

" 'Look,' he said to the operator, 'I'm at the airport. Where am I going to get seven-fifty in change?'

" 'Maybe there's a store nearby,' Eddie the operator suggested. 'Maybe they'll give you some change.'

" 'Dutch,' I said forcefully, 'we've gotta go right now!'

" 'I gotta go,' Dutch finally said. 'Listen, just put it on my bill.'

" 'Don't you dare hang up this phone,' Eddie told him. 'Listen, you made that call and now you're going to pay for it. If you don't deposit seven dollars and fifty cents, we're going to have to fine you twenty-five dollars.'

" 'Dutch, this is ridiculous,' I said.

"He didn't know what to do. Finally he said to Eddie, 'Let me speak to your supervisor.'

"Eddie pressed a few more buttons, then said in an entirely different voice, 'This is the supervisor. May I help you?'

" 'Look,' Dutch said in a weary voice, 'I made a collect call and now the operator wants me to pay seven-fifty.'

" 'That's correct, sir,' Eddie the supervisor continued, 'the billing on your call did not go through. You'll have to deposit seven dollars and fifty cents right now.'

" 'But I don't have that much in change.'

" 'I'm sorry, sir, but—'

" 'Dutch, c'mon, the plane's leaving—'

"He put his hand over the receiver. 'They want seven-fifty for my call.'

"I told him, 'You'd better go get some change.'

" 'I can't,' he said. 'I'll miss the plane.'

"I shook my head. 'Boy,' I told him, 'I don't know what to tell you. You know what the phone company can do to you.'

"Finally Dutch said to supervisor Montague, 'I gotta hang up right now to catch a plane. Just send the bill, that's all.'

" 'I wouldn't do that if I—' Eddie started to warn him, but Dutch hung up. He spent the entire flight to St. Louis trying to figure out why his wife wouldn't accept the charges. Naturally, we never told him the truth. That way we can do it again."

Baseball teams spend almost as much time waiting in airports as umpires—and end up using the telephones for the same reasons. Once, for example, the Orioles landed in Texas at 3:00 A.M. and the chartered bus scheduled to meet their plane had not arrived. No restaurants, shops, or newsstands were open at that hour, so while the traveling secretary scrambled to provide transportation, the players had nothing to do but sit around and grumble. The fact that they had just dropped three straight games in Kansas City did not lighten the mood. Then Jim Palmer and Tony Muser got an idea.

It is important to know that Earl Weaver is approximately five feet, six inches tall and somewhat sensitive about his height—which is why I was always careful to call him things such as "Mickey Rooney." While the players waited, Earl stood next to a telephone situated very low on the wall to be used by handicapped people and children. Muser found something to discuss with Earl and, while doing so, took the number of that phone. Then he walked away.

A few minutes later that telephone started ringing. And ringing. It was the only sound in that entire airport at that time of night, and the ringing just blasted throughout the entire building. Weaver was standing right next to it but refused to answer it. The whole team was pretending not to watch him pretending not to hear it ringing. Finally Palmer, with whom Earl had a relationship that made Weaver and Dempsey look like pals, sighed, stood up, and answered the telephone. "Hello," he said, then listened for a moment. "Sure," he continued, "he's standing right here." With that, he handed the phone to Earl, telling him, "It's for you."

The entire squad broke into laughter. Even Weaver couldn't help laughing. That broke the tension of the losing streak, and the Orioles swept a three-game series from the Rangers.

Probably no manager has been the butt of more practical jokes than Tommy Lasorda. Once in spring training, for example, while Tommy was asleep in his Dodgertown villa, his players nailed shut all the windows, secured the door to a palm tree so it couldn't be opened, and removed the speaker from his telephone. Then they called to wake him up.

If the security guard hadn't been strolling by an hour later and heard Lasorda calling for help, he might still be in that house.

When Lasorda was the buttee, Jay Johnstone usually could be identified as the butter. Once he and Jerry Reuss trailed Lasorda for miles to a restaurant, waited till Lasorda was seated, then walked in, cut off his tie, and left. On another occasion Johnstone, Reuss, and Don Stanhouse went into Lasorda's Dodger Stadium office and removed from his walls hundreds of framed photographs of Tommy with Hollywood stars. Lasorda and Sinatra was taken down. Lasorda and Don Rickels was taken down. Lasorda and just about every television and movie star in California was taken down. In fact, only three photographs were left hanging—Lasorda and Johnstone, Lasorda and Reuss, and Lasorda and Stanhouse.

During the postgame celebration after the Dodgers had won the 1981 World Series, Bobby Valentine slipped out of Lasorda's office with Tommy's Dodgers jacket. Lasorda knew Valentine well enough to suspect he would play this kind of prank—Tommy had been surprised to see his World Series shirt from '78 hanging in Bobby's restaurant—and called to ask him if he had the jacket. Valentine remembers telling him, "Tommy, am I the kind of guy who would steal your favorite jacket? The jacket you wore while winning your first World Series? Okay, so maybe I am. But in this case, no, I didn't take it. There were a lot of people in the clubhouse that day. . . .

"Tommy was really sad about losing the jacket, and I knew I had to return it. The problem was how to do it best. During the winter we were doing a banquet tour in Pennsylvania and got up early one Sunday morning to go to church. Tommy went in first while I parked the car. I waited until just before the service was ready to begin, then walked in wearing Tommy's Dodgers jacket. He couldn't mistake it—it had 'Lasorda' written on the back.

"He couldn't believe it. But just as he opened his mouth to tell me what he thought of me, the priest walked in and the service began. He didn't get out the first word, and he had to sit there fuming throughout the entire service. Every time he looked at me, I would smile pleasantly at him."

Among players, Johnstone is known as one of baseball's premier practical jokers. When he was with the Dodgers his friend Steve Garvey was a particular target. "I used to put all sorts of things inside his glove while he was batting," Jay explains, "sunflower seeds, shaving cream, whatever was available. Once, though, we were in San Francisco and a ladies' group had brought us some fresh, thick chocolate brownies. They were just oozing chocolate, just perfect for either eating or putting in Steve Garvey's glove.

"So when he was at bat in the first inning, I took one of these brownies and gently placed it in the pocket of his first baseman's glove. I did not put it inside the glove it was too soft for that. Then I gently laid the infield ball on top of it, the baseball Steve took out to first base to throw warm-up grounders to the infielders. He popped out to end the first inning, came into the dugout, and picked up his glove and sunglasses and trotted out to first base. AND HIS SUNGLASSES! I hadn't figured on the sunglasses. What happened next was inevitable.

"When he got to first base he stuck the glove underneath his arm and squeeeeeeezed it tightly while he used his hands to adjust his sunglasses. I watched. I didn't even want to imagine what was happening to that soft, chocolate brownie. Sunglasses adjusted, he slipped his glove onto his hand and reached into its pocket for the infield ball . . . and grimaced. That baseball was covered with chocolate brownie. His glove was covered with chocolate brownie. His hand was covered with chocolate brownie. In general, I would have to say that at that moment Steve Garvey was not a happy man.

"I knew someone was going to have to take the blame for this, so I began figuring out exactly who that should be. My eyes settled on Jerry Reuss. I still had some chocolate on my hands, so I went over and sat down next to my friend Jerry. 'Hey, buddy, how ya doin'?' I asked as I rubbed some chocolate on the leg of his uniform pants. Then I had to make good my escape. 'The bullpen,' I decided, 'I'll go to the bullpen and warm up.'

"Meanwhile, Garvey had called time and was jogging over to the dugout. I ran out of the dugout right past him. As I trotted by first base, I whispered to umpire Paul Runge, 'Watch what Garvey does.' In the dugout, Steve picked up a towel and began cleaning his hands and his glove while looking down the bench trying to figure out who the culprit was. Everybody looked innocent—everybody *was* innocent. Then Garvey spotted the chocolate on Reuss's uniform. 'I didn't do it!' Reuss screamed when Garvey confronted him. 'I didn't do it!'

"I could hear Garvey screaming from the outfield. 'Yeah? Then how'd that chocolate get on your uniform?'

" 'I don't know,' Reuss insisted, 'but I didn't do it!' Runge was laughing so hard he had to turn his back to the dugout.

"I thought Garvey was going to kill Reuss. All the way out to the bullpen I could hear Jerry claiming, 'I'm telling you I didn't do it!' And neither of them ever did find out who was responsible for the crushed brownie."

There is perhaps no one in baseball more likely to be voted Least Popular Hotel Guest than shortstop Chris Speier. Teams can't take him anywhere. "When I was with the San Francisco Giants we often wore ties and jackets while traveling," he explains. "I'll tell you something, you can get away with a lot more dressed in a tie and jacket than you can in an old sweat shirt.

"We were staying at the Shamrock Hilton in Houston. The Shamrock has a large ballroom and my teammate, my roommate, my friend, the notori-

ous Chris Arnold and I walked into that ballroom
just as a group of singers and dancers were setting
up to audition. We must have looked pretty snazzy
in our ties and jackets, because two men came over
to us and said, 'Mr. Simpson, we're ready for the
audition now.'

"Now, what would any person with a little
good sense have done? The same thing I did. 'Fine,'
I told him, 'whenever you're ready.' So Chris and I
sat down and they went through part of their routine.
They were really working hard, singing and tapping
their hearts out. When they finished, Chris and I
both applauded, but then I had to tell them the
truth. 'Listen,' I said, 'you've got a good tap-dance
routine there, but you just won't be able to hear it
in the back. There's gonna be at least five hundred
people in this place. You think maybe you could
liven it up a little?'

" 'Oh, sure,' they replied. 'We've got some plywood staging in the back.'

"So they went and got their plywood, put it
down, and went through their entire routine again.
They were really working very hard, they were
sweating. I admired them. I finally felt so bad about
fooling them that I had to tell them the truth.
'Listen,' I said, 'this is going to be a younger crowd,
not a bunch of old people. Have you got anything to
kind of cheese up your costumes a bit, you know,
make them a little more risqué?'

" 'Oh, sure,' they replied. 'We've got some . . .
some other costumes in the back.'

"So they went and got their other costumes,
and then they went through the entire routine again.
By the time they were finished they were huffing
and puffing, leaning on scenery, lying on the floor.
Now I *really* had to tell them the truth. 'Listen,' I
said, 'we're really impressed and we're gonna talk
to the general manager right now.' Then we got up
to leave. And as we walked out of the ballroom,

who did we pass coming in? His nametag read: Mr. Simpson. We did not stay for that audition.

"They knew Chris and I very well at the Shamrock, probably from the day we walked into the kitchen with efficiency charts attached to clipboards and proceeded to rearrange the entire place, including making some important additions and deletions to the menu. But compared to what we did at the Queen Elizabeth in Montreal, that really wasn't very much.

"We arrived at the Queen Elizabeth on the first day of a two-week road trip and as we were registering we heard band music on the promenade level. We went upstairs and discovered a dental convention in progress. Tables had been arranged around the room, and the long, rectangular dais was set up directly in front of the bandstand.

"We were just standing there, minding our own business, bothering no one, with no plans, not even thinking about a prank, when this extremely distinguished-looking gentleman approached us and asked, '*Excusez-moi.* May I help you?'

"Talk about a leading question. 'Yes,' I said, 'we're with General MacArthur's party and we're here to secure the dais for him. He apologizes for being late and has asked us to inform you that he will be bringing the entire group of twenty-five guests!'

"He looked at me a bit strangely. 'General MacArthur?'

" 'Yes, General MacArthur. You do know that he is going to be representing the President tonight to accept his honorary membership in the Dental Society, don't you?'

"Obviously he did not know that, but he also did not want to admit that he did not know that. He disappeared, and returned a few moments later with the headwaiter. I repeated the entire spiel.

"As I was telling him the story, Chris walked out the door. He came back about a minute later and reported, 'The party is in the limos. They should be here in about fifteen minutes.'

"The headwaiter claimed he knew nothing about General MacArthur's party. 'You may not know anything about it,' I told him, 'but our jobs depend on us securing that head table.'

"Chris again left and returned moments later. 'They're at the traffic circle,' he said, 'maybe twelve minutes.'

"I looked the headwaiter straight in the eyes. 'What are you going to do about this?'

"The headwaiter quickly located the woman who had mailed out all the invitations and brought her over to us. Meanwhile, the dental convention guests were filling up the room and taking our seats at the dais. 'This is simply not going to do,' I told the woman. 'This can't be allowed.' Then I again explained that we were General MacArthur's representatives and his party was due to arrive at the ballroom in . . . seven minutes.

"She thought for a few seconds, then said, 'General MacArthur? Isn't he dead?'

"Naturally, I became indignant. 'What is this?' I demanded, 'some kind of silly joke? Not that General MacArthur. *That* General MacArthur is dead, yes. Look, maybe this is funny to you, but my job depends on those seats being there when the general and his guests walk through those doors. Here . . .' I reached into my pocket and pulled out all the money I was carrying for the road trip, then I started peeling off twenty-dollar bills.

" 'That won't be necessary,' she said. 'Just a minute.' She began giving orders to clear the dais. Various waiters started running around, moving people to other tables.

"Chris had left once again. He returned just as the people at the dais were moving. 'The limos are here,' he said in an almost panicked voice.

" 'That's okay,' she replied, 'we'll have everyone moved in a minute.'

" 'Fine,' I said, 'wonderful. We'll go meet the general and stall him. We'll be back in five minutes, sharp.' We shook hands, turned around—and just took off.

"Then there was the time we stole the bellmen's luggage carts and they ended up chasing us through the entire hotel. We finally escaped by pretending to be members of a band that was just packing up their equipment. Naturally, we requested another cart to help us carry the instruments. Eventually they had to padlock their carts. None of this had anything to do with putting hot balm in pitcher Ron Bryant's shoes when he was scheduled to pitch, but that's another story."

Of course, the last laugh was on Speier. After all that, he was traded to Montreal.

Surprisingly, before the beginning of free agency, when players gained the right to sell their talents to the highest bidder, general managers of baseball teams used to play wonderful practical jokes—but they called them contract negotiations. Bobby Valentine, for example, seriously injured his knee during the winter and had to have an operation. "I had just come out of the recovery room," he remembers, "and I was lying there in the hospital, my entire leg in a cast, suspended in midair. I had nothing to do but wonder if I was ever going to be able to play baseball again. Among my first guests were Al Campanis of the Dodger front office and his secretary, Marge. Marge just happened to have a blank contract for the next season with her. I didn't care that it was blank, I signed it anyway and told Campanis to fill in whatever he thought was fair. I was just so pleased somebody wanted me to play baseball."

A few years earlier Valentine had ripped up the contract the Dodgers had offered and mailed the tiny pieces back to general manager Peter Bavasi. Bavasi carefully taped the pieces together and returned them to Valentine. He signed.

Gary Carter had a terrible season in 1976. He was hitting .219 when he broke his hand, and he too was worried about his future in baseball. The Expos invited him into the front office. "I thought they were going to send me home," he remembers. "Instead, they offered me a contract for 1977. I couldn't even hold a pen in my broken hand, but I signed that contract."

When pitcher Lee Stange refused to sign a contract offered by the Cleveland Indians, general manager Gabe Paul suggested a compromise: If, at the end of the season, Stange had really helped improve the Indians, Paul would give him a three-thousand-dollar bonus. Stange agreed. In midseason, he was traded to the Boston Red Sox. Two days after he arrived in Boston, Gabe Paul sent him a check for the three thousand dollars.

Of course, there are some people who believed *I* was the biggest joke in baseball. For some reason they believed the job of an umpire was to call balls and strikes, safes and outs, fair and foul. I don't know where they got that idea. I know where they *didn't* get that idea—from me.

About the only part of baseball I liked better than being on the field was being off the field. No one yelled at you off the field. Maybe they banged on the door a little, but it wasn't the same as being a standing target. The best time to be off the field was all winter. The only way anyone could yell at you during the winter was by long distance, and no one I knew in baseball would do that unless they could call collect.

Being an umpire is a part-time job, and that part lasts about six months a year. Unfortunately, the salary structure—which has improved since I've retired, no connection—makes it necessary for umpires to work during the off-season. Lee Weyer, for example, does some promotional work for Pontiac. Davey Phillips used to referee college basketball games but now is the supervisor of basketball offi-

THE TOP OF THE NINTH

cials for the Metro Conference. Doug Harvey also
used to referee basketball games as well as work for
the Santa Fe Railroad, but his wife's success in real
estate has enabled him to spend much of the winter
working on improving his golf game. Dale Ford
does public relations for Pepsi, and Eddie Montague
does the same for the Marchants Stordor Corporation,
a trucking company. Rocky Roe is in marketing for
Computer Methods Corporation, a company that
produces software and provides trained personnel
for the computer industry. Eric Gregg has his own
sports segment and sometimes cohosts Philadelphia's
Evening Magazine, a television program. He is also
a spokesperson for Philly Franks. Eric and food, a
perfect match.

And Kenny Kaiser wrestles for charity. One
year, for example, he wrestled the fabulous Gonzo
Sisters. "They were mean mothers," he remembers,
"and I had to pin them right in front of their
children." He got into wrestling after being introduced to professional wrestler André the Giant. "This
man is seven-six tall, weighs four hundred seventy-
five pounds, and there is not an ounce of fat on
him," Kenny says. "His head is bigger than most
people's body. We went out for dinner the night we
met. I had a nice eighteen-ounce steak and a big
salad. The person who introduced us had the same.
André had a salad about the size of a swimming
pool, eleven baked potatoes, and two twenty-ounce
steaks. Then he drank a keg of beer. André speaks
very little English, so we got along well because
neither do I, and toward the end of the meal he said
something in French. I asked what he'd said. My
friend explained, 'He just wanted to tell you that
he'll pick up the check.'

"I looked at the remnants of eleven potatoes,
two steaks, and a pool of salad. 'No kidding,' I
said."

I spent my first few winters in baseball working as a substitute teacher. And I hated it. As far as

I'm concerned, the only thing wrong with schools is children. Get rid of those kids, you won't have any problems in the schools. I was the only substitute teacher who was absent more than the students. Finally I just couldn't do it anymore. I was only six-four, two hundred eighty pounds—the eight-year-olds were winning.

I had realized right at the beginning of my major league career that I'd better start planning for the end of my major league career. I decided to open a sporting goods store. Unfortunately, I knew as much about retailing as Jackie Onassis knows about couponing. Still, I pushed ahead, and on December 15, 1977, Ron Luciano's Sports World opened in Endicott, New York, just after all of central New York had finished buying their Christmas presents. It turned out to be a very brief world.

To publicize the opening of my store I decided to hire two ballplayers to make an appearance. Endicott is Yankee territory, so I invited two of the most popular Yankees, Roy White and Mickey Rivers. Both of them agreed to appear and sign autographs.

Now, Mickey Rivers is a very nice person with a very short memory. So during the season, every time I saw him I would remind him, "You're going to be there, Mick, right? December fifteenth."

"I'll be there, Ronnie."

If I didn't see the Yankees for a while I would call and remind him. "December fifteenth, Mick, my store is opening, right?"

"I'll be there, Ronnie."

When the season ended I called him every few weeks. He told me, "I'll be there, Ronnie."

But just to make sure he would be there, I arranged to have a limousine pick him up at his house, drive him to the airport, and deliver him to a stewardess. The stewardess would make sure he got on the plane, and when the plane landed in Binghamton, deliver him to another driver, who would bring him directly to the store. It wouldn't go wrong. It couldn't. And Earl Weaver didn't argue about half swings, either.

On December 12 I began calling Mickey at home. No answer. I called all day and all night. No answer. I called the next day and the next night. No answer. I called until the last possible minute and never found him.

The store opened without him. Roy White was there and was wonderful. Months passed. In February I went to Arizona for spring training. Mickey went with the Yankees to Florida, so I didn't see him before the season opened. I wasn't scheduled to work any Yankee games in April or May, so it was early June when I finally caught up with him. I came out of the locker room long before the game and spotted him leaning against the batting cage. I walked right up to him, put my hand on his shoulder, and said, "Mickey, what about the opening of my sporting goods store?"

"Oh, yeah, Ronnie," Mickey said enthusiastically, "when is that again?"

I suppose I should've taken that as an omen. But, as it turned out, a more accurate omen would have been an earthquake. Before I opened that store I stocked it with every item I thought a sporting goods store had to have. I thought we'd bought the whole world—in every size. The second day we were opened a man came in asking for a pink karate suit for his girlfriend. Extra small. I searched every shelf. We had karate suits in eight colors, none of them pink. This was practically my first customer and I didn't have what he wanted. So from then on, any time a customer asked for something we didn't have, I immediately ordered a stock of them, in all sizes.

I hated to lose a single sale. Once, for example, a man came in looking for an eight-pound shot put. I tried to explain to him that shot puts weighed sixteen pounds. He insisted on an eight-pounder. I spent half the day on the telephone trying to locate a supplier of eight-pound shot puts. Successful stores, I eventually learned, stocked few items. Carvel sells ice cream. McDonald's had perhaps fifteen different items. Ron Luciano's Sports World had five hundred thirty-seven different items. Five hundred thirty-seven by inventory count.

Then, our location was not ideal, either. As soon as I opened, the largest store in the mall, a department store that attracted most of the mall's customers, went out of business. That was a bad sign. Then the road in front of the entrance collapsed and the construction company hired to fix it went out of business. There was a blockade in front of that driveway for nine months.

Everything went wrong. The store next door to me was an exotic pet store. They had bad pets. Snakes, spiders, lizards, things like that. My store would get the overflow from that store, the kind of people who would drop down to the mall on a Saturday afternoon to browse at spiders. Once, one of the pythons escaped and my help refused to come to work because they were afraid it had crawled into my store through an air-conditioning duct. I knew it couldn't happen— the air-conditioning ducts were blocked and we didn't have air conditioning.

When NBC hired me, I realized it was time for my World to come to an end. Things were so bad that when we had our going-out-of-business sale, the first thing we sold, to the owner of another store nearby, was our going-out-of-business-sale sign.

As it turned out, compared to my ability as a color commentator on the backup *Game of the Week*, I was a retailing genius. I had never before realized talking could be so difficult. Other people get tongue-tied; I got tongue-knotted. The only way I could have made it as a broadcaster is if NBC sent each listener a written translation. There was some discussion about having our games closed-captioned for the deaf and hard-of-hearing, but the deaf and hard-of-hearing voted against it.

The transition from the playing field to the broadcasting booth, I quickly discovered, was not as easy as it looked. I also discovered that I was not the first person to discover that. "In all honesty," Phil Rizzuto says, "I would have to describe the beginning of my broadcasting career as tragic. I broke in sitting between Mel Allen and Red Barber, two men who spoke the King's English. I spoke your basic Brooklyn. During my first game I had Yogi Berra hitting a foul pop-up, and Yogi Berra settling under it and catching it. Then I would say things like, 'The pitcher, the catcher, and the batter, all trying to outsmart each other.' I didn't understand the technical aspects, either. When the director would talk to me through my headphones, I would talk back to him through my microphone. Listeners would hear half a conversation. I learned. I still didn't get it right, but I learned."

Another former Yankee infielder, Jerry Coleman, also had problems learning the broadcasting business. He would say things like, "A fly ball to center field. Winfield is going back, back ... he hits his head against the wall. It's rolling toward second base," and "The relief pitcher is throwing up in the bullpen."

Even nonathletes like Harry Caray make mistakes. Caray, now working for the Chicago Cubs, has been broadcasting baseball games for decades. "A few years ago the White Sox had a young girl sitting along the foul line picking up foul grounders," he remembers. "She is a very attractive woman and usually wore shorts on warm days. After a long hot spell in Chicago we suddenly had a cool night, and she came out of the dugout wearing a warm-up suit. So naturally I told our listeners, 'And there's our ballgirl. And this is the first time I can recall seeing her without her pants on.' "

After my career in broadcasting ended, which

was just after my career in retailing ended, which was not too long after my career as an umpire ended, during which time my teaching career had ended, and even before that my professional football career had ended, I discovered that I was basically the same person I was before going into baseball—unemployed.

The first thing everybody advised when I thought about my future was that I should not make any quick decisions. That made me feel good—for fifteen years as an umpire, about the only thing I learned how to do was make quick decisions.

Fortunately, before I could find another career to end, I began to get offers to do television commercials. I was told, "People like to see you." It didn't take me long to figure out why. They looked at me and thought, "No matter how bad things are going in my life, it could be worse. I could look like that guy."

The beer company with its own all-star squad asked me to audition for them, explaining I was a natural for their product. They said I had the good looks, the smooth delivery, the positive public recognition and, most important of all, the beer belly.

However, they explained, they already were using an umpire on their commercials, and he did the bad-vision gags. Jim Honochick. "Jim Honochick!" I said. "I used to solder his shinguards together. I used to put his plate shoes in the deep freezer."

The advertising agency producer told me that Jim Honochick had done a number of commercials that were running frequently and that he was collecting hefty residuals from the commercials. When Jim and I had worked together I had noticed that he laughed at the most unusual times. Finally, after all these years, I had discovered what it was he had been laughing about.

So they had to find a new "character" for me to play. They tried nine different approaches. In one, I was in a disco doing a new dance, "The Umpire," which consisted of all the signals an umpire uses on the field. I told them I couldn't dance. They told me they had heard me on the *Game of the Week*, and the fact that I couldn't speak hadn't stopped me from broadcasting.

Next, they teamed me with an actor standing in for Billy Martin. Billy and I were supposed to be in an Italian restaurant talking about how we liked each other and agreed on everything, then we argued about the menu. I ended up ejecting him from the restaurant.

Next they type-cast me—they had me start an argument with millions of television viewers, and this one ended with me throwing everybody out of their living rooms. That didn't work, they explained, because they were afraid I would scare their customers.

Next they had me sitting at a bar explaining, "One of the things I've spent the last fifteen years of my life doing is making decisions." Then they showed a clip of me calling people safe or out or, unfortunately, both. Then I continued, "So if there is one thing I can do very well, it's making decisions, and that's why I choose—"

The bartender then interrupted me and asked, "You want this in a glass or the bottle?"

"A glass," I answered firmly. "No, wait, maybe you'd better give it to me in the bottle. Nah, I'll take the glass. Okay, the bottle. Wait. . . ." I paused, looked directly at the camera, and said, "I think I'd better get another opinion."

I have not mentioned the name of the beer company because I have a firm rule I follow about commercials. I will not do a commercial unless I honestly believe in the product and use it myself. Or unless they pay me. Luckily, the next offer came from United Airlines. They wanted me to be an executive traveler. If there is one thing umpires know about, it is airlines. I have flown on every one of them. I have flown on airlines that flew so low the pilot had to pay tolls on the thruway. I agreed to do the commercial, but I made it clear that this was a one-time-only situation and I would not be one of those people who dropped the name of the company, United Airlines, every time he could in hopes that he would be used on a second commercial. And United Airlines understood. They explained that United Airlines does not operate that way, and I told them that made me glad I was doing this commercial for United Airlines.

In that commercial for United Airlines, I was seated on a United Airlines wide-body 747 when a United Airlines stewardess served my meal. That's when I said some nice things about United Airlines, concluding with, "And they always look good from behind the plate." Get it? The stewardess was serving me dinner and I was a former umpire—behind the plate!

I also began my career as a television actor during this period. I had my audition. When NBC was looking for someone to play a bartender on the new comedy *Cheers*, they decided they wanted a heavyset former athlete. Talk about a perfect role. They searched all over for a heavyset former athlete. Here I am. They auditioned former basketball star and coach Tommy Heinsohn. Here I am. They tried to get former football coach and broadcaster John Madden. Yoo-hoo, over here. Finally they ran out of candidates. That's where I came in. I auditioned. I don't want to claim that I was superb, because I wasn't. I was good. I was so good, in fact, that they realized they had to use a professional actor in the role.

The woman who was doing the casting was optimistic, however. "You know, you're very talented," she told me, "and I think I have the perfect role for someone with your looks."

"That's great," I said.

"Yes," she finished, "and I think you and the chimp will get along very well."

Chimp? What chimp? The only thing I hate more than kids are chimps. Chimps make kids look nice. But, on the other hand, we all must make sacrifices for our art. So because of my "look," she recommended me for the voice of the chimp on a show called *Mr. Smith*, about a chimp who practices law. I thought that guy defended me once.

I didn't get any NBC shows, but I did get my own show, *Ron Luciano's Lighter Side of Sports*. It was a wonderful show. It lasted one segment. I should have realized it wasn't going to work when I met the announcer. He is one of the few Tibetans working in American television. We were taping in July and he was wearing a fur hat—with the ear-flaps down. Even that would have been okay if he had spoken English. "But he works cheap," the producer explained.

The two best things about the show were the song written especially for umpires by Steve Goodman and Sean Kelly entitled, "It Ain't Easy Being Perfect, But I Am," and Fred Newman, a man who makes mouth sounds. He can sound like a rock 'n' roll band, the Queen's Guard, or a stampede. The show might not have been successful, but at least I met a man who can sound like an orchestra.

So, once again, I find myself at a crossroads. Which road shall I follow? Shall it be the one with the sign reading "Dead End," or shall it be the other, the one with the sign proclaiming, "Detour—Use Other Road"?

Whichever path I follow, I know I have been very fortunate. I have had the loyal support of my fan club—although I must admit my fan is starting to get a little old—and I have fifteen years of wonderful memories of a life in baseball.

People ask me if I miss being part of baseball. I tell them that baseball will always be part of me. The people I've met, the friendships I've made did not end when I blew my last call. I still attend games, watch games, and recently umpired a game in the Class A New York–Pennsylvania League. I don't think I realized how much I enjoyed being off the field until I went on the field again.

The best way I can describe my feelings about baseball is to quote a woman I met in Atlanta, Georgia, Pearl Sandow. Pearl may well be the ultimate fan. She started attending Atlanta Cracker games in 1934 and has not missed a single Braves game since they arrived in Atlanta in 1966. She was in Yankee Stadium the day Don Larsen pitched his perfect game in the World Series and was in the Polo Grounds when Bobby Thomson won the pennant with his home run—sitting four seats away from the spot the ball hit. "I've seen a lot of baseball," Pearl told me, "and I believe that the best thing in the entire world is to watch a winning baseball team."

And the second best thing? I asked her.

She smiled. "Watching a losing baseball team!"

THE END

". . . did I mention the home run I hit off Bobby McClure in Anaheim? That one was unreal. I hit that ball and it just . . ."

THE AUTHORS
RON LUCIANO & DAVID FISHER

Ron Luciano, whose first book THE UMPIRE STRIKES BACK was on *The New York Times* hardcover bestseller list for over four months, was an American League umpire from 1968 to 1979. Upon retirement, he joined NBC for a period of time as a sports commentator on the Saturday Game-of-the-Week.

David Fisher, who co-authored THE UMPIRE STRIKES BACK, once worked in the baseball commissioner's office. He is the author of more than 20 books, including his most recent novel, *The War Magician*, and the reference book *What's What*.

Hey There Sports Fan!

We have something just for <u>you</u>!

SPECIAL
MONEY SAVING
OFFER

Now you can have an up-to-date listing of Bantam's hundreds of titles plus take advantage of our unique and exciting bonus book offer. A special offer which gives you the opportunity to purchase a Bantam book for only 50¢. Here's how!

By ordering any five books at the regular price per order, you can also choose any other single book listed (up to a $4.95 value) for just 50¢. Some restrictions do apply, but for further details why not send for Bantam's listing of titles today!

Just send us your name and address plus 50¢ to defray the postage and handling costs.
